CROSS-LINGUISTIC STRUCTURES
IN SIMULTANEOUS BILINGUALISM

STUDIES IN BILINGUALISM (SiBil)

Volume 21

Susanne Döpke (ed.)

Cross-Linguistic Structures in Simultaneous Bilingualism

CROSS-LINGUISTIC STRUCTURES IN SIMULTANEOUS BILINGUALISM

Edited by

SUSANNE DÖPKE
Monash University, Australia

JOHN BENJAMINS PUBLISHING COMPANY
AMSTERDAM/PHILADELPHIA

™ The paper used in this publication meets the minimum requirements of American National Standard for Information Sciences — Permanence of Paper for Printed Library Materials, ANSI Z39.48-1984.

Library of Congress Cataloging-in-Publication Data

Cross-linguistic structures in simultaneous bilingualism / edited by Susanne Döpke.
    p.   cm. -- (Studies in Bilingualism, ISSN 0928-1533 ; v. 21)
    Includes bibliographical references and indexes.
    1. Bilingualism in children. 2. Language acquisition. I. Döpke, Susanne. II. Series.
P115.2.C75   2000
404'.2'083--dc21   00-034225
ISBN 90 272 4131 7 (Eur.) / 1 55619 953 8

John Benjamins Publishing Co. • P.O.Box 75577 • 1070 AN Amsterdam • The Netherlands
John Benjamins North America • P.O.Box 27519 • Philadelphia PA 19118-0519 • USA

Table of Contents

List of Contributors

Susanne **Döpke**
P.O. Box 11A (Linguistics)
Monash University VIC 3800, Australia
e-mail: susanne.dopke@arts.monash.edu.au

Ira **Gawlitzek-Maiwald**
Anglistische Linguistik
Universität Mannheim
D-68131 Mannheim, Germany
e-mail: Gawlitzek@t-online.de

Ulrike **Gut**
Lankwitzer Weg 2
33619 Bielefeld, Germany
e-mail: gut@pool.uni-mannheim.de

Aafke **Hulk**
French Department/HIL & IFOTT
University of Amsterdam
Spuistraat 134, 1028VB
Amsterdam, The Netherlands
e-mail: aafke.hulk@let.uva.nl

Elisabeth **Lanza**
Department of Linguistics
University of Oslo
Post Box 1102 Blinder
0317 Oslo, Norway
e-mail: elizabeth.lanza@ilf.uio.no

Johanne **Paradis**
Department of Linguistics
University of Alberta
4–46 Assiniboia Hall
Edmonton AB T6G 2E7, Canada
e-mail: johanne.paradis@ualberta.ca

Christina **Schelletter**
Dept Linguistics
Watford Campus, Aldenham
Watford Herts WD2 8AT, UK
e-mail: C.Schelletter@herts.ac.uk

Indra **Sinka**
Department of Humanities
Faculty of Humanities,
Languages and Education
University of Hertfordshire
Watford Campus, Aldenham
Hertfordshire WD2 8AT, UK
e-mail: I.Sinka@herts.ac.uk

Rosemarie **Tracy**
Fakultät für Sprach- und
Kulturwissenschaften
Universität Mannheim, Schloss E.W.
D-68131 Mannheim, Germany
e-mail: rtracy@rumms.uni-mannheim.de

Elisabeth **van der Linden**
French Department/HIL & IFOTT
University of Amsterdam
Spuistraat 134
1028VB, Amsterdam, The Netherlands
e-mail: elinden@hum.uva.nl

Preface

The present volume brings together a group of researchers with a shared interest in the simultaneous acquisition of two languages in early childhood. We share a curiosity in cross-linguistic structures and dissatisfaction with the treatment that they have received in the literature. We are delighted by the commonalities of our findings in spite of the fact that we are all working in different structural areas and with different languages. We are committed to finding far-reaching explanations for the various facets of bilingual development in the hope that these will eventually lead to a comprehensive picture of this type of language development.

Some of us met for the first time at the 1st International Symposium on Bilingualism in Newcastle-upon-Tyne in 1997. The idea for this book was conceived then. I would like to thank Li Wei and his team for organising such a stimulating event. The rest of the authors came on board through cross-contacts. During the production of the book, we all got to know each other very well through intensive internet contact.

In 1998 several of us had the chance to meet again at the International Conference of Infant Studies, which was held in Atlanta. I would like to thank Elena Nicoladis for organising the symposium on "One language theory or two? Toward a unified theory of language development" at this conference. The parallels between the Atlanta event and this book were quite by chance but very much welcomed.

Special thanks go to Kees Vaes at John Benjamins and the editors of this series for their patience during the rather lengthy process of getting all the contributions together and their help with finalising the product.

Susanne Döpke
Department of Linguistics
Monash University, Australia
October 1999

Introduction

On the Status of Cross-Linguistic Structures in Research on Young Children Growing Up With Two Languages Simultaneously

Susanne Döpke

Monash University

Most people who have contact with young bilingual children at times notice structures in their speech which are atypical of monolingual children of the same age. More often than not atypical structures sound as if they are coming from the child's other language. In the aftermath of severe prejudices against bilingualism, such structures are still being viewed with suspicion by parents, teachers and health professionals. An important question to be answered by linguists is: What is the status of atypical structures produced by bilingual children?

In the debate during the last decade of whether simultaneously bilingual children start out with one unified structural system or immediately differentiate between their two languages, crosslinguistic structures in the children's output have become marginalised. Such structures were either not reported, were seen as too few in number to be of interest, or were disregarded as indications of early second language acquisition and therefore not of interest to research in simultaneous bilingualism.

That notwithstanding, the search for evidence against an initially unified structural system has convincingly shown that bilingual children predominantly produce language-specific structures at all stages of their development. This indicates that the simultaneous acquisition of two languages proceeds within the structural scope of each of the target languages. This is a very reassuring outcome of the research into bilingualism during the primary language acquisition process.

It is time now for us to take a fresh look at the more unusual structures produced by bilingual children and to assess them for the insights they can provide into the process of acquiring two languages simultaneously.

The aim of this book is to make crosslinguistic structures the focus. The contributors to this book are interested in discovering reasons for their presence or absence. In their analyses, they want to treat crosslinguistic structures as a legitimate feature of bilingual development and explain them within the core of their chosen theoretical framework.

There are a number of issues which have been common to studies on childhood bilingualism over recent years and which are reflected in the contributions to this volume as well.

A consistent thread through all the contributions to the present volume is the acceptance that even the earliest grammatical structures of bilingual children indicate that their two languages develop along the language-specific lines which are to be expected for each language. At the same time, all contributors have an active interest in accounting for those structures which seem to be motivated through cross-language influences. They do not see them as disproving the separate development hypothesis, but take them as a means for tracking the cognitive processes involved in the simultaneous acquisition of two languages. As Paradis (this volume) rightly argues, it is the extent to which crosslinguistic structures are evident which supports one or the other of the hypotheses. Limited appearance of cross-language influences should actually be expected even if the children do successfully distinguish between their languages.

Comparisons with monolingual children as requested by Tracy (this volume) are a feature of several of the articles in the present volume. It is heartening to see and fully within the predictions of the separate development hypothesis that the bilingual data by-and-large fall within the range of variation also evident in the monolingual development of the respective languages. Differences between monolingual and bilingual children are mostly small, but need to be considered in the light of claims that comparable structures "never" appear in monolingual children or in only very low quantities while their appearance under bilingual conditions is more frequent and more widespread.

Paradis (this volume) crystallises recent developments in the research of bilingual children into a new hypothesis: the "interlanguage ambiguity" hypothesis. While she is the only one to use this term, it is implicitly the guiding hypothesis for several of the contributors to the present volume. It reconciles the obvious evidence for structural separation between the languages in young bilingual children's spontaneous utterances with the evidence for cross-language influences, which is equally impossible to ignore.

It is no accident that all papers are based on longitudinal investigations of small numbers of children. Such studies provide insights into the normal course of development and have been a feature of research into monolingual development for a long time. It is the accumulative effect of many such studies which will eventually do justice to the full scope of the complexity of bilingual first language acquisition. Crosslinguistic structures are intricate aspects of a bilingual child's normal course of development. They surface at points of productive crises or, at least, points of difficulties and represent the extremes to which the developing systems of the young language learners can be pushed. Often times, such evidence is only available sparingly as routine productions predominantly reflect the separateness of the development of the two languages. The relationship between target and non-target structures both in quantitative and qualitative terms is important for understanding the motivations for their appearance. This can best be detected in the naturalistic settings of longitudinal investigations.

Since crosslinguistic structures are for the most part scarce and in some cases fairly minor in frequency even in the papers presented in this volume, I would like to spend a moment on the issue of frequency in studies of language development. Lack of quantity has been the leading argument in the marginalisation of difficult to explain structures in the study of monolingual and bilingual children alike. They have been treated as performance errors and, therefore, as not representative of the child's structural competence. While the distinction between competence and performance has occupied an important place in linguistic theory building, it does not necessarily follow that everything that remains below a certain threshold of frequency is unsystematic and therefore cannot contribute any insights to our research interests. Roeper (1992: 340 and fn.33) acknowledged this when he suggested that not every aspect of language development is accessible to the researcher; but in some places of development or for some children, major developmental steps might happen too rapidly or even silently. Therefore we might have to draw on "apparently minor overt signs of systematicity as possible indications of fundamental underlying principles" (p. 340). This is echoed by Radford (1996: 62) who argues that it is fallacious to generalise from the lack of evidence for a certain stage at a certain point in time that this stage does not exist. The researcher might simply have missed it because it preceded the period of observation. Therefore, minor occurrences in some children should not be disregarded while, at the same time, important theoretical points are made on the basis that structures do not occur at all in other children. Roeper asserts that the "significant fact is that some children exhibit [a certain] pattern, not that some children do not." (p. 363 fn.33).

It is in relation to this ambivalence between rejecting numerically minor evidence on one hand but wanting to find missing links in the children's language development on the other that Radford's (1996: 81) by now famous (and for some people infamous) utterance "Every example counts" *needs* to be taken seriously. In fact, if structures are frequent enough to show up repeatedly in randomly collected data, they are unlikely to do so accidentally. Atkinson

(1996: 475) suggests that their multiplication into tokens for the relevant period of a child's development would provide an estimate of actual occurrence and would make it more difficult to dismiss them as irrelevant.

The reliance on infrequent occurrences in order to prove major theoretical points is not always considered unacceptable (Clahsen 1991; Meisel & Müller 1992; Wexler 1994; Roeper 1996).[1] Atkinson (1996: 483 fn.19) believes that one needs to exercise "sensitivity" as to whether to include minor frequency examples. This opens the door to the type of theoretical bias which Tracy (1995: 198) must have had in mind when she wrote: "What one counts as an exception is not just defined by some quantitative feature but by the fact that it lies in conflict with our theory."

Tracy (1995: 204) raises the issue of relativity for what is too little or enough evidence to be of interest. To prove her point, let us consider the following: Poeppel & Wexler (1993: 8) reckon that 6 out of 43, ie. nearly 14%, of nonfinite verbs in an unpredicted syntactic position are a "relatively small number of exceptions" which do not "require [Poeppel & Wexler] to restructure [their] theory explicitly to account for them", and Harris & Wexler (1996: 20) deem 6% to be "extremely close to zero". Roeper (1992: 365 fn.44), on the other hand, questions whether 2.7% is a "small amount", admittedly not in his own data but someone else's. Related to this is the issue of what the occurrences of an unusual structure are being calculated against. Any phenomenon can be relegated to insignificance by splitting the data up into too many cells or by including too wide a base against which they are calculated.[2]

The other side of the coin is the status of target structures in the children's output. The majority of the forms young children produce are likely to be correct as per input. But whether they are indications of the children's grammatical competence just because they are high in quantity is not at all clear. There is evidence of forms and structures appearing in children's output as a direct reflection of the input through delayed repetitions and holistic chunks (Clark 1974; Speidel & Nelson eds. 1989). Many of the target structures might actually be reproductions based on the input rather than competence based child creations.[3] For the most part this is not verifiable for the researcher although some safeguards have been put in place over the years, such as excluding imitations of the adult input within a certain number of turns prior to the child's utterance or verifying that forms or structures are productive through their appearance in alternative combinations somewhere else in the transcript. Unfortunately these are meagre attempts at solving this problem in the light of some children's, especially some of the early talkers', exceptionally good memory capacities.[4]

While I am in no way suggesting that target forms are always reproductions of the input, I believe that they cannot inform us very well of what is happening inside the child's mind. For instance, we cannot really ascertain the independent use of a verb affix until it shows up on verbs which were not modelled in the input or in positions where we would not expect it. Overgeneralisations, even if they only happen once or twice in our transcript, are very powerful sources of information that the child is actively using a grammatical form or a syntactic structure.

If there is one thing we can say about crosslinguistic structures, then it is that they are the children's own creations because the children could not possibly have heard them from their interlocutors.[5] It is in the nature of crosslinguistic structures, just as it is in the nature of overgeneralisations, that they will not necessarily manifest themselves systematically since the child does not receive any re-enforcing input. Crosslinguistic structures often remain "experiments", but experiments which are based on the child's momentary analytic capacities. A purely quantitative account of clearly creative structures at the edge of the child's momentary abilities hides more than it reveals if the creative structures are calculated against large numbers of possibly routine productions and reproductions of the input.

A stumbling block to overcome at the moment is to reconcile the diverse evidence we have gained from bilingual children's language development ranging from no apparent differences to monolingual development in some children to pockets of systematic variation in others. In part, this might be due to the combination of languages to which various bilingual children are exposed, as some language combinations generate greater structural ambiguities than others (Tracy 1995: 85; and several of the authors in this volume). Another reason for this might be found in individual differences between children. It is, therefore, important not to make general claims on just one or two children and to use the evidence from such small numbers of children to negate someone else's findings. Instead, we need to integrate the diverse range of evidence into a comprehensive picture of bilingual development. It is reasonable to suspect that what one child does frequently and another does only occasionally occurs for the same cognitive reasons. In other words, we should strive to find encompassing explanations across children. I concur with Tracy (1995: 199) when she argues that "if one child's exception can be another's well-documented pattern, we may have to re-evaluate our theory."

In conclusion to this elaboration on the frequency issue in studies of language development, I would like to stress that rather than negating minority cases of non-target structures as unimportant we need to adopt Hulk's (this volume) position and ask: "Why do these bilingual children make precisely these errors that seem to reflect characteristics of the other of their two languages?" and consider the possibility raised by Paradis (this volume) that "the marginal number of [...] constructions in one child [...] might indicate that for other [...] children systematic and sustained use of crosslinguistic structures could occur".

If we pay particular attention to the unusual, we may find out more about the more occult operations of the language learning mind.

A further issue which is being addressed by the present volume is the importance of the language combination and language module. In their explorations of the extent of the validity of the question "one system or two", several authors find that both the question and the answer need to be much more differentiated. What the reader will gain from this volume is the impression that the degree of cross-language influences crucially depends on the degree of inter-language ambiguity which is being generated by a particular language combination for a particular language module.

Predictions as to where cross-language influences are likely to occur would, however, be difficult to make. While some researchers might find this hard to accept because they see their ability to make predictions as proof that their theory is correct, others will agree with me that there is still much uncertainty about how the minds of children work with respect to language acquisition. In making predictions we assume that we already have a very clear picture of the role of the child's cognition in this process. In many cases this might be premature. If predictions do not prove correct that does not necessarily mean that the theory or the acquisition model are incorrect. We might just not have a clear enough picture of the child's role in the acquisition process for making this type of specific predictions. In other words, we are still not quite able to adequately assess the role of learning and the transition from no language knowledge to the ability to structure complex sentences.

The study of cross-language influences in relation to varying linguistic complexities is well suited to contributing to our understanding in this regard because bilingual acquisition situations appear to produce more unusual and un-expected child structures than monolingual acquisition situations tend to do. Thus the similarities, and differences, between monolingual and bilingual children might prove to be of considerable value for language acquisition research in general.

Lastly, there has so far been no clear order as to majority and minority language in the naming of hyphenated acquisition situations in the literature. I have taken the liberty to always place the minority language in front of the language of the country. Where that was not possible, as for example with respect to Canada, I have placed the language spoken in the home before the language of the immediate community outside the home. This may function as an easy reminder to the reader of some gross sociolinguistic features of the children's environments.

The contributions to this volume are loosely ordered by the language combination and the language module they address. The article by **Tracy** opens the discussion by taking the reader through a range of difficulties typical for analysing young bilingual children's production data. She argues that the analytic problems we have with adult bilingual data are even more severe when it comes to analysing young children's speech. Tracy recommends that we compare the bilingual acquisition data with the range of variation found in monolingual children and that we interpret utterances which are clearly motivated by crosslinguistic influences in relation to what the developing language systems in each of the child's languages are capable of at the time. She argues that the superb abilities of the mind to deal with structural ambiguities are responsible for young children being able to integrate conflicting evidence into two discreet language systems. Many of Tracy's threads are picked up by the other contributors to this volume.

Van der Linden compares the behaviour of bilingual adults and children with respect to crosslinguistic influences on lexical choices. From the example of two bilingual French-Dutch speaking children, van der Linden argues that the cognitive interaction we commonly find in the lexicon of bilingual adults is also found in bilingual youngsters. In fact, to expect otherwise would be unreasonable. In rejecting the lexical gap hypothesis, van der Linden makes some interesting suggestions regarding the reasons for variation in the degree of cross-language activation in different children.

Hulk extrapolates the principles of the acquisition and use of the lexicon in the same two French-Dutch bilingual children to their development of syntax. She argues that indirect influences of Dutch on French increase the frequency of those structures in the children's French which superficially overlap with Dutch. It is important to note that this view is very different from the position of one language dominating the other. It reconciles the findings of language-specific development and cross-language influences in an account of "cognitive permeability" between the languages.

The theme of indirect influences of one language on the other is also reflected in the paper by **Döpke** on German-English bilingual children. She draws on the Competition Model in order to explain the cross-language processes which become activated at points of superficial overlap between the structures of the two languages. She argues that contrasts between the languages enable the child to keep the development of the languages separate. However, at points of structural similarities, the cue competition otherwise operative within one language extends across languages. This affects the strength of structural cues within each of the languages and might modify the path of development.

Schelleter looks at unusual negation structures in the English of a German–English bilingual child. She argues that the language contact situation motivated the child to analyse the negation as a substantive rather than a functional category. Thus, like Hulk and Döpke, Schelleter suggests indirect influences on the processing of the language-specific input.

Gawlitzek-Maiwald focuses on infinitival constructions in the development of English-German bilingual children in relation to the children's development of IP and CP. She finds that asynchronous development can be explained as due to systematic differences in the syntactic structures of the two languages. Mixed utterances appear at times when the children restructure their syntactic systems or when one system is significantly ahead of the other in terms of development. Gawlitzek-Maiwald argues that bilingual data help us to reconsider preconceptions about monolingual acquisition and provide arguments in favour of "system thinking", that is, to see the complex relationships between the part and the whole.

Sinka asks whether lack of structural overlap between the two languages a child is acquiring would result in the absence of crosslinguistic structures. Her young subjects are simultaneously exposed to Latvian and English, with Latvian being the syntactically freer and morphologically richer of the two languages. Sinka finds that crosslinguistic influences are, indeed, very rare. When they do occur, they involve syntax rather than morphology, which is congruent with a range of other studies.

Paradis considers the disparate results in her own studies of French-English bilingual children's morpho-syntax on the one hand and their phonological processing on the other. She argues that at points of structural similarities ambiguities may arise for the young child, which in turn may lead to cross-language interaction during the acquisition process. She speculates that various subcomponents of language, like morpho-syntax, lexicon or phonology are affected by cross-language interaction in different ways.

The study by **Gut** on two of the children already reported on by Gawlitzek-Maiwald supports the hypothesis that various modules of language are not affected equally. She finds that her informants show no crosslinguistic influences in the phonological systems of their English and German in spite of a high degree of similarities of the two systems in this respect. Thus ambiguities and similarities may interact with the relative complexity of the system to be acquired.

Lanza provides the concluding remarks to this volume. She reminds us of the sociolinguistic dimension of mixed utterances. This provides an important extension to the largely psycholinguistic perspective taken by the other contributors.

Together the papers in this volume show that crosslinguistic structures have a psycholinguistic basis which is closely connected with the process of acquiring language for the first time. This stresses the similarities between monolingual and bilingual children. At the same time, crosslinguistic structures are features of language production. This unites very young bilinguals with mature bilinguals. These psycholinguistic aspects of cross-language influences are complicated by environmental factors. The papers in this volume pay tribute to this complexity.

Notes

1. Meisel & Müller (1992) and Roeper (1996) argue for the structural connection between underlying and derived positions on the basis of a few exceptional examples in which children have filled both these positions in the same utterance. Wexler (1994) cites a few secondary examples to prove the OI hypothesis for a range of languages. Clahsen (1991) and Déprez (1994) argue that the occasional finite verbs in final position in main clauses provide evidence that Infl occupies a Head–Final position in German.

2. The percentage of raised non-finite verbs in Rohrbacher & Vainikka (1995:490f.) would drastically increase if one excluded ambiguous forms from the calculation. In the case of Poeppel & Wexler (1993:7f.), finite verbs were calculated differently to non-finite verbs for which reason the 14% never appeared in their paper.

3. Hamann (1996:81) reduced the Andreas data on negated infinitives to insignificance by excluding "normal adult" forms from the count.

4. I was not really able to appreciate the extent to which this can be possible until I became the mother of one such child. Because he is growing up bilingually, we were usually able to trace his most advanced sounding utterances back to their sources. Those could be as far as a week apart from him using the structure in his own speech and were at times so cleverly combined with other structures that the outsider would be hard pressed to suspect they were not original.

5. This assumes, of course, that the input which the children received was not mixed. For the contributions to the present volume as well as many other recent studies on childhood bilingualism, this has been the case.

References

Atkinson, Martin. 1996. "Now, hang on a minute. Some reflections on emerging ortho-doxies". In H. Clahsen (ed), *Generative Perspectives on Language Acquisition.* Amsterdam: John Benjamins, 451–485.

Clahsen, Harald. 1991. *Child Language and Developmental Dysphasia.* Amsterdam: John Benjamins.

Clark, Ruth. 1974. "Performing without competence." *Journal of Child Language* 1: 1–10.

Déprez, Viviane. 1994. "Underspecification, functional projections and parameter setting." In B. Lust, M. Suñer & J. Whitman (eds), *Syntactic Theory and First Language Acquisition: Crosslinguistic Perspectives.* Vol. 1: Phrase Structure. Hillsdale, NJ: Lawrence Erlbaum, 249–271.

Hamann, Cornelia. 1996. "Negation and truncated structures". In M. Aldridge (ed), *Child Language.* Clevedon: Multilingual Matters, 72–83.

Harris, Tony & Kenneth Wexler. 1996. "The optional-infinitive stage in child English. Evidence from negation." In H. Clahsen (ed), *Generative Perspectives on Language Acquisition.* Amsterdam: John Benjamins, 1–42.

Meisel, Jürgen M. & Natascha Müller. 1992. "Finiteness and verb placement in early child grammars. Evidence from simultaneous acquisition of French and German in bilinguals". In J. Meisel (ed), *The Acquisition of Verb Placement.* Dordrecht: Kluwer, 109–138.

Poeppel, David & Kenneth Wexler. 1993. "The full competence hypothesis of clause structure in early German". *Language* 69: 1–33.

Radford, Andrew. 1996. "Towards a structure building model of acquisition". In H. Clahsen (ed), *Generative Perspectives on Language Acquisition.* Amsterdam: Benjamins, 43–89.

Roeper, Tom. 1992. "From the initial state to V2: Acquisition principles in action". In J. M. Meisel (ed), *The Acquisition of Verb Placement.* Dordrecht: Kluwer, 333–370.

Roeper, Tom. 1996. "Is bi-lingualism universal? A view from first language acquisition". ms.

Rohrbacher, Bernhard & Anne Vainikka. 1995. "On German verb syntax under age 2". *Proceedings of the 19th Annual Boston University Conference on Language Development* Vol. 2: 487–498.

Speidel, Giesela E. & Keith E. Nelson. eds.1989. *The Many Faces of Imitation in Language Learning.* Springer: New York.

Tracy, Rosemarie. 1995. *Child Languages in Contact: Bilingual Language Acquisition (English–German) in Early Childhood.* Habililitationsschrift, Universität Tübingen.

Wexler, Kenneth. 1994. "Optional infinitives, head movement and the economy of derivation". In D. Lightfoot & N. Hornstein (eds), *Verb Movement.* Cambridge: Cambridge University Press, 305–350.

Language Mixing
as a Challenge for Linguistics

Rosemarie Tracy
University of Mannheim

1. Introduction

This essay invites the reader to take new perspectives on a number of long-standing issues. As a preparatory exercise, consider M.C. Escher's description of his famous woodprint "Day and Night":

> Grey rectangular fields develop upwards into silhouettes of white and black birds; the black ones are flying towards the left and white ones towards the right in two opposing formations. To the left of the picture the white birds flow together and merge to form a daylight sky and landscape. To the right the black birds melt together into night. The day and night landscapes are mirror images of each other, united by means of the grey fields out of which once again the birds emerge.[1]

Like Necker's cube, Rubin's Peter-Paul goblet, and all ambiguous or impossible figures, Escher's art challenges our cognition, as the division of a plane causes potentially endless shifting back and forth of foreground and background properties. Despite clearest lines in wood or on paper, conceptual distinctions become blurred and, as indicated in the quote, they 'merge' and 'melt'. As linguists we have grown familiar with similar fuzzy categories, believing them safely dealt with by theories of logic and semantics. There are, however, other areas where both fuzziness and vacillation between different perspectives catch us off guard. Consider the following examples:

(1) *Va chercher Marc <u>and bribe him</u> avec un chocolat chaud*
    go fetch   ...   with a hot chocolate
    <u>*with cream on top*</u>   (from Grosjean 1982: 145)

(2)   *Nachdem ich mir den hamstring ge-pulled hab*
        after   I   me the ...   pref-   have
        'after I pulled my hamstring muscle'

(3)   *Für heaven(')s Willen!*
        for ...   sake

(4)   *Ich cover mich(-)self up.*   (H. 2;4)
        I   ...   my ...

Examples (1)–(3) were produced by adult bilinguals. Both (1) and (2) allow us
to trace their lexical items to the languages involved in a more or less straightforward fashion. In (1) the speaker switches from French to English to French
and back to English again, with switch sites appearing to coincide with phrasal
boundaries, if we ignore the issue of assigning the proper name *Marc*. In (2), the
situation gets complicated by the fact that an English verb and its complement
(*pull (my) hamstring (muscle)*) surface in a German nonfinite VP[2], exhibiting
various morphological markers required for German, including case and gender
in a definite article and part of a German participle.[3] Example (3) is the fuzziest
of them all. In addition to the blending of German *Um Himmels Willen!* and
English *For heaven's sake!*, the English *for* surfaces in the shape of its German
cognate *für*, which does not figure anywhere in the German idiom. And who
could be sure about the status of the possessive? To make things worse, what we
cannot see from the orthography is that the pronunciation of *Willen* was English.

Cases such as (1) and — with some doubt because of its degree of integration — (2) are usually categorised as intra-sentential codeswitching which allows
the bilingual speaker to construct his or her bi-ethnic and bi-cultural identity. In
contrast, utterances like (3) are often considered to be the result of interference
and hence irrelevant from a sociolinguistic perspective.[4]

The last example of the set, (4), was produced by a bilingual child. Here,
almost every other morpheme jolts us from one language to the other, which
raises the question of whether this particular child really knows two languages or
has instead developed a single, fused system.

This paper focuses on a number of problems that arise in our attempts to
apply our linguistic know-how to the fuzzy nature of mixed utterances. I shall
take my departure from what I consider to be unsolved problems in current
approaches to language mixing in both adults and children and then tackle
selected conceptual and methodological stumbling blocks affecting the reliability
and validity of our studies. Despite these problems, the paper finishes on a decidedly
positive note, highlighting what the study of language mixing has to offer to
linguistic theory and to the familiar odd couple of competence and performance.

2. Perspectives on adult language mixing

Recognition that language mixing is a common feature in conversations among bilinguals has been slow to develop within the linguistic community. Nevertheless sociolinguistic research has eventually led to the appreciation of both the linguistic competence and the skill required for the production of utterances like (1) and (2). Quite a number of researchers have investigated how bilinguals used their two (or more) languages in order to satisfy a variety of socio-symbolic functions and sought to determine what became known as formal, possibly universal, constraints on codeswitching (cf. Pfaff 1979; Poplack 1980; Woolford 1983; Joshi 1985; di Sciullo et al. 1986; Milroy & Muysken 1995). This search for the principles according to which languages alternate or where elements from one language get inserted into the matrix frame of another (cf. Myers-Scotton 1990, 1993) reached a point that led Gardner-Chloros to express the fear that a new orthodoxy would replace the old orthodoxy of monolingual norms, since it aimed at distinguishing skilled codeswitching from "the aberrant manifestations of bilingualism which involve one language influencing another" (1995: 68), such as in (3) above.

As investigators tested various constraints for many language pairs 'in contact', it became increasingly obvious that, while the codeswitching behaviour involved showed similar tendencies regardless of the language pair involved, whatever constrained it was, at the same time, much more tolerant than had been predicted. It was also recognised that except for (arguably) clear cases like (1), distinctions between different types of contact phenomena (alternational and insertional codeswitching, various types of borrowing, interference, etc.) were hard to maintain on theoretical grounds and the dividing line was often empirically impossible to draw. As pointed out by Muysken (1995), in any given situation, more than one type could be involved, as we saw above in (3), with both its blending of idiomatic expressions and the *for/für* translation.

To complicate matters, neither current views on borrowing nor on codeswitching contribute to our understanding of expressions in which the *for/für* type of interaction reaches yet another magnitude. These are cases where, even though most (or all) of the lexical items are drawn from the word stock of one language, the overall format appears to be that of another. Structures like those in (5), an example from a handwritten corpus (cf. Lattey & Tracy in print), are usually considered to be loan translations:

(5)   *für eine car zu parken*
        for a   car to park

To date we still know very little about 'crossover' phenomena of this kind,[5] and a new approach to language-contact should be able to deal with them as well.

As I hope to be able to show, the language mixing that we encounter during the simultaneous acquisition of two languages in early childhood also calls for a wider perspective than existing codeswitching approaches have so far provided.

3.   Children's language mixing

On the one hand, recognition of the need for new perspectives on adult code-switching and the renouncement of deterministic constraints make it harder to answer the question raised by Lanza (1992) as to whether two-year-old children can codeswitch. On the other hand, the good news is that if our current ideas about principles governing adult behaviour lack validity, we need not trouble ourselves with attempts to explain how they could have been acquired.

The study of language mixing in children has received special attention within the larger issue of language differentiation (cf. the overviews in De Houwer 1990 and Lanza 1997). While we cannot rule out the possibility that, depending on the similarities and differences of the languages involved, children start out with a fused system, there is sufficient evidence available to show that bilingual children (implicitly) know that they are acquiring two languages by the time they are two years old. Nevertheless they may still engage in pragmatic and intra-sentential mixing for reasons yet to be discovered. Reseachers have suggested various explanations, arguing in favour of factors such as dominance, access to mixed input, the need to fill gaps by syntactic and lexical borrowing and of competition because of partially overlapping formats (Petersen 1988; Lanza 1992, 1997; Genesee *et al.* 1995; Gawlitzek-Maiwald & Tracy 1996; Tracy 1995, 1996; Döpke 1998; Meisel 1989; Köppe & Meisel 1995; Müller 1998; van der Linden, this vol.).

While many of the mixed utterances produced by children may still lead us to believe that what is going on can be regarded as either alternational or insertional codeswitching, there are other phenomena which reveal much more subtle interactions of the kind referred to as 'crosssover' above, cf. example (6) from the same child, Hannah, who also produced (4). At the time she was 2;8.

(6)   M: you are reading the newspaper, are you?
         C: *don't stör   mich, nicht mich stören,   in English or German.*
               ...   bother me,   not   me   bother, ...

Several structural features suggest that the child indeed knows what she is talking about. First, there are unambiguous negation operators taken from each language; second, there is word order, ie. one of the nonfinite verbs governs to the right, as in English, the other one governs to the left, as required for German; in each case, the negative operator is in its appropriate canonical position to the left of the VP. Furthermore, the verb appears in its appropriate morphological shape: stem for English, stem + *en* for German. Quite obviously, then, the child knows a lot about relevant English-German contrasts, true to her claims. Should we let it bother us too much that the lexicon appears overly flexible? Actually, we probably should, given our current ideas about the division of labour between the syntax and the lexicon, but that is an issue to which I return in a later section.

There is one more point which, I believe, has not received adequate attention so far. There are children who, in spite of bilingual input and their obvious ability to understand both, choose to speak only one of their languages.[6] As investigators dependent on verbally cooperative subjects, we may not be overly happy about this. However, a change of perspective may be called for: what superficially looks like underperformance should be recognised as the result of impressive proactive control which successfully prevents mixing.

4.   Problems of switch detection

Investigators who attempt to identify switch sites should be aware that they are part of a bilingual experiment. I found that in my own coding of phonetically transcribed data from bilingual children, there were about two out of 20–40 mixed utterances per corpus (about 200–400 utterances) which I did not recognise as such at the first go, and these were not just cases with cognates or homophonous diamorphs. While problems of reliability should not be underestimated in any case (cf. Pye *et al.* 1988 for phonetic transcriptions, Howe 1976 for thematic interpretation), the issue takes on a particularly crucial dimension with respect to bilingual data where we are often limited to very small sets of mixed utterances. This failure to pick up relevant distinctions underscores the ease with which our own processor smoothes over potential clashes even in cases where we are preattuned to their existence and are actually looking for them.

Similarly, researchers may fail to notice ambiguities and therefore only consider — and, consequently, count — one of (at least) two possibilities. This is particularly interesting given what we know from experimental studies with adult bilinguals (cf. contributions in Schreuder & Weltens 1993), namely that even when bilinguals are faced with a monolingual task (such as reading a text written in only one of their languages), their 'other' language is never completely turned off, and slight hesitations in reading-aloud experiments correlate significantly with points of lexical ambiguity. The following examples show that consequences of non-detection in our data may be anything but trivial.

By way of illustration consider Redlinger & Park's (1980:345) list of supposed single-noun mixes produced by a German-English bilingual boy, Danny (aged 1;11,22 and 2;8,7) with italics highlighting the relevant items.

(7) *From up in Himmel*
    ...   heaven

(8) *She's in Kirche*
    ...   church

Both (a) and (b) contain an ambiguous preposition *in*, which could belong to either language. Because of the ambiguity of language assignment, we cannot tell whether the switch includes or excludes the preposition. This means that we may just as well be faced with a phrasal mix involving PP. On the basis of similar cases with unambiguous prepositions like *aus* ('out (of)'), we can at least decide whether mixes after and before prepositions are possible *in principle*.

This is not the end of ambiguities yet, since even the copula in (8) could be German. Redlinger & Park (1980:348) cite the following as a case of pronoun substitution in an otherwise English format by the same child, where the same ambiguity with respect to the copula obtains, cf. (9).

(9) *Der   is a monkey*
    that-one ...

The authors do not provide phonetic transcriptions, but even if they had done so, only a voiced [iz] could have provided an unambiguous cue since monolingual English-speaking children are known to use final devoicing (cf. Ingram 1986), otherwise a very distinctive feature of German. So, as the example stands, we might as well be dealing with German as the base language of the sentence. It would be helpful to find out whether Danny already uses any other forms of the copula paradigm in either language. In the ideal case we would find evidence for a few unambiguous cases in one of the languages, such as *die sind müde* or its English equivalent *they are tired,* or various mixes (*die/they are/sind müde/tired*). While this may not help us disambiguate the individual case at hand, *der is a monkey*, it would at least establish where mixing could occur *in principle*.

Whenever languages are very similar this will be a constant problem, aggravated by the fact that the developmental period under discussion is well known for its phonetic and phonological instability. In the contact situation German-English, for example, substitution of the interdental fricative by a stop merges the English article with the neutralised German form [də], which is stripped of its number, case and gender marking. Similarly, English *there* and the German demonstrative *der* ('that one', 3SG) cannot be reliably distinguished. Redlinger & Park's *der* in (9), which they interpret as a German demonstrative, is ambiguous for the same reason. Given these uncertainties, Danny might actually have produced an unmixed, perfectly well-formed English sentence (*there is a monkey*), phonological detail apart.

Lanza (1997) experienced similar difficulties in her study of Norwegian-English bilingual children, with English *that* and *there* hard to distinguish from their Norwegian equivalents. While she mentions that she "excluded from any analysis of language mixing forms for which it was impossible to determine the source language" (p. 106), the appendix shows that almost all occurrences of the deictic in the data of the child Siri were taken to be tokens of Norwegian *der*. The consequence is that in single-word or two-word utterances in conversations with Siri's English-speaking mother, *der* is considered to be an item chosen from the inappropriate language. In many cases (cf. *der* fall, p. 332, *der* boy, p. 333, *der* money, p. 335 etc.) the status of the whole utterance would therefore change quite radically to 'appropriate' language, if what Lanza renders orthographically as *der* turned out to be *there* or a neutral blend.

How should cases of ambiguity be handled, then, provided we detect them in the first place? One safe recommendation would be to assign them to a temporary category of their own, hoping that subsequent syntactic and morphological analyses will confirm one or the other interpretation or open up yet another perspective such as, for instance, hypotheses concerning cross-linguistically merged forms and formats.

5.   In search of the base or matrix language

Researchers have made various proposals for determining which of a bilingual's languages supplies the format for individual utterances (a modern sequel to Weinreich's belief that "each utterance is in a definite language" 1953: 7), none of which are uncontested (cf. Joshi 1985; Myers-Scotton 1990, 1993; Muysken 1995). For adult language mixing, one of the most relevant models is the Matrix Language Frame model by Myers-Scotton, according to which one of the languages makes available the system morphemes (ie. functional categories) and thereby the frame into which elements from the other language can be integrated.

In the case of bilingual children it is typically assumed that the base language can be determined by considering (a) the language requirements of the situation or conversation, in particular the language of the interlocutor, and (b) sentence- or utterance-internal criteria, such as the language of the majority of words or morphemes or the types of categories involved, as in the Matrix Language Frame model.

It is easy to see why investigators adopt the language of conversation criterion as a base-line: It can be extended to single words as well, ie. to cases where the interlocutor says something to which the child reacts with a one-word utterance in the other language. A consequence, however, is that once it comes to multi-word utterances, it is often impossible to tell whether and how consistently investigators distinguish cases of utterance-internal mixing from pragmatically unmotivated language choice.

As an illustration of the criterion 'language of the conversation' let us consider the following utterances from a French-German bilingual boy, Ivar.[7] In (10) the language of the interlocutor is German, hence the base language is considered to be German as well, with *bateau* ('boat') the inserted element. In (11), the interlocutor speaks French (and has just asked *Et c'est quoi?* 'and what's that?'), hence *das* (that) is considered to be the inserted element despite formally equivalent expressions.

> (10)   *das bateau* (pointing)   (2;0,2)

> (11)   *das vache*   (2;4,3)

This means that in (10) a noun, in (11) a pronoun/deictic element would be added to the count of the respective categories. In this case, no harm would be done since both learner varieties (ie. Ivar's German and his French) appear to make equational formats available, and both the open and the closed class would get a boost.

The major problem with the criterion 'language of the conversation' is that children may have an altogether different perspective of what the language of the conversation should be (cf. Meisel 1989; Köppe & Meisel 1995; Köppe 1997; Tracy 1995), a point to which I will return later.

The second criterion, ie. the majority rule, is particularly problematic as long as children's utterances are short (cf. also Veh 1990), which they usually are in the early phases of language acquisition. Obvious problems arise in any of the following cases: if there happens to be the same number of elements from each language, if utterances contain ambiguous parts, or whenever additional aspects (such as word order, functional architecture) threaten to upset the count.

In the case of the examples from Ivar, the majority rule does not help. Let us therefore consider a more complex case. In her case study of an English-and-Dutch-speaking child De Houwer (1990: 90ff.) assigns utterances to categories like *mixed mainly Dutch, mixed mainly English,* and *Dutlish,* depending on the number of morphemes in either language, with Dutlish representing a draw, as in Ivar's (9)–(10).

The following table illustrates the outcome of calculations for a set of three utterances from Hannah at the age of 2;3, who was trying to get her parents to switch on the television set so that she could watch a puppet show, hence *puppet* should be interpreted as a complement of *gucken* (look) (# indicates morpheme boundaries, *-en* = German infinitival suffix, L-category = language category according to De Houwer, s. above).

Table 1

	Example	No. of morphemes		L-category
		English	German	
(12)	Puppet#guck#en	1	2	mixed mainly G
(13)	Puppet#s#guck#en	1 or 2	2 or 3	DRAW or mixed mainly G
(14)	Də # puppet#s #guck#en	1,2 or 3	2,3 or 4	mixed mainly G or mixed mainly E

The right column shows that slight variation in length shifts the result from *mixed mainly German* in (12) to an even distribution in (13), provided the *-s* is taken to represent an English plural. If the plural morpheme comes from German, the majority rule speaks in favour of *mixed mainly German* (3 to 1). Now, consider (14) where we encounter the same problem with respect to plural — *s*. In addition we need to reach a decision concerning the article [də]. As already mentioned above, we know that monolingual English children tend to replace interdental fricatives by alveodental consonants, and we also know that German children start with a neutralised, case- and genderless form of the article (Tracy 1983, 1986). This means that [də] could be either. Faced with a choice, the overall outcome would either be *mixed mainly English* or *mixed mainly German*.

At this point, at the latest, we come to recognise that the counting exercise illustrated above may become quite arbitrary. The ambiguities mentioned cannot be resolved locally, ie. by looking at individual utterances or even utterance-context pairs. Practically any decision concerning the status of individual morphs and morphemes presupposes an analysis of the rest of the child's system(s). With respect to the examples at hand, we would have to determine whether there is any plural or an article in either language in unmixed utterances. As a matter of fact, Hannah uses [də] in otherwise unmixed German and English utterances alike, which means that, with respect to the article, the ambiguity cannot be resolved; but at least we can be certain that both interpretations are justified.

Interestingly, all three utterances by Hannah were produced in a situation in which the language of her interlocutors, her parents, was English. Therefore, if we added the 'language of conversation' criterion we might feel compelled to opt for a solution treating *guck+en* ('look') as the inserted items and English as the base language. All things considered we end up with a case where the criteria mentioned before (language of conversation and morpheme count), are in potential conflict.

Consideration of additional factors might force us to distinguish between the language of the ongoing conversation (English) and the child's perception of the language of the interlocutors. In Hannah's case, there was a shift in language policy from the 'one person-one language' pattern to English as the language of the home when Hannah was about eighteen months old. Could not then the presence of the father, who used to be Hannah's most important source of German, have made German the 'language of the conversation' for (12)–(14), from Hannah's point of view? Fortunately, for Hannah the question of how much the presence of her father tended to influence her language choice can be answered. As our overall corpus shows (cf. the tables in Tracy 1995), Hannah uses just as many German or mixed utterances with her mother when her father is *not* around.

Returning one last time to (12)–(14), we see that the overall syntax with its head-complement order is German. That adds a further criterion to the set considered so far. In Ivar's examples this aspect did not enter the picture because the syntax of French and German does not diverge in this case — assuming unmixed utterances like French *ça bateau* or German *das boot* (both meaning *that (is a) boat*.)[8]

In summary, then, many factors have to be taken into consideration in any attempt to identify the base language. Language of the conversation and majority rule have been widely employed, sometimes with shifts between them. Lanza (1997), for instance, considers a Norwegian item in a conversation with the English-speaking mother and an English item in conversations with the Norwegian-speaking father to be 'mixes' but adopts a different baseline in situations where both parents are present: "In interactions with both parents, the decision will be based on considerations of context and the linguistic composition of the utterance. In other words, in an utterance of three or more words, the main language of the utterance will be considered the one containing more words." (p. 182). What this means, though, is that in conversations with both parents, utterances containing fewer than three morphemes remain ambiguous, unless the addressee can be clearly identified.

What my step-by-step reasoning about the examples in (12)–(14) attempts to show is that whatever criteria we employ, they need not converge in any simple way and may be contradictory. While some of these problems are simply due to the nature of the data, others arise because of methodological inconsistencies. 'Language of the conversation' leaves us completely helpless in situations where parents negotiate a bilingual context along the lines proposed in Lanza (1992, 1997), and application of the majority rule might be a waste of time, first of all because small changes in the morphology lead to radical but arbitrary shifts in language assignment, as in the progression from (12)–(14), and second, because the mixing involved in utterances like (6), *Don't stör mich, nicht mich stören* ('Don't bother me'), would simply be invisible. There is, then, no easy way out of this impasse besides the recommendation to remain open to the idea that Weinreich might have been wrong after all, ie. there may well be utterances without "a definite language" but rich in multiple representations instead. In any case we have to try to avoid what I will here call the *Daisy principle* ('S/he loves me, s/he loves me not') applied to language: English, German, English, German etc. up to an arbitrary last leaf.

6. Problems of categorisation

Problems of identifying the degree to which different languages cooperate in utterance production are easily matched by problems of assignment of lexical or morphological items to various grammatical categories. Following Vihman (1985), many investigators have recognised an early preference for the mixing of functors (closed-class elements) vs. elements from open classes of the lexicon (cf. Veh 1990; Köppe & Meisel 1995; Lanza 1997). When we look at the way in which individual researchers have assigned elements to various form classes, we see considerable inconsistencies, which once more makes it hard to compare results. Lindholm & Padilla (1978: 31), for instance, count *maybe* as a conjunction, alongside coordinating conjunctions and complementisers like Spanish *porque* ('because'), and Lanza (1997: 216) counts *down* as a grammatical morpheme.

Redlinger & Park (1980: 347) claim that in their data adverbial expressions are frequently mixed, quoting cases such as *da big truck* from Danny in (15), with German *da* ('there') assumed to be the mixed element in a conversation with an English-speaking interlocutor. However, if we look at further examples (also from Danny, p. 347) we find that *da* has been analysed (and counted) as a pronoun ('that') as well; cf. (16).

(15)   <u>da</u> *big truck*   translated as 'there'   (1;11–2;0)

(16)   <u>da</u> *too big*   translated as 'that'   (1;11–2;0)

Sometimes miscategorisation on part of the child is a possibility as well. In Gawlitzek *et al.* (1992) we present data from a monolingual German-speaking child who consistently and for many months uses the preposition *wegen* ('because-of') as a subordinating conjunction, which is not an option in the adult target.

Having myself underscored the function of *da* as a convenient placeholder in the utterances of German children (Tracy 1991, 1995), I have no objection against its potentially dual role in the case mentioned by Redlinger & Park. However, any classification needs to be justified on distributional grounds, which requires a detailed analysis of the overall system(s) available to the child at the time.

7.   Directionality of mixing: dominance, asymmetry, asynchrony?

The issue of dominance of one language over another has received a lot of attention in bilingualism research (cf. the overview in Romaine 1989, Grosjean 1982). From a linguistic point of view it is a problematic concept, since too many factors may interact and get confounded: from degree of proficiency to amount of opportunity to speak both languages to personal preference, to list but a few.

In acquisition research, the issue is often related to what has been called 'directionality of mixing' (cf. Petersen 1988; Schlyter 1993; Lanza 1992, 1997), which has to some extent already been implicit in the section above on the determination of the matrix language. What warrants separate treatment here is the fact that the matrix language could in principle be locally reset for each utterance while dominance suggests some more principled imbalance apart from individual utterances.

In order to compensate for problems of comparability of the calculations on which previous investigators based their assessment, Genesee *et al.* (1995) suggest taking into account four dominance indices: MLU (mean length of utterance) and UPPER BOUND (ie. MLU of longest utterance) for each language, percentages of multi-morphemic utterances and word types. Taken together they yield a more comprehensive assessment of potential asymmetries between the child's systems. While this is certainly an important step towards an improvement in standards, I will briefly address two conceptual fallacies which must be dealt with before any calculations can be made. The first threatens whenever we fail to take into consideration the nature of contrasts between the two target languages. The second arises from potential developmental asynchronies, a point related to what was said above about the need to determine which categories and structural formats a child has available.

Asymmetries in the formal inventories of the languages involved may tip our calculations in undesirable ways. This can easily happen when we compare German and English. If we granted individual 'bonus' points for each overt case, gender and number feature, the bilingual adult who produced (2), *den hamstring gepulled*, would end up with a German score which English could simply never match.

In addition to typological contrasts, there is the critical issue of developmental asynchrony. Because of the frequency with which Norwegian grammatical morphology and other closed classes appeared in the utterances of the child Siri, Lanza (1992, 1997) concluded that Norwegian was her dominant language. At the same time, however, Lanza also points out that English lagged behind Norwegian in several areas of the grammar involving exactly the same elements, ie. pronouns, auxiliaries, negation, etc. (cf. Lanza 1997: 157, 167, 169, 174 etc.). Her observation of this temporary asynchrony makes it impossible to separate dominance from unequal mastery. The issue could, potentially at least, be decided by checking what happens after Siri's English has had a chance to catch up.

Similar problems arise with respect to Redlinger & Park's (1980: 345) claim that nouns and adverbs are mixed more often than prepositions and conjunctions. Without information about the overall frequency of occurrence of these items in mixed and unmixed utterances alike, we are unable to say whether prepositions or conjunctions are just not likely to be mixed or whether they are still unavailable at this point. Given what we know about the development of these items in monolinguals, the latter is highly probable.

In Gawlitzek-Maiwald & Tracy (1996), Gawlitzek-Maiwald (1997), and Tracy (1995, 1996) we dealt with similar asynchronies. The contributions of German and English to the mixing observed in Hannah, for instance, could be traced to the respective developmental stages in the two systems. Hannah produced utterances with German auxiliaries, modals and generally inflected verbs as in (17)–(19) alongside simple, untensed English VPs several months earlier than (20). From this and related patterns (for instance the initial absence of the infinitival particle *to*) we concluded that Hannah's English needed more time to build layers of structure on top of the VP. This, however, did not stop her from pooling her resources.

(17)   *ich hab   ge-<u>climbed</u> up*   (2;4)
         I   have prefix- ...

(18)   *soll   ich <u>hit it</u>?*   (2;6)
         shall I   ...

(19)   *mama kannst du   <u>do it up</u>*   (2;8)
         ... can   you ...

(20)   *he should <u>warten</u> for us*   (2;10)
         ...   wait   ...

Faced with contrasts between languages — such as richer vs. poorer morphology, more vs. less restricted word order — bilingual children do not automatically go for the 'cheaper' solution. This becomes clear from the different studies that have produced evidence for developmental asynchronies.

8.   Monolingual and bilingual fictions

For a long time, researchers in bilingualism had it easy. Whenever expressions departed from monolingual standards, this could be blamed on transfer from the other language or, if no direct transfer seemed possible, on general confusion. Results from various studies looking into intra- and interindividual variation in monolingual language acquisition show that this conclusion may not be warranted (cf. Fritzenschaft *et al.* 1990; Gawlitzek-Maiwald *et al.* 1992; d'Avis & Gretsch 1994; Hohenberger 1996). The fact that there are monolingual German-speaking children who produce deviant subordinate clauses (with the verb not in the required final position), which look superficially very much like imports from SVO languages, suggests that other factors than direct cross-linguistic transfer have to be considered in our attempts to explain deviant patterns in the subordinate clauses of German-speaking bilinguals as well. As has been claimed by Müller (1998), transfer could still play a role in a more indirect fashion, as when ambiguities within one system (German) are resolved by taking recourse to a structural option made available in the other. Other researchers have also drawn attention to patterns which could have arisen on the basis of partial overlapping of the bilinguals' languages (cf. Döpke 1998; Hulk this vol.).

   In her 1998 study of bilingual children growing up with German and English in Australia, Döpke found sentences with lexical items drawn from German whose syntax, however, is reminiscent of the 'crossover' phenomena mentioned before, in which the overt string looks very much like a relexified version of an underlying pattern from the other language. In many cases these involved negative (*nicht*, 'not') and adverbial particles (*auch*, 'too/as well') and resulted in sentential formats in which the German finite verb was 'pushed' out of its second position in main clauses, cf. (21) from Döpke (1998: 569).

(21)   *und dies   auch schreibt rot*   (JH-G2;5)
       and this-one also   writes   red

On the basis of recent investigations of the acquisition of focus and negative particles, we know that patterns such as (21) are also produced by the monolingual child. Penner, Tracy & Weissenborn (in print) and Penner, Tracy & Wyman (1999) attempt to explain why sentences with *auch* ('also/too') and the negator *nicht* exhibit peculiarities, including the verb's resistance to being raised to the left, ie. to the V2 position of the German main clause, cf. the following examples. For some children, all attested early multiword utterances with *auch* were deviant.[9]

(22)   *Papa   geht arbeiten*
       Daddy goes (to) work
       Nina AUCH geht arbeiten.
       N.   also   goes (to) work   (Julia 1;11)

(23)   *das auch weint*   (Julia 1;11)
       that also cries

(24)   *dies auch passt*   (Florian 2;8)
       this also fits

(25)   *dies nicht passt*   (Florian 2;8)
       this not   fits
       'this one doesn't fit'

The fact that we cannot appeal to influence from other languages in these cases suggests that transfer and overlap may not be the only factors to consider in the case of the bilinguals either. It would certainly be interesting to find out whether bilingual children need more time to correct misanalyses. Ivar's extended struggle with German subordinate clauses led Müller (1993, 1998) to suggest that he worked out the word order of German subordinate clauses in an item-by-item fashion for each complementiser.

As a last parallel between monolingual and bilingual development to be addressed here, consider Redlinger & Park's (1980: 349) "[...] duplication of items first in one language and then in the other", cf. (26)–(27).

(26)   *I put it das up.*   (Danny, p. 350)
       ...   it   ...

(27)   *Il fait   macht die Wasser*   (Henrik, p. 350)
       he makes makes the water

Given the adjacency of the doubled items, these examples may simply result
from lexical competition. Hannah also produced structures as in (28)–(31), which
look like attempted compromise solutions.

(28)   *mama hat das fix it*   (2;3)
       mama has that ...

(29)   *ich habe die tortoise throw it away*   (2;3)
       I   have the ...

(30)   *du mußt es hol it*   (2;6)
       you must it get ...

(31)   *du mußt das nicht wipe my face*   (2;6)
       you must that not   ...
       'you mustn't wipe my face'

Patterns like these, which have also been documented by other researchers (cf.
already Leopold 1949), appear to blend features of both German and English
VPs, with the result that at least superficially the verb is no longer at the left or
right periphery of its projection.
       Except for the lexical mixing, reduplications are also attested in the speech
of monolinguals, cf. (32)–(34) which were produced by monolingual children
between the ages of two and three (from Tracy 1989).

(32)   *das$_i$ mach ich' s$_i$ auch*
       that make I   it also
       'I'll also make that one'

(33)   *die ham$_i$ das schön gemacht hatten$_i$*
       they have that nicely made   had
       'they did that nicely'

(34)   *julia$_i$ brauch ich$_i$ das*
       julia need   I   that
       'I need that'

At first sight it is difficult to decide whether these are *nonce* blends or whether
they arise on the basis of a temporarily overgenerating syntax, where several
coexisting, abstractly available positions are simultaneously filled. In Tracy
(1989), I entertained the latter interpretation because some patterns were
restricted to specific developmental phases. In addition, it was shown that learners

seemed to develop preferences for one or the other type of structure.

Reduplication as such is therefore by no means a privilege of the bilingual. We should welcome its occurrence since it informs us about what is simultaneously active (as in slips of the tongue) and therefore also about an initial lack of effective proactive controls that could intercept these blends before they reach the point of articulation. They also help us recognise domains in which the learner may actually attempt to reconstruct a common underlying schema. In the case of the monolingual examples the overt version is a faithful reflection of the complete underlying potential. In the bilingual blend of German and English VPs, however, real system convergence should be prevented by the crucial German-English contrast in head directionality. It is for this reason that I favour an analysis in which the English verb and the complement that follows are reanalysed as a complex verb, an option which also suggests itself for cases like (35), where adjacency requirements between the English verb and its complement would otherwise be violated.

(35)   *Papa,   kannst du*   [$_V$ *move a bit*] *your feet away.*
       Daddy, can   you   …

Given what we know today about the extent of intra-individual variation in the monolingual, it should be only a small step to abandoning the belief that monolingual children limit themselves to only one coherent, unitary system. Any child who has available different and (temporarily) unrelated structural formats which may also be tied to different functional contexts and to different interactional routines is, *de facto*, 'bilingual'. Children acquiring German could then be seen as developing one grammar for productive verb-end formats (*Mama bus fahrn*, 'mummy bus ride'), while other expressions cluster around some V2-prototype (initially mainly formulae like [*dazə*] *ball*, 'there-s-the ball'). Once the same verbs appear in both patterns, and especially when both verb positions are filled simultaneously, we can conclude that the learner has managed to (re-)construct an underlying representation in which his or her original grammars can be derivationally linked within a new grammatical system (cf. Tracy 1991, 1995 for proposals concerning the mechanisms involved).

This suggests that young monolinguals initially behave very much like 'ideal' bilinguals (or, rather, multilinguals). Instead of trying to explain why a child with dual input comes to have *two* systems, we might then ask how a (supposedly) monolingual but (in effect) multilingual child comes to reanalyse and restructure his or her independent subsystems to a point where they can be integrated on increasingly abstract levels of representation. According to this view, initial fusion or non-differentiation of languages (as proposed by Volterra

& Taeschner 1978; Taeschner 1983) would not be an option open to the learner. What distinguishes the 'traditional' bilingual from this conceptualisation of the multi-system monolingual is that somewhere throughout the individual's development potential convergence should be blocked, as in the case involving both a Head-Initial (English) and a Head-Final VP (German) mentioned above.

9. Multiple representations, coactivation and coproduction

As linguists we are used to describing utterances on many coexisting levels of representation, and in on-line speech production and perception intensive coactivation and competition appear to be the norm, not the exception (cf. Frauenfelder & Tyler 1987; Garman 1990; Levelt 1989; Schreuder & Weltens 1993; Grosjean & Soares 1986; Grosjean 1995). Our cognitive system is superbly capable of dealing with many simultaneously accessible representations, and often — as in the successful recognition of irony or the interpretation of metaphor — it is the conflict between different representations which points to the actual message. Even under ordinary circumstances spontaneous reanalyses lead to the recognition of ambiguity, as in our linguistic standard examples like "the man with a wooden leg named X" and the "terrible shooting of the hunters." Bilingualism and, with it, language contact phenomena contribute further to our understanding of the scope of our ability to perform more than one task at a time.

The language mixing under discussion here implies that at some point during encoding two (or more) languages are activated in parallel. At least two candidate utterances (or, rather, fragments thereof with representations on various levels) arise *in tandem*, and there may be many more, including further alternatives from within each language. All of these might be part of a whole cohort of candidates made available by the speaker's *Formulator* (cf. Levelt's 1989). In the case of the bilingual no setting of switches need be involved. Eventually some candidates will be inhibited while others (regardless of language) are kept on and are eventually 'coproduced' within a single utterance. While our knowledge of what exactly increases or inhibits the activation of various candidates is still limited, we know more about what happens afterwards. Based on slips of the tongue and other production phenomena, psycholinguistic research with monolinguals has produced ample evidence for mechanisms which proactively repair on-line problems especially via lexical control and other phonological or morphological adjustments (cf. Levelt 1989). Yet, as long as we restrict ourselves to the study of competition in monolingual speech production, we may underestimate the extent of pre-articulatory patching and repair involved for the simple reason that potential conflicts and contrasts between options considered by the speaker are less visible than in bilingual language mixing.

Utterances exhibiting cross-linguistic features therefore offer excellent opportunities for increasing our understanding of coactivation and coproduction in general. Ideally, what we currently conceive of as different types of contact phenomena (involving various degrees of integration in borrowing, alternational and insertional codeswitching and interference) will eventually become related to different stages of the overall encoding process. 'Crossover' phenomena (ie. loan translations) may turn out to be particularly telling: since they most flagrantly violate the grammar of one language (as in *für eine car zu parken* in example (5)), they must have successfully circumvented it in the first place and should owe their existence to late relexification.

There may not even be any need for appealing to extra constraints on codeswitching. Again, what we perceive as tendencies to maintain formal equivalence in language mixing (cf. Poplack 1980; Muysken 1995) could result from the fact that coactivated parallel formats strengthen each other more than divergent patterns, regardless of which language wins out in the end. More importantly, perhaps: equivalence should help avoid disruptions which one's own control system finds it hard to cope with. This could make the equivalence constraint more useful as a constraint on performance than on competence.

It is important to realise that nothing which has been said so far belittles the job left to the grammatical knowledge systems available to the speaker. Grammars, to be of any use at all, must be conservative (as in the case of the direction of verbal head government mentioned above), and it is the very clash between different formats (ie. VO *vs.* OV) that teaches the child that he or she is acquiring two languages in the first place. Nevertheless, we should also consider the possibility of there being additional cognitive levels of abstraction where requirements of individual grammars can be more or less playfully suspended, possibly not unlike what we, as linguists, do all the time when we (voluntarily, to be sure) create ungrammatical examples.

Over the past several years our conception of what a 'grammar' might look like has changed in a direction which has proved highly fruitful for acquisition research. This is particularly true for generative grammar (cf. Chomsky 1981, 1995), with X-bar theory deriving structural formats from a single prototype and highly restricted procedures ensuring structure-building (by merging) and the elimination of non-converging representations (by feature checking). In addition, parameter theory has significantly contributed to our understanding of the critical dimensions along which natural languages may be seen to contrast, and it has thereby offered us a clearer vision of the search space available to the learner.

Given a theoretical approach, then, for which cross-linguistic similarities and differences are of utmost theoretical relevance, it is quite surprising that the question of how bilinguals deal with potential conflicts and forced choice has not received more attention. It is to be hoped, then, that both linguistics and psycholinguistics will recognise what they stand to gain from the evidence bilingual adults and children have to offer.

10. Conclusion

As in the initial quote from Escher, this paper has dealt with two opposing formations and various continua. In his case rectangular fields turn into birds, white birds merge into daylight, black birds melt into night. In our case, the conceptual pull in two opposing directions has come from two languages, the grey areas being domains which resisted assignment to any definite language (in the sense of Weinreich) or to any unambiguous category of language mixing (such as different types of borrowing, codeswitching and interference). Stretching the analogy a bit, we could even catch a reflection of Escher's "mirror image" in the binary opposition of the Head-Parameter, with German nonfinite verbal heads governing to the left, English heads governing to the right.

Bilingual children (implicitly) know very early what dealing with the opposing formations entails: Within the limits of their grammars *en route* to adult competence they know what it takes to make individual expressions look more like night or day, as we saw in *Don't stör mich, nicht mich stören* in (6) above. Sometimes they appear to go through considerable trouble in their attempt at getting it right, as in the following utterances from an episode in which Hannah, aged 2;3, tried to secure her mother's help in strapping her doll into her buggy (\ signals falling intonation).

(36)   a.   die dolly [ənstræpən] \
       b.   die dolly [əntræp] \
       c.   dəs eins-[stra:p i:n] die puppe\
       d.   die ein-[stra:p i:n] die dolly\
       e.   die mama helf mir [tap] it [i:n] \
       f.   mama (= voc.) [tʰap] it [i:n]\ die dolly\

The child starts with what looks like a German VP, (a)–(b), with the verb in the latter case already on its morphological way to an English infinitive, the form required for the English constructions with which she ends up in (e) and (f). In (c) and (d) we witness some blending of both German and English with respect to syntax and morphology. Throughout, the long vowel of *in* appears to retain phonological properties of the separable German particle *ein* (including stress).

Note that *strap* is not a verbal stem in German, but this is an accidental, not a systematic gap. Also, in this particular instance, there is no other equivalent German expression with the separable prefix *ein*. The most idiomatic translation for the set (a)–(f) into German would require *anschnallen* (or *festschnallen*), and actually, for all we know, the *an* might well be on its way in the 'grey', ambiguous onset of the first syllable of the verb in (a) and (b). On top of the contrast involving the positioning of the verb with respect to its complement (OV *vs.* VO) and the contrasting morphological design of an English *vs.* a German infinitive (stem+Ø *vs.* stem+*en*) there is, then, from the child's perspective, an additional conflict involving a (virtual) German particle verb (*einstrappen*) and an English phrasal verb (*strap in*). The overall groping pattern shows two things: uncertainty about the homebase of the verb and, nevertheless, expertise in conjuring up the contexts appropriate to both languages, with the blends in (c) and (d) offering us a particularly good glance at on-line competition and conflict resolution. This resolution, however, is not a permanent option for the child's grammars, which can contain only VO *or* OV.

It is impressive how early bilingual children become experts at handling what they perceive to be crucial design features of each language. If, as we believe, children know that all languages are instantiations of one and the same universal prototype anyway, the care they take spelling out the contrasts is even more remarkable.

Acknowledgments

The bilingual acquisition data were collected in projects supported by the "Deutsche Forschungs-gemeinschaft" (DFG Grants Tr. 238/1 and 2).

Notes

1. From Escher, M. C. (1975). *The Graphic Work of M. C. Escher*. New York: Ballantine Books, p. 11.
2. Comparable with the Panjabi-English mixes involving 'helping' verbs discussed in Romaine (1989).
3. The speaker, a linguist, reports having been at a loss for the German equivalent for *hamstring muscle* and was very much surprised about *pull* coming along; the participle ended in an English, ie. voiced, suffix.

4. Reference to *mixing* as a cover term is sensible in a field where terminological problems more or less directly reflect serious conceptual trouble.

5. A metaphor borrowed from the domain of music denoting the reappearance of a piece in a new genre.

6. It is clear that this kind of passive bilingualism needs to be tested experimentally. In some cases it is possible to find out why children choose not to produce one of their input languages. In our Tübingen project one child whose parents had chosen a liberal *one person-one language* schedule (liberal in the sense that the child experienced his American mother, who addressed him mainly, but not exclusively, in English, as a competent speaker of German as well) could only be moved to speak English when he engaged in role play and had to take the part of a female doll. In his environment only women spoke English, including our project member, who did the taping and also became his babysitter, and his visiting grandmother, who spoke nothing else. Several researchers have mentioned hypotheses entertained by children about who talks what. Leopold (1949: 59) reports that his daughter Hildegard (4;1–2) asked: "Mother, do all fathers speak German?".

7. Ivar took part in the Hamburg DUFDE study. The examples were taken from Veh's MA thesis (1990: Appendix pp. 5,18; her ref. I51 and I258).

8. There is an alternative interpretation for this German expression as an NP fragment, translatable as *the boat*.

9. Early sentences with *auch* verbs tended to be nonfinite or missing a verb altogether, cf. Penner et al. (1999, 2000).

References

Chomsky, Noam. 1981. *Lectures on Government and Binding*. Dordrecht: Foris.

Chomsky, Noam. 1995. *The Minimalist Program*. Cambridge Cambridge, MA: MIT Press.

D'Avis, Franz & Petra Gretsch. 1994. "Variations on 'variation': on the acquisition of complementizers in German". In R. Tracy & E. Lattey (eds), *How Tolerant is Universal Grammar? Essays on Language Learnability and Language Variation*. Tübingen: Narr, 59–109.

De Houwer, Annick. 1990. *The Acquisition of Two Languages from Birth: A Case Study*. Cambridge: Cambridge University Press.

DiSciullo, Anne-Marie, Pieter Muysken, & Rajendra Singh. 1988. "Government & code-mixing". *Linguistics* 22: 1–24.

Döpke, Susanne. 1998. "Competing language structures: the acquisition of verb placement by bilingual German-English children". *Journal of Child Language* 25(3):555–584.

Frauenfelder, Uli & Lorraine Tyler. (eds) 1987. *Spoken Word Recognition*. Cambridge, MA: MIT Press.

Fritzenschaft, Agnes, Ira Gawlitzek-Maiwald, Rosemarie Tracy & Susanne Winkler. 1990. "Wege zur komplexen Syntax". *Zeitschrift für Sprachwissenschaft* 9: 52–134.

Gardner-Chloros, Penelope. 1995. "Codeswitching in community, regional and national repertoires: the myth of the discreteness of linguistics systems." In L. Milroy & P.

Muysken (eds), *One Speaker, Two Languages: Cross-Disciplinary Perspectives on Codeswitching*. Cambridge: Cambridge University Press, 68–89.

Garman, Michael. 1990. *Psycholinguistics*. Cambridge: Cambridge University Press.

Gawlitzek-Maiwald, Ira. 1997. *Der monolinguale und bilinguale Erwerb von Infinitivkonstruktionen*. (Linguistische Arbeiten 370) Tübingen: Niemeyer.

Gawlitzek-Maiwald, Ira, Rosemarie Tracy & Agnes Fritzenschaft. 1992. "Language acquisition and competing linguistic representations: the child as arbiter". In J. M. Meisel (ed.), *The Acquisition of Verb Placement: Functional Categories and V2 Phenomena in Language Development*. Dordrecht: Kluwer, 139–179.

Gawlitzek-Maiwald, Ira & Rosemarie Tracy. 1996. "Bilingual bootstrapping". In N. Müller (ed), *Two Languages. Studies in Bilingual First and Second Language Development*. Special Issue of *Linguistics* 34(5): 901–926.

Genesee, Fred. 1989. "Early bilingual development: one language or two?" *Journal of Child Language* 16: 161–179.

Genesee, Fred, Elena Nicoladis, & Johanne Paradis. 1995. "Language differentiation in early bilingual development". *Journal of Child Language* 22: 611–631.

Grosjean, François. 1982. *Life with Two Languages: An Introduction to Bilingualism*. Cambridge, MA: Harvard University Press.

Grosjean, François. 1995. "A psycholinguistic approach to codeswitching: the recognition of guest words by bilinguals". In L. Milroy & P. Muysken (eds), *One Speaker, Two Languages: Cross-Disciplinary Perspectives on Codeswitching*. Cambridge: Cambridge University Press, 177–198.

Grosjean, François & C. Soares. 1986. "Processing mixed language: some preliminary findings". In J. Vaid (ed), *Language Processing in Bilinguals,* Hillsdale, NJ: Lawrence Erlbaum, 145–179.

Hoffmann, Charlotte. 1991. *An Introduction to Bilingualism*. London: Longman.

Hohenberger, Annette. 1996. *Functional Categories and Language Acquisition: Self-Organization of a Dynamic System*. PhD University of Frankfurt; to appear in Tübingen: Narr.

Howe, Christine. 1976. "The meaning of two-word utterances in the speech of young children". *Journal of Child Language* 3: 29–47.

Ingram, David. 1986. "Phonological Development". In P. Fletcher & M. Garman (eds), *Language Acquisition*. Cambridge: Cambridge University Press, 223–239.

Joshi, A. K. 1985. "Processing of sentences with intra-sentential codeswitching". In D. Dowty, L. Kartunen & A. Zwicky (eds), *Natural Language Processing: Psychological, Computational and Theoretical Perspectives*. Cambridge: Cambridge University Press.

Köppe, Regina, 1997. *Sprachentrennung im frühen bilingualen Erstspracherwerb Französisch/Deutsch*. Tübingen: Narr.

Köppe, Regina & Jürgen M. Meisel. 1995. "Codeswitching in bilingual first language acquisition". In L. Milroy & P. Muysken (eds), *One speaker, Two Languages*. Cambridge: Cambridge University Press, 276–301.

Lanza, Elisabeth. 1992. "Can biligual two-year-olds codeswitch?" *Journal of Child Language* 19: 633–658.

Lanza, Elizabeth. 1997. *Language Mixing in Infant Bilingualism. A Sociolinguistic Perspective*. Oxford: Clarendon Press.

Lattey, Elsa & Rosemarie Tracy. In print. "Language contact (English-German) in the individual: a case study based on letters from a German immigrant to the Northeastern United States". In S. Ureland (ed), *Language Contact in North America — Migration, Maintenance, and Death of the European Languages*. Tübingen: Niemeyer.

Leopold, Werner. 1949. *Speech Development of a Bilingual Child: A Linguist's Record*. 4 vols. New York: AMS Press.

Levelt, Willem. 1989. *Speaking: From Intention to Articulation*. Cambridge, MA: MIT Press.

Lindholm, Kathryn & Amado Padilla. 1978. "Child bilingualism: report on language mixing, switching and translations". *Linguistics* 211: 23–44.

Meisel, Jürgen M. 1989. "Early differentiation of languages in bilingual children." In K. Hyltenstam & L. Obler (eds), *Bilingualism Across the Lifespan: Aspects of Acquisition, Maturity and Loss*. Cambridge: Cambridge University Press.

Milroy, Lesley & Pieter Muysken. (eds) 1995. *One Speaker, Two Languages: Cross-Disciplinary Perspectives on Codeswitching*. Cambridge: Cambridge University Press.

Müller, Natascha. 1993. *Komplexe Sätze. Der Erwerb von COMP und von Wortstellungsmustern bei bilingualen Kindern (Französisch-Deutsch)*. Tübingen: Narr.

Müller, Natascha. 1998. "Transfer in bilingual first language acquisition". *Bilingualism. Language and Cognition* 1: 151–171.

Muysken, Pieter. 1995. "Codeswitching and grammatical theory". In L. Milroy & P. Muysken (eds), *One speaker, Two Languages*. Cambridge: Cambridge University Press, 177–198.

Muysken, Pieter & René Appel. 1987. *Language Contact and Bilingualism*. London: Arnold.

Myers-Scotton, Carol. 1990. "Codeswitching and borrowing: interpersonal and macrolevel meaning". In R. Jacobson (ed), *Codeswitching as a Worldwide Phenomenon*. New York: Lang, 85–110.

Myers-Scotton, Carol. 1993. *Duelling Languages: Grammatical Structure in Codeswitching*. Oxford: Clarendon Press.

Penner, Zvi, Rosemarie Tracy, & Karen Wymann. 1999. "Die Rolle der Fokuspartikel *auch* im frühen kindlichen Lexikon: eine Studie zum Erwerb des Deutschen im Vergleich mit dem doppelten Erstspracherwerb Deutsch-Englisch und dem verspäteten Sprechbeginn". In J. Meibauer & M. Rothweiler (eds), *Das Lexikon im Spracherwerb*. Tübingen: Francke, UTB, 229–251.

Penner, Zvi, Rosemarie Tracy, & Jürgen Weissenborn. 2000. "Where scrambling begins: triggering object scrambling in early language acquisition". In C. Hamann & S. Powers (eds), *The Berne Volume: Papers from the Workshop on L1-L2 Acquisition of Clause-Internal Rules, Scrambling, and Clitization*. Dordrecht: Kluwer, 127–164.

Petersen, Jennifer. 1988. "Word-internal codeswitching constraints in a bilingual child's grammar". *Linguistics* 26: 479–493.

Pfaff, Carol. 1979. "Constraints on language mixing: intrasentential codeswitching and borrowing in Spanish-English". *Language* 55: 291–318.

Poplack, Shana. 1980. "Sometimes I'll start a sentence in Spanish y termino en Español". *Linguistics* 18: 581–618.

Pye, Clifton, Kim Wilcox, & Kathleen Siren. 1988. "Refining transcriptions: the significance of transcribers' errors". *Journal of Child Language* 15: 17–37.

Redlinger, Wendy E. & Tschang-Zin Park. 1980. "Language mixing in young bilinguals". *Journal of Child Language* 3: 449–455.

Romaine, Suzanne. 1989. *Bilingualism*. Oxford: Basil Blackwell.

Schlyter, Susanne. 1993. "The weaker language in bilingual Swedish-French children." In K. Hyltenstam & Å. Viberg (eds), *Progression and Regression in Language*. Cambridge: Cambridge University Press, 289–308.

Schreuder, Rob & Bert Weltens. (eds) 1993. *The Bilingual Lexicon*. Amsterdam: John Benjamins.

Taeschner, Traute. 1983. *The Sun is Feminine: A Study on Language Acquisition in Bilingual Children*. Berlin: Springer.

Tracy, Rosemarie. 1983. "Cognitive processes and the acquisition of deixis". In G. Rauh (ed), *Essays on Deixis*. Tübingen: Narr, 99–148.

Tracy, Rosemarie. 1986. "The acquisition of case morphology in German". *Linguistics* 24: 47–78.

Tracy, Rosemarie. 1987. "The acquisition of verb placement". In P. Griffith, J. Local, & A. Mills (eds), *Proceedings of the Child Language Seminar*. York: University of York, 81–94.

Tracy, Rosemarie. 1989. "Projektionsprobleme". *Zeitschrift für Literaturwissenschaft und Linguistik* 19: 75–113.

Tracy, Rosemarie. 1991. *Sprachliche Strukturentwicklung: Linguistische und kognitionspsychologische Aspekte einer Theorie des Erstspracherwerbs*. Tübingen: Narr.

Tracy, Rosemarie. 1994. "Raising questions: formal and functional aspects of the acquisition of *wh*-questions in German". In R. Tracy & Elsa Lattey (eds), *How Tolerant is Universal Grammar? Essays on Language Learnability and Language Variation*. (Linguistische Arbeiten 281) Tübingen: Niemeyer, 1–34.

Tracy, Rosemarie. 1995. *Child Languages in Contact: The Simultaneous Acquisition of Two Languages (English-German) in Early Childhood*. Habilitationsschrift University of Tübingen.

Tracy, Rosemarie. 1996. "Vom Ganzen und seinen Teilen: Fallstudien zum doppelten Erstspracherwerb". *Sprache und Kognition* 15 (1–2): 70–92.

Veh, Brigitta. 1990. "Syntaktische Aspekte des Codeswitching bei bilingualen Kindern (Französisch-Deutsch) im Vorschulalter", MA thesis, University of Hamburg.

Vihman, Marilyn M. 1985. "Language differentiation by the bilingual infant. *Journal of Child Language* 12: 297–324.

Volterra, Virginia & Traute Taeschner. 1978. "The acquisition and development of language by bilingual children". *Journal of Child Language* 5: 311–326.

Weinreich, Uriel. 1953. *Languages in Contact: Findings and Problems*. 1968 Edition: The
    Hague: Mouton de Gruyter.
Woolford, Ellen. 1983. "Bilingual codeswitching and synctactic theory". *Linguistic
    Inquiry* 14(3): 520–536.

Non-Selective Access and Activation in Child Bilingualism

The Lexicon

Elisabeth van der Linden
University of Amsterdam / IFOTT

1. Introduction

In this chapter, I investigate some phenomena of non-selective access and activation, resulting in crosslinguistic influence in the utterances of Anouk, a French-Dutch bilingual child growing up in the Netherlands. Crosslinguistic phenomena have been described by others for bilingual children in different kinds of language pairs. Several researchers have reported on the use of words or constructions in one language from the other. As a matter of fact, the phenomenon is not limited to child language but is also encountered in adult bilinguals. It is then often discussed as an example of 'code switching' or 'transfer'.

While psycholinguistic studies on bilingualism have been focusing on lexical acquisition and the interaction between languages in the lexicon, the acquisition of syntax has been the main concern for linguists. The mutual interaction between these two approaches has been limited. And yet, although their methods may differ, they converge on one of their central questions, namely the nature of the relationship between the two developing languages of bilingual subjects in the course of the acquisition process. One of the main objectives at the lexical as well as the syntactic level has been to find out if the two language systems are stored separately or together and what the effects are of the simultaneous acquisition of two languages in the bilingual brain.

In the utterances of our French-Dutch bilingual subject, we find examples of mixing at the lexical as well as the syntactic level. In this chapter, I will concentrate on the lexical development. I will show that the existence of lexical mixing does not necessarily mean that the child is unable to differentiate between the two languages, but rather that crosslinguistic influence plays a role in bilingual first language acquisition.

The paper is organised as follows: in section one, I discuss what is known about the interaction between languages at the lexical level in bilingual adults. In section two, I will discuss what is known about interaction at the lexical level in bilingual children. I will then confront these facts to the data of our own French-Dutch bilingual subject and suggest a way of interpreting crosslinguistic evidence as the consequence of several interacting factors.

2.   Interaction at the lexical level in adult bilinguals

Psycholinguists have used several types of experimental techniques to study the interaction at the lexical level in adult bilinguals. For child bilingual acquisition, the data are generally gathered in longitudinal case studies. The outcomes of both types of studies point, as we will see, in the same direction.

Research into lexical access in ADULT bilinguals has shown that, although activation of one of the bilingual's languages inhibits the other language, it is not possible to suppress this other language entirely. In this type of research, the bilingual subjects are not always bilinguals from birth, as is generally the case in the research on child bilingualism. Several types of adult bilinguals are studied, without specification of their personal history of development of bilingualism. Implicitly, it is assumed that from a certain level of proficiency onward, one may suppose that there is no difference in the organisation of the bilingual mental lexicon between bilinguals with various acquisition routes. Evidence about lexical activation and access in adult bilinguals comes from several sources like the study of aphasic bilingual patients and experimental research with normal bilinguals, including priming effects, Stroop tests, and word recognition.

As for aphasics, Perecman (1984) presents a case study of a German-French-English aphasic trilingual who was unable to separate his languages. In answer to the question, put to him in German, to point to the 'clock' (*Uhr*), he answered: *la vyur, la vyur, I don't know how much to tell*. Paradis (1983, 1996) gives several examples of bilingual aphasics who are not able to separate their two languages. Of course, it may be surmised that in these cases, the lack of inhibition of the 'other' language is caused by the aphasia of the subjects in question. However, the fact that these subjects produce mixed utterances, suggesting that their languages are not stored separately but in a common — or closely interconnected — lexical store, could be an indication that lexical storage in 'normal' subjects is common as well.

Cross-language priming experiments with bilingual subjects, on the other hand, have typically shown that words in different languages prime each other in semantic priming tasks (Altarriba 1992; Schwanenflugel & Rey 1986).

Presenting a Dutch word like 'koe' (*cow*) to a Dutch-English bilingual subject leads to faster reaction times in lexical decision about an English word like 'farm' compared to 'chair'. The transfer in these semantic priming tasks has been taken as support for a common memory model for the two languages (see also Kolers 1973; Potter et al 1984). Grainger (1992) goes so far as to claim that in word comprehension, all words of both languages are activated during the search for recognition of the lexical item. It would be only after scanning the whole word that the choice is made as to which language the word belongs. For those word forms which exist in both languages of the bilingual, like *four* for a French-English bilingual, it is (after scanning of the word) the language context which disambiguates it. Grainger's position is not the general one: most psycholinguists hold the view, exposed by Paradis (1996), that

> "the activation of a linguistic item implies concomitant inhibition of all its possible competitors. As a consequence, in order to keep the two languages separate and to prevent interference from one language when one speaks the other one, the neuronal substrate of the language that is not used at the moment is inhibited while the substrate of the language in use is activated. [...] the degree of inhibition varies depending on the frequency of need to speak [this other language]" (Paradis 1996: 60; translation ours)

But Paradis equally shows that, even if the bilingual chooses one language mode to communicate in a specific situation, (s)he is not able to suppress entirely the 'other' language; it is always partially activated.

Recent psycholinguistic research on *access* to the mental lexicon in adult bilinguals has confirmed this view on the relationship between the two lexicons (de Groot 1993; Kroll & Sholl 1992). In these studies, refinements are proposed of the general principle of inhibition. It is shown that concrete words are more easily accessed in the 'other' language than abstract words. The same holds — not surprisingly — for cognates. In these studies, a distinction is made between the lexical (word form) level and the conceptual (word meaning) level. They show that at both levels, items may be stored in a common store across languages while others may be stored separately.

Stroop tests have equally pointed in the direction of imperfect inhibition of the second language. In a classical Stroop test, subjects are given colour words printed in a colour which does not always correspond to the referent of the colour word (like *blue* written in red ink). They have then to name the colour of the ink. This is an old test in monolinguals, which shows that the verbal information interacts with the visual information. Repeated attempts with this experimental paradigm in a bilingual setting have shown that bilinguals cannot game out one of their languages. The magnitude of Stroop interference in the second language appears to be related to the bilingual's proficiency: when the subject becomes more proficient in L2, the interference becomes stronger. This result shows that beginning bilinguals are able to disregard the meaning attached to the word form in the test, while more advanced bilinguals are no longer capable of doing so: they cannot so easily disregard the meaning of the item they are presented with. Inevitably, they link the form of the written word to its meaning which is equally linked to the word form in the 'other' language. The major part of this type of research has been done with adult bilinguals who were not necessarily bilingual from birth: they learned the second language at a later stage. This makes the lack of inhibition more surprising in a way. The learning of a second language could be expected to lead to a 'coordinate' system in the terms of Weinberg (1953), which is very similar to the separate systems proposed in the above mentioned experiments.

Finally, additional evidence for these findings, all of which suggest mixed lexical storage, comes from bilingual speakers who produce blends such as 'Springling' (English *spring* + German *Frühling*). This kind of blend can only be explained by admitting that there is indeed interaction between the two systems.

3.   Interaction at the lexical level in bilingual children

If adult bilinguals sometimes have problems in keeping the words from their two languages apart, it would be natural to expect children to have the same problems. Like for adults, this is not to say that their two lexical stores are in a state of fusion, but simply that children probably have the same — or stronger — problems with the inhibition of the 'other' language. Investigation of this question however cannot take the same form as the experimental research used with adults: the nature of the tasks described in the previous paragraph makes them impossible to use in bilingual first language acquisition by little children. Mostly, bilingual first language acquisition, like monolingual language acquisition, has been studied longitudinally by collecting child utterances in a natural setting. Of course, bilingual children as well as monolingual children find themselves confronted with the same huge task of mapping word forms to meanings, while simultaneously acquiring the concepts underlying these meanings. Aitchison (1994) calls this the 'labelling' problem, Clark (1993) uses the term of 'mapping'. As for this task, bilingual children have the same problem as monolingual ones. But in addition to this mapping problem within languages, bilingual children have to discover that they are confronted with two different language systems simultaneously, which they have to differentiate from each other. For monolingual lexical learning, Clark (1993) states that, in learning words, children rely on the principles of 'conventionality' and 'contrast'. The principle of conventionality helps them to understand that a word form is related to its meaning by the conventions in the community of language users. This relation is arbitrary, but once fixed, it is very reliable. The principle of contrast implies that every meaning has a corresponding specific word form, and that different word forms must have different meanings. This has sometimes been called the principle of "one form, one meaning". According to Clark, children, like adults, have no problems with homonymy (one word form may have several meanings) but, again like adults, children hate synonyms: "Speakers do not tolerate complete synonyms" (Clark 1993: 70). Clark states that this principle could explain rather nicely a phenomenon observed in some bilingual children: the fact that they start building up a lexicon where cross-language synonyms are rare or non-existent. She cites as an example the research by Taeschner (1983), who reports that her German-Italian bilingual daughter Lisa assigned a different meaning to the cross-language synonyms *specchio* (It) and *Spiegel* (German), both meaning *mirror* in the respective adult languages. In view of the principle of contrast, it looks as if Lisa simply refused to have something as inefficient as two words for the same meaning. According to Taeschner, this behaviour is related to the lack of differentiation between the two languages in Lisa: she would possess only one language system in the first stages of her linguistic development. We may conclude that a discussion about differentiation of languages in the bilingual child is related to the question of the principle of contrast.

3.1 *The principle of contrast*

As a matter of fact, the principle of contrast has been challenged in recent research. As for homonyms, where Clark claimed that this is not a big problem for language users, Peters & Zaidel (1980) found that (monolingual) children do have problems with homonyms. In a recent replication of this study, however, Backscheider & Gelman (1995) have shown that the results of Peters & Zaidel (1980) are at least partially caused by the cognitive and metalinguistic complexity of the task the children had to perform. In their own study, Backscheider & Gelman (1995) find that children show a slight reluctance to assign two different meanings to the same word form, but that in the majority of cases they are ready to accept them.

For synonyms, on the other hand, Quay (1995) has shown that the English-Spanish bilingual child she studied had no problems with crosslinguistic synonyms: from the onset on, she learned and used translation equivalents in her first words: her third word was a Spanish equivalent for a word she had first produced the week before in English (Quay 1995: 370). Between age 1;5,13 and 1;10, Manuela had at all stages the possession of a percentage of equivalents varying between 38% and 42%. In the same vein, Pearson, Fernandez & Oller (1995) report that, in a survey of the lexical development of 27 English-Spanish bilingual children, most of their children equally know translation equivalents from the first stage of word learning. The mean proportion of translation equivalents at all stages in their investigation is 30%. This seems to show that the contrast principle should be abandoned: children appear to use crosslinguistic synonyms from the very beginnings of their language development. But if we take a closer look at the data of Pearson et al (1995), we see that the situation is not as clear cut as the overall numbers suggest. The tables presenting the data in their paper are far from clear, but in any case they show that there are enormous individual differences between the children, some using a very small number of 'doublets', some using many more. For the younger children (number of words < 100), the minimum number of doublets per child is 0, the maximum percentage is 100%. For the more advanced children, the minimum percentage of translation equivalents is 9%, the maximum is 76%. We may wonder what these figures tell us. In the first place, of course, it could be that the number of doublets is related to the proficiency of the children in each of the languages. The authors tell us that there are enormous differences between the children; balanced bilinguals are rare. The bilingual situation of the children is described as very diverse and the degree to which one language is dominant varies immensely from child to child. The presence or absence of doublets could therefore be caused by degree of proficiency and dominance in one of the two languages. But the authors do not provide information about this relationship. Besides proficiency, other factors like the nature and quantity of the input may play a role in the development of the two languages. Döpke (1992) found that the strictness with which parents apply the 'one person one language' strategy influences strongly the degree to which the children in her study stick to one language. Strict appliance of the 'one person one language rule' could offer clearer cues to the children about the bilingual situation they are placed in and thus help them to develop crosslinguistic equivalents. Because of the variation between children, the data of Pearson, Fernandez & Oller (1995) do not show very convincingly that the contrast principle must be abandoned. Rather the results suggest that the contrast principle is a *strategy* rather than a *constraint*: some children seem to use it, others don't. Quay's subject would be an example of a bilingual child that does not use the contrast strategy, while the subject described by Nicoladis (1998) does use this strategy: she does not learn any translation equivalents until the moment when she 'realises' that she has to use a different language to different interlocutors.

A 'contrast strategy' is certainly useful in monolingual acquisition. Indeed, if there would be no contrast principle, objects could get several names and the child would never know if there is a 'best match' in the mapping procedure. That would mean that every day, a new word form for a familiar object could be expected. For bilingual children, the situation is of course different, because they have to learn precisely that the meaning of an object may be attached to two word forms across languages. Once they have learned this, crosslinguistic synonyms should not be a problem any more. Indeed, Davidson et al (1997) have shown that bilingual children are more permissive than monolingual ones when it comes to assigning novel labels to familiar objects in a (monolingual) experimental task. This effect is stronger for five- and six-year old children than for three- to four year olds. But even if they are more permissive, bilingual children reject these novel names in the majority of cases: in the disambiguation task as well as in the rejection task described by Davidson et al, 4 and 6 years old bilingual children, like monolingual children of the same ages, prefer to assign novel names to novel objects rather than to assign them to known objects. The fact that this tendency is stronger for monolingual than for bilingual children suggests that bilingual children are more ready to accept that one object may have several names. But they still prefer them not to. If bilingual children prefer referents to have only one word form attached to them in a monolingual language context, it should not be excluded that this preference plays a role between languages as well. This would lead them to assign one word form to words in the two languages. Of course, the contrast strategy has to be abandoned relatively soon after the moment when they start acquiring synonyms. Moreover, I would like to suggest that relations of subordination and superordination may play a role in this development: while these relations may be rather clear in adult knowledge of the lexicon, for children, words like 'animal' and 'dog' could at first very well function as synonyms. So the acquisition of superordinates and subordinates may be a step towards the rejection of the 'contrast strategy'.

3.2 *Language differentiation at the lexical level*

In the first stage of word learning at least, there is a strong relationship between the two languages of the bilingual child, as is evidenced in mixed utterances. This mixing is not limited to the lexical level, but is evidenced also in the domains of morphology, syntax and pronunciation (for a wealth of examples, see Déprez 1994). Some researchers, like Meisel (1989), Vihman (1985), Taeschner (1983) have proposed that in this first stage (under age 2), children would have a mixed system for the two languages, while only in later stages, the two languages are clearly separated (Meisel introduces the term of 'fusion' for this very early mixed system). In producing utterances in this first stage, children would consider translation equivalents as synonyms which can be used regardless of the matrix language and indifferently from the fact if they know the appropriate word in the appropriate language.

According to Meisel (1989, 1990, 1994), Parodi (1990) and others, language differentiation would be triggered by syntactic development: they state that differentiation is evidenced by the appearance of subject-verb agreement.

Quay (1995) on the other hand seems to suggest that language differentiation is active from the first moment of language production. The fact that in the first stage children do not use the appropriate word in the appropriate context may be caused simply by the lack of crosslinguistic equivalents:

> "Studies which interpret mixing as showing a lack of language differentiation do not take into account the fact that bilingual children may lack the appropriate vocabulary and NOT have a choice in their language use". (Quay 1995: 370)

In other words, when a child uses a word from the 'other' language, he may do so because he fills a lexical gap, it is not necessarily a sign of lack of differentiation between languages. The lexical gap explanation may hold especially in the very first stages (up to 50–100 words), when children do not always have doublets in their two languages. It does not seem to hold any more from the moment on when children accept and know crosslinguistic equivalents, a moment well before their second birthday: in the lexicon of Raivo, for example, the Estlandic-English bilingual child described by Vihman (1985), the first crosslinguistic equivalents appeared around 1;6 and at 2;0 he had achieved a fairly complete dual lexicon, 76% of the words represented overlap between the two languages (Vihman 1985: 302). For the child studied equally by Quay (1993), Deuchar (1997) points out that differentiation is made earlier for content words than for function words. She suggests that the child achieves complete differentiation about age 1;10.

Nicoladis (1998) suggests that differentiation is not a yes or no question. She studies the appearance of translation equivalents in an English-Portuguese bilingual child. The little boy was late in acquiring translation equivalents. According to Nicoladis , his first translation equivalents could be compared to the knowledge of synonyms by monolingual children of the same age. Nicoladis' paper addresses the question of pragmatic versus lexical differentiation. She defines pragmatic differentiation as the use by the bilingual child of the appropriate language to the interlocutor addressed. She shows that the child she studies seems to acquire a large number of translation equivalents only after the moment (around age 1;5, when the child possesses some 50 words) when he realises that he has to address a different language to each parent. It is a month after this moment that the number of translation equivalents grows dramatically. Nicoladis concludes that

> "given these results, it seems reasonable to conclude that this child did not initially show lexical differentiation and than clearly showed such differentiation around session 19 (when he was about 1;5)." (Nicoladis 1998: 111)

Nicoladis explicitly relates the use of translation equivalents to the more general question of the development of language differentiation. She suggests that in different domains of the language, differentiation could be achieved at different moments. If we follow this idea, then the appearance of crosslinguistic equivalents could be considered as a first step to language differentiation. Syntactic differentiation would come later.

The utterances of bilingual children show that, even after the moment when differentiation between languages is achieved, the inappropriate use of words from the 'other' language continues, as we see in the following examples:

(1)   M   (French):   *Oh, qu'est-ce qu'il y a là?*   (Anouk 2;3,13)
                         'Oh, what is there?'
       C   (Dutch):   *huis*
                         'house'

(2)   M   (French):   *sale, qu'est-ce qui est sale?*   (Anouk 2;3,13)
                         'dirty, what is dirty?'
       C   (Dutch):   *neus*
                         'nose'

(3)   *il est red, le book*   (Anthéa 2;6)
            it is red, the book

(4)   *ya no puede bouger*   (Corinne 3;0)
            not any can   move

(5)   *ik   deux jambes*   (Anouk 2;7)
            me two legs

(6)   *il faut faire un stapel*   (Anouk 3;7)
            it is necessary to make a stack

These examples for the language pairs French-English, French-Spanish and French-Dutch (the examples (3) and (4) are from Déprez 1994: 114) are certainly not rare in the utterances of little bilingual children. Some authors like Leopold (1970), Swain (1972), Volterra & Taeschner (1978), Taeschner (1983), Vihman (1985) have taken this as an indication that even after the age of two, bilingual children are not able to distinguish well between their two languages and, for that reason, they go on mixing their vocabularies. Indeed, the examples (1) to (6) cannot all be considered as lexical gaps. In (5), for example, the reason for using the word *ik* (me) cannot be that the French equivalent *je* would not be known, as the lexical gap approach would predict. On the other hand, it is not probable that children really still have a mixed language system at this point. De Houwer (1990) points out that real confusion between the two languages would result in a 50–50 distribution of words from the two languages in the utterances of the child. This is not what we find: the matrix language provides a large majority of the words in the child utterances. Also, it has been shown (Lanza 1992; Nicoladis 1998) that 2 year old children differentiate clearly between their two languages: they use each language correctly in contact with different interlocutors. They are even able to give crosslinguistic synonyms when asked for as in the following fragment:

(7) F (Dutch): *park, en wat hebben we nog meer?*
  'parc, and what more?'
  wat is dit?
  'what is this?'

  C (Dutch): *boot*
  'boat'

  F (Dutch): *en wat zegt mama hiervoor?*
  'and how does mummy say this?'
  wat zegt mama?
  'what says mummy?'

  C (French): *bateau*
  'boat' (Anouk 2;5,20)

This shows that there is a first metalinguistic awareness of the fact that more than one language is involved. That means that fusion of the language systems can certainly not explain lexical mixes at this stage any more.

Children may have several different reasons to use in one matrix language elements from their two languages. Although the child is aware that her two languages differ at the phonological, lexical and syntactic level, and conforms generally to the 'rules' of the matrix language, there may be occasions when nevertheless elements from the 'other' are activated and preferred.

From the moment on when differentiation between the lexicons is achieved, mixes from the 'other' language in the matrix one mostly take the form of the insertion on one lexical element into an utterance in the 'other' language: they look more like borrowing or *code switching* from this moment on. There has been a lot of discussion about code switching in the literature on bilingualism (for an overview, see Romaine 1989). Starting with Poplack (1980), efforts have been made to formulate constraints on code switching. Although there are indications that code switching is rule governed behaviour, no rules have been found which are able to describe the linguistic and sociolinguistic constraints underlying it. For the moment, it seems possible only to formulate tendencies for code switching, such as: single nouns are the elements that are most easily inserted in the matrix language; clitics are almost never to be mixed; at the place of the switch, the surface strings of matrix and other language must be parallel. As for quantitative aspects of code switching, Poplack suggested already that a higher level of proficiency in both languages leads to more ease in code switching. And Paradis (1996) states that the inhibition of the 'other' language will be weaker in situations where many bilinguals are together and where there is no taboo on code switching (Paradis 1996: 61). Döpke (1992) found in her study of 6 cases of child bilingualism, that the child who performed best in separating the two languages was the one whose parents were strictest in applying the principle of one parent one language. In other words, the degree of code switching, in children as in adults, is influenced by input: children who are exposed to input in which a lot of mixing and code switching takes place, will be much more tempted to reproduce these same patterns in their own speech. The little girl Line, studied by Tabouret-Keller (1962), is an example of this case. Tabouret-Keller reports that, by 2 years of age, 60 percent of Line's utterances are mixed. The input she is exposed to by her mother is of the same mixed kind. As a consequence, both languages of the child are continuously activated and she does not feel the need to suppress one of the languages in her output. Our own subject, Anouk, who is educated along the (strictly respected) principle of 'one person-one language' is an example of the contrary. Indeed, we find only a small set of lexical mixes in her utterances. Instead, in the utterances of Machiel, another child we started to study recently, we find a larger number of lexical mixes. We equally see that his (French-Dutch bilingual) mother uses many more mixes in her utterances. We will discuss this in more detail below.

It seems that reasons for inserting single words from the 'other' language may be multiple for bilingual children. In the first place, words from the 'wrong' language can be used as a relief strategy (Meisel 1989) when the child does not know the correct word yet. This is also what happens equally in adult borrowings. As I showed before, this filling of lexical gaps is evidenced from the first stages of acquisition, with very young children.

Children could equally use words of the 'other' language (as we saw for bilingual adults) because of the impossibility of inhibiting completely the activation of one of the two languages. This lack of inhibition could very well be strong in the case of bilingual children. The word of the 'other' language could be activated earlier because of its phonological simplicity, or its higher frequency in the other language, etc. In the next section, I will look more closely into lexical mixes in the utterances of our French-Dutch bilingual subject in order to find out which mechanisms could be at work.

4.   Lexical activation and access in Anouk

In the utterances of our own bilingual subject Anouk, we find, as I mentioned before, a relatively small number of lexical mixes. Anouk has been living in Amsterdam from birth and is being brought up bilingually by her French mother who speaks French to her and her Dutch father who speaks Dutch to her, in agreement with the principle of "une personne une langue" (one person-one language) which is strictly applied. Anouk's mother understands Dutch and speaks it reasonably well. She addresses Anouk only in French. Anouk's father understands some French but speaks it poorly. As shown by Döpke (1992), this situation is apt to stimulate the achievement of successful language differentiation and of inhibition of the other language in a monolingual context.

From about 6 months of age, Anouk attended a Dutch kindergarten for three days a week. The corpus was collected by making audio recordings in both languages. Recordings were made by the mother for French, and by the father — and a native Dutch student — for Dutch. They were made approximately every three weeks, starting at 2;3,13 (MLU 1.4) for French and at 2;5,20 (MLU 1.7) for Dutch. Anouk's language development is late in both her languages: at the first recordings, she still produces mostly one word utterances.

Lexical mixes in Anouk undergo quantitative and qualitative changes during the period of observation (2;3 till 3;11). In the first recordings, when Anouk is still mainly in the one word stage, lexical insertions are relatively frequent, especially in the French matrix situation. In the very first recording, for example (French matrix language, age 2;3,13), we have 56 child utterances, containing 42 French words and 26 Dutch words. The frequency of lexical switches decreases dramatically in the first months of observation and becomes almost non-existent in later recordings. Table 1 and 2 give an illustration of this evolution

Table 1. *Word use in the French matrix situation*

	French	French-Dutch	Dutch	unintelligible
Age 2;3,13 MLU 1.41	42	10	26	4
Age 2;5,20 MLU 2.1	114	12	4	4
Age 2;11,23 MLU 2.67	120	0	8	4

Table 2. *Word use in the Dutch matrix situation*

	French	French-Dutch	Dutch	unintelligible
Age 2;5,20 MLU 1.73	6	13	153	5
Age 2;11,23 MLU 3.19	0	3	137	3

In these tables, 4 types of words are distinguished: French words, Dutch words, words of either language (French-Dutch) and unintelligible words. The 'either' category consists of words that could belong to either French or Dutch, such as proper names or interjections (Anouk, Stella, oooh). 'Mama' and 'papa' were counted as part of either language in the first recording, where no translation equivalents existed. Later, they were counted as language specific, because both 'mama'(Dutch) and 'maman' (French) appeared and for 'papa' phonological differentiation was made according to language.

As we see, between 2;3,13 and 2;5,20 the use of Dutch words in a French context diminishes drastically, from 32% at 2;3,13 to 3% at 2;5,20. As for the use of French words in a Dutch context we find more or less the same situation. Only we do not have Dutch matrix language observations from the first month. At age 2;5,20 we see 3.4% French words in a Dutch context, which is comparable to the use of Dutch words in a French context.

At age 2;11,23 we find 6.7% Dutch words in a French context and 0% French words in a Dutch context. The 6.7% of Dutch words in a French context seem an augmentation. In fact, they are all instances of the use of "ja" instead of "oui". In the same file, we find one instance of French "oui", so we cannot conclude that Anouk does not know the French word for "yes". Nevertheless, she shows a strong preference for the use of "ja" instead of "oui". It is only at 3;3,17, after a summer holiday in France, that Anouk chooses to use "oui" instead of "ja" in her French. After this moment, we do not ever see 'ja' appear in a French context.

Table 1 shows that it is only in the first recording (age 2;3,13) that we see an extensive use of translation equivalents from the other language. A closer analysis may help to discover for what reasons these equivalents are used.

In this first recording, with French as the matrix language, we have 56 utterances and 82 words, to be distinguished as follows:
−   42 French words (25 different ones);
−   26 Dutch words (10 different ones;
−   10 words which are neutral between the two languages;
−   4 unintelligible ones.

As Anouk produces still mainly one word utterances, most of the Dutch words are evidenced as switches between turns. There are only 4 intra-sentential switches, all consisting of the use of Dutch 'nee' to express negation, like in the following example:

(8)   *Anouk chaud nee*   (Anouk 2;3,13)
        'Anouk warm no'

The 22 other Dutch words are used mainly in one word turns, answering a French question, like the use (8 times) of 'ja' (yes) or 'nee' (no):

(9)   M: *Le soleil est couché?*   (Anouk 2;6,11)
            'the sun is setting?'
        C: *ja*
            'yes'

Indeed, 'ja' and 'nee' are consistently used by Anouk instead of their French equivalents until the age of 3. The 12 other Dutch words are of two types: 4 Dutch words are part of a Dutch song Anouk starts to sing; the other 8 words appear in utterances like the following:

(10)   M   (French):   ⟨knocks on the table⟩
                        c'est quoi?
                        'what is this?'
        C   (Dutch):   *tafel*
                        'table'

(11)   M   (French):   *le petit lapin, qu'est-ce qu'il fait?*
                          'the little rabbit, what does it do?'
       C   (Dutch):   <u>*uile*</u>
                          'cry'

In all eight cases, the child names an object or an action in answering a question.

This type of crosslinguistic influence is not limited to French; we see it also in the settings where Dutch is the matrix language:

(12)   F   (Dutch):   *kijk eens, wat is dat?*   (Anouk 2;5,20)
       C   (French):   <u>*cochon*</u>

For these cases of lexical mixing we can reject the hypothesis that they are examples of the filling of lexical gaps, as suggested by Quay (1995). In the first file, where we found the Dutch word 'huis' in a French matrix situation, we find equally the French equivalent 'maison':

(13)   M   (French):   *c'est une table, oui. Et ça c'est?*
                          'that is a table, yes. And this is?'
       C   (French):   *maison*
                          'house'

The same holds for the word 'konijn' (rabbit), which in the same file is present with the French equivalent 'lapin' and for 'ja' (yes) which is also present as 'oui'. So of the 22 occurrences of Dutch words (the 4 words of the Dutch song are of course not expected to trigger French equivalents), 7 have their French equivalent in the same file. For these words, the lexical gap explanation does not hold. We cannot be sure of course if it holds for the other Dutch words, because we have no evidence to tell us whether their French equivalents are known to the child or not. It does not seem probable that she does not know the highly frequent word 'table' in French. It is equally improbable that the 10 occurrences of the frequent word 'nee', used instead of the French 'non', are cause by a lack of lexical knowledge. Both the use of 'ja' instead of 'oui' and 'nee' instead of 'non' could be linked to the ease of pronunciation of the Dutch versus the French words and to the extremely high frequency of these words in the language of Anouk's peers in the Dutch kindergarten. If this is correct, then only two Dutch words remain as candidates for the lexical gap explanation: 'huilen' (to cry) and 'uit (out). Here, we could indeed suspect there to be examples of gap filling, especially in the case of 'out', which cannot be translated in a straightforward way by a comparable French adverb. It would normally be equivalent with a verbal form like '(veux) sortir'.

If the filling of lexical gaps does not constitute the most important explanation for the lexical mixes of the first recording, there has to be another reason. It seems tempting to suggest that in this first recording we witness the last moment before the complete achievement of lexical differentiation by Anouk. This means that differentiation is achieved very late. Indeed, I already pointed out that Anouk's language development is late: the first words appeared long after her first birthday and her slow development was one of the reasons why our recordings started only after age 2. In another paper (Hulk & van der Linden 1996) we showed that complete syntactic differentiation appears only at age 2;7. Taking into account this slow development as well as the respective percentages of French and Dutch words in the first recording (51% of French words, 32% of Dutch words) and the fact that several words are present with their equivalents of both languages in this first recording, it seems legitimate to suggest that at this age Anouk still considers crosslinguistic equivalents as synonyms which can be used regardless of the language context.

When we look at the use of crosslinguistic lexical items in later recordings, we see that there is a fast quantitative as well as a qualitative evolution. While at 2;3,13, the use of Dutch words forms 31.7% of the total number of words used by Anouk, at 2;4,17 this percentage drops to 11% and at 2;5,20, it has gone down to 3%. The percentage of French words in a Dutch context never exceeds 3.4%. So from age 2;5,20 on, we may safely say that the number of lexical mixes is negligible: lexical differentiation is achieved and the 'other' language is properly inhibited under the influence of the strictly separated language input.

From a qualitative point of view, there is also a difference. Apart from the use of Dutch 'ja' and 'nee' which we discussed before, the use of crosslinguistic equivalents seems to be in most cases an instance of the filling of a lexical gap or a 'relief strategy', as in (13):

(14)   *Il faut faire un stapel*   (Anouk 3;7)
        'we must make a stack'

Anouk uses Dutch words in the French context because she does not know the French equivalent or because the Dutch one comes to her mind much quicker. This has been shown to be one of the reasons for code switching in children as well as adults. So we assume that after the age of 2;5,20, Anouk's use of crosslinguistic equivalents is no more a sign of lack of language differentiation, but has turned into examples of code switching. In other words, in the first few months of observation of Anouk's utterances, we witness the fascinating moment of the emergence of language differentiation at the lexical level.

When we compare the data of Anouk to those described in the literature, we see that Anouk's development is very late compared to that of other children described. While differentiation of the lexicons of the two languages is reported to be achieved between 1;5 (Nicoladis) and 1;10 (Deuchar, Vihman), it seems that Anouk achieves lexical differentiation only at about 2;5,20. This late differentiation is surprising when we look at the socio-linguistic conditions Anouk grows up in, with two parents applying the principle of 'one parent-one language' very strictly. Döpke (1992) showed that this linguistic environment is apt to stimulate early successful language differentiation. Anouk's late differentiation can probably be explained by her overall late language development, which is equally described in Hulk & van der Linden (1996), van der Linden & Hulk (1998) and by Hulk (this volume). Our findings suggest that indeed, as proposed by Nicoladis, differentiation is not simultaneous for all language domains, and that pragmatic and lexical differentiation come before syntactic differentiation.

5. Conclusion

We have seen that bilingual subjects (adults as well as children) are generally successful in inhibiting words from the language other than the matrix language in their utterances. However, both languages remain accessible in children as well as adults, as is shown by psycholinguistic experimental research. This incomplete inhibition leads to the occasional use of words of the other language in a monolingual context.

For children, the situation is different from that of adults, because they first have to learn that they are exposed to two different language systems and that their utterances have to conform to these respective systems. It is this pragmatic competence that comes first in bilingual language acquisition, immediately followed by the competence of lexical differentiation. Syntactic differentiation comes only later. It is not clear whether a principle of contrast plays a role in the first stages of language development. Perhaps we should rather think of a strategy of contrast as being useful for beginning language acquisition. This strategy, which may be useful for a monolingual acquisition situation, has to be adapted to the bilingual language situation from the moment when pragmatic language differentiation is achieved.

This development is evidenced by our French-Dutch bilingual subject, who achieves pragmatic and lexical differentiation around age 2;5 while syntactic differentiation comes only at around 2;7. In the first stage she seems to consider crosslinguistic equivalents as synonyms which can be used interchangeably. After a few months, however, the use of crosslinguistic equivalents diminishes dramatically, showing that pragmatic differentiation is achieved, and the remaining cases of crosslinguistic language use becomes more similar to that of adult code switching behaviour.

Acknowledgments

The investigation reported on in this chapter has been carried out in collaboration with Aafke Hulk of the University of Amsterdam, who wrote the chapter in this volume on access and activation in the syntactic domain.

References

Aitchison, Jean. 1992. *Words in the mind: An introduction to the mental lexicon.* Oxford: Basil Blackwell.

Altarriba, J. 1992. "The representation of translation equivalents in bilingual memory". In R. Harris (ed), *Cognitive Processing in Bilinguals.* Amsterdam: Elsevier, 157–174.

Backscheider, Andrea & Susan Gelman. 1995. "Children's understanding of homonyms". *Journal of Child Language* 22(1): 107–127.

Bates, Elizabeth & Brian MacWhinney. 1989. "Functionalism and the competition model". In B. MacWhinney & E. Bates (eds), *The Crosslinguistic Study of Sentence Processing.* Cambridge: Cambridge University Press.

Clark, Eve. 1985. "The acquisition of Romance with special reference to French". In D. I. Slobin (ed), *The Crosslinguistic Study of Language Acquisition.* Vol. 1. Hillsdale, NJ: Lawrence Erlbaum.

Clark, Eve 1993. *The Lexicon in Acquisition.* Cambridge: Cambridge University Press.

Davidson, D., D. Jergovic, Z. Imami, & V. Theodos. 1997. "Monolingual and bilingual's children's use of the mutual exclusivity constraint". *Journal of Child Language* 24: 3–24.

De Groot, Annette M. B. 1993. "Word-type effects in bilingual processing tasks: support for a mixed-representational system". In R. Schreuder & B. Weltens (eds.), *The Bilingual Lexicon.* Amsterdam and Philadelphia: John Benjamins, 27–52.

De Houwer, Annick. 1990. *The Acquisition of Two Languages From Birth: A Case Study.* Cambridge: Cambridge University Press.

Déprez, Viviane.1994. *Enfants Bilingues: Langues et Familles.* Paris: Didier.

Döpke, Susanne. 1992. *One Parent, One Language. An Interactional Approach.* Amsterdam and Philadelphia: John Benjamins.

Grainger, Jonathan. 1992. "Visual word recognition in bilinguals". In R. Schreuder & B. Weltens (eds.), *The Bilingual Lexicon.* Amsterdam and Philadelphia: John Benjamins, 11–27.

Hulk, Aafke C. J. & Elisabeth van der Linden. 1996. "Language mixing in a French-Dutch bilingual child." *Toegepaste Taalwetenschap in Artikelen* 55 (EUROSLA 6, A selection of papers): 89–103.

Kail, Michèle. 1989. "Cue validity, cue cost and processing types in sentence comprehension in French and Spanish". In B. MacWhinney & E. Bates (eds), *The Cross-linguistic Study of Sentence Processing*. Cambridge: Cambridge University Press.

Kolers, A. P. 1973. "Interlingual associations". *Journal of Verbal learning and Verbal Behaviour* 2: 291–300.

Kroll, J. F. & A. Sholl. 1992. "Lexical and conceptual memory in fluent and non-fluent bilinguals". In R. Harris (ed), *Cognitive Processing in Bilinguals*. Amsterdam: Elsevier, 191–204.

Lanza, Elizabeth. 1992. "Can bilingual two year olds codeswitch?" *Journal of Child Language* 19: 633–658.

Leopold, Werner. 1949–1970. *Speech Development of a Bilingual Child: A Linguist's Record*. Vols. 1–4. New York: AMS Press.

MacWhinney, Brian. 1987. "Applying the competition model to bilingualism". *Applied Psycholinguistics* 8: 315–327.

Meisel, Jürgen M. 1989. "Early differentiation of languages in bilingual children". In K. Hyltenstam & L. Obler (eds), *Bilingualism Across the Life Span. Aspects of Acquisition, Maturity and Loss*. Cambridge: Cambridge University Press, 13–40.

Meisel, Jürgen M. (ed) 1990. *Two First Languages. Early Grammatical Development in Bilingual Children*. Dordrecht: Foris.

Meisel, Jürgen M. (ed) 1994. *Bilingual First Language Acquisition: French and German Grammatical Development*. Amsterdam and Philadelphia: John Benjamins.

Nicoladis, Elena. 1998. "First clues to the existence of two input languages: pragmatic and lexical differentiation of a bilingual child". *Bilingualism* 1(2): 105–116.

Paradis, Michel. 1983. "Le neurologie du bilinguisme: représentation et traïtment de deux langues dans un même cerveau." *Langages* 4: 7–15.

Paradis, Michel. 1996. *Evaluation De L'Aphasie Chez Les Bilingues*. Paris: Hachette.

Parodi, Teresa. 1990. "The acquisition of word order regularities and case morphology". In J. M. Meisel (ed), *Two First Languages. Early Grammatical Development in Bilingual Children*. Dordrecht: Foris: 157–193.

Pearson, Barbara Z., Sylvia Fernandez & D. Kimbrough Oller. 1995. "Cross-language synonyms in the lexicons of bilingual infants: one language or two?" *Journal of Child Language* 22: 345–368.

Perecman, J. 1984. "Spontaneous translation and language mixing in a polyglot aphasic". *Brain and Language* 23: 43–63.

Peters, Ann & E. Zaidel. 1980. "The acquisition of homonymy". *Cognition* 8: 187–207.

Poplack, Shana. 1980. "Sometimes I'll start a sentence in English y termino en español; toward a typology of codeswitching". *Linguistics* 18: 581–616.

Potter, M. C., K.-F. So, B. von Eckart & L. B. Feldman, 1984. "Lexical and conceptual representation in beginning and proficient bilinguals". *Journal of Verbal Behaviour and Verbal Learning* 23: 23–38.

Quay, Suzanne. 1995. "The bilingual lexicon: implications for studies of language choice". *Journal of Child Language* 22: 369–387.

Romaine, Suzanne. 1989. *Bilingualism*. Oxford: Basil Blackwell.

Schreuder, Rob & Bert Weltens. (eds) 1993. *The Bilingual Lexicon*. Amsterdam and Philadelphia: John Benjamins.

Schwanenflugel, P. J. & M. Rey. 1986. "Interlingual semantic facilitation: evidence for a common representational system in the bilingual". *Journal of Memory and Language* 25: 605–618.

Slobin, Dan. I. 1985. *The Crosslinguistic Study of Language Acquisition*. Hillsdale, NJ: Lawrence Erlbaum.

Swain, Merrill. 1972. *Bilingualism as a First Language*. PhD dissertation. University of California: Irvine.

Tabouret-Keller, Andrée. 1962. "Vrais et faux problèmes du bilinguisme". In M. Cohen (ed), *Etudes Sur Le Langage De L'Enfant*. Paris: Editions du Scarabée, 161–192.

Taeschner, Traute. 1983. *The Sun is Feminine. A Study of Language Acquisition in Bilingual Children*. Berlin: Springer.

Van der Linden, Elisabeth & Aafke Hulk. 1998. "Access and activation in lexical and syntactic acquisition". AILE, numero spécial: *Actes du Colloque EUROSLA 8*. Paris. Vol I: La Personne Bilingue: 33–51.

Vihman, Marilyn. 1985. "Language differentiation in the bilingual child". *Journal of Child Language* 12: 297–325.

Volterra, Virginia & Traute Taeschner. 1978. "The acquisition and development of language by bilingual children". *Journal of Child Language* 5: 311–326.

Weinreich, Uriel. 1953. *Languages in Contact: Findings and Problems*. New York: Linguistic Circle of New York. Reprinted in 1974 by Mouton de Gruyter, The Hague.

Non-Selective Access and Activation in Child Bilingualism

The Syntax

Aafke Hulk
University of Amsterdam / HIL

1. Introduction

In this chapter phenomena of non-selective access and activation in the domain of syntax are investigated. We will discuss examples of cross-linguistic influence in the utterances of Anouk, the French-Dutch bilingual child whose lexical production has been studied in the preceding chapter.

The syntactic structures of the utterances of bilingual children have been studied in a number of publications in the last two decades. A central question in these publications concerns the differentiation between the two languages of the bilingual child. We see here a parallel with the discussion of lexical storage and access: for the lexicon, the question is whether the words of the two languages are stored separately or together, and what the consequences are for retrieval and inhibition. For syntactic acquisition the question is whether the two systems are acquired as one system or as two distinct ones. While several researchers in the eighties have argued that bilingual children begin language acquisition with a mixed language system for the lexicon as well as for syntax (Taeschner 1983; Vihman 1985; Leopold 1949–1970), most syntactic studies in the last decade of bilingual language acquisition have sustained the contrary thesis that bilingual children differentiate between their two languages from very early on.

Investigations into large corpora of bilingual children's utterances such as in the DUFDE project (Meisel 1990, 1994) have shown that children differentiate their languages both at the lexical and at the syntactic level. The same has been argued for by De Houwer (1990) for English-Dutch bilingual children. Lanza (1992) showed that formal aspects of language mixing by bilingual two-year-olds, which has often been interpreted as a sign of the child's lack of language differentiation, demonstrate that children do differentiate their language use in a contextually sensitive way. In arguing — convincingly — against the idea that bilingual children first have a unitary language system, these linguists tend to overlook examples of crosslinguistic influence. They sometimes even deny that there is any influence from one language on the other and they state that bilingual language acquisition is the same as monolingual acquisition. Schlyter & Håkansson (1994) claim that in their study of French-Swedish bilinguals they do not find any signs of transfer of word order from one language into the other. The same claims have been made by Meisel (1989) and Parodi (1990).

Recently, Paradis & Genesee (1996) raised the question whether there is any influence of one language on the other in their data of French-English bilingual children. They conclude that these children show no evidence at all of transfer. Interestingly, however, they do mention some puzzling data which at first sight look like transfer data, but they qualify them as follows: "these aberrant examples are most likely performance errors". Although it may be true that at least part of these data are performance errors, this does not mean that there is no need to explain them in a more satisfactory way. Why do these bilinguals make precisely these errors that seem to reflect characteristics of the other of their two languages?

Partly unpublished studies of the syntactic development of bilingual children (Döpke 1996, 1998; Tracy 1995; Gawlitzek-Maiwald & Tracy 1996; Hulk & van der Linden 1996; Hulk 1997; Hulk to appear) have revived the interest in such "mixed" utterances which appear in different language pairs. Having established that bilingual children are able to differentiate between their two languages at a very early age, we are now at the point that we can address in a more precise way the question of crosslinguistic influence.

In studying bilingual language acquisition we witness the emergence of grammars of two languages at the moment of creation, when they are in close contact with each other. This study can reveal interaction between the two languages at the pragmatic, phonetic, lexical, and the syntactic level. If we just consider word order we know, for example, that a French-Dutch bilingual child has to be able to react to word order cues in one way when processing Dutch and in another way when processing French. As suggested already by MacWhinney (1987) the bilingual child may attempt to make short cuts and allow strategies of one language into the other (cf. the relief strategies discussed in the preceding chapter on the acquisition of the bilingual lexicon). We especially expect such "short cuts" when the child has to cope with problematic input, which is ambiguous and contains evidence for more than one grammatical analysis. The bilingual child is exposed to a much wider range of syntactic possibilities than the monolingual child and he/she is offered structural possibilities which monolinguals do not have. A complicating factor is the fact that the input of each of the languages separately is probably smaller for the bilingual child than for the monolingual child. It has sometimes been hypothesised that for that reason, language development is slower in bilingual children. Assuming that for bilinguals just as for monolinguals language acquisition, in particular as far as syntax is concerned, is constrained by the principles of Universal Grammar, crosslinguistic phenomena can also teach us a lot about possible grammars and linguistic theory.

2. The acquisition of syntax

In this section we take a closer look at syntactic phenomena involving word order in the acquisition of French by bilingual French-Dutch children. We discuss spontaneous production data. Most data are from Anouk, who has been recorded between age 2;3,13 and age 3;10,7. Some data are from one other child, who we are still in the process of recording, Machiel.

What makes the syntax of French-Dutch bilinguals particularly interesting is the fact that on the one hand, the basic word order of French and Dutch sentences differs quite a lot: in terms of parameter setting, for a number of parameters French and Dutch have different values. On the other hand, superficially a lot of sentences in Dutch and French seem to have the same word order. We will see that this may create some problems for the bilingual child.

First we will give a brief overview of the main characteristics of French and Dutch (adult) syntax which play a role in our research.

2.1 Adult syntax

Dutch is generally analysed as a Head-Final (XP_V) language. This basic word order shows up most clearly in embedded sentences

(1)   *Jan zegt [dat hij een koekje wil]*
                             O   V
        'John says that he a cookie wants'

In root sentences the finite verb has to move to the second position: Dutch is a so-called V2 language. Therefore, root sentences with a simplex verb seemingly have SVO order:

(2)   *ik   wil   een appel*
        S   V   O
        'I want an apple'

When there is a verbal complex, consisting of an auxiliary and a past participle, however, the underlying OV order shows up again:

(3)   *ik heb   een appel gegeten*
        Aux O   V
        'I have an apple eaten'

Another property of V2 language is that the first position in the root sentence is open not only for the subject (as in (1) to (3)), but for all kinds of other arguments and adjuncts. As a result, in sentences with such a fronted constituent, the subject is in postverbal position:

(4)   *appels lust ik niet*
        O   V S Neg
        'apples like I not'

(5)   *morgen   ga ik naar Amsterdam*
        Adv   V S PP
        'tomorrow go I to Amsterdam'

In generative syntax, the landing site of the finite verb in root clauses is generally taken to be the head of the left most functional projection, C. The fronted constituent is then in SpecCP.

French, on the other hand, is a Head-Initial (V_XP) language with finite verb movement to Infl both in root and non-root clauses:

(6)   *Jean a   mangé un gateau*
                Aux V   O
        'John has eaten a cookie'

(7)   *Jean dit qu'il a   mangé un gateau*
                       Aux V   O
        'John says that he has eaten an apple'

In all (declarative[1]) sentences the subject precedes the finite verb. Fronting of constituents is only possible for adjuncts: they are adjoined to the sentence in such a way that the SVO order is maintained:

(8)   *Hier   Jean a   mangé une pomme*
        Adv   S   Aux V   O
        'Yesterday John has eaten an apple'

If one wants to front an object, a completely different construction must be used:[2] either a left dislocation, when the object is a topic, expressing old or shared information, or a cleft construction, when the object is focalised and expresses new or contrastive information:[3]

(9)   *Les pommes,*   *Jean les a déjà mangées*
       LEFT DISLOCATION
       'the apples,   John them has already eaten'

(10)   *Ce sont les pommes*   *que Jean a mangées*
       CLEFT
       'It are the apples   that John has eaten'

2.2 *The emergence of early syntax*

Now, we will examine how the structure of the clause emerges in the syntax of (bilingual) children and illustrate this with examples from Anouk (and some from another child, Machiel). We will distinguish three periods in the data collected from Anouk. The first period goes from age 2;3,13 to age 2;7,5, her MLU is between 1.38 and 2.38 for French, and between 1.57 and 2.57 for Dutch. The second period goes from age 2;7,5 to age 3;6,25, when the MLU is between 2.5 and 4.5 for both languages. The last period goes from age 3;6,25 to age 3;10,7, when the MLU is above 4.5. The data from Machiel all belong to one period, corresponding to what has been called "early syntax" (MLU < 2).

We adopt the idea that clause structure is gradually acquired (cf. Radford 1990; Wijnen 1995; Ferdinand 1996; Roeper 1992). In this view, the first two word combinations take the form of a binary branching structure, sometimes referred to as a Small Clause:

(A)   [YP XP]

Some combinations clearly express a subject predicate relation, where particles can function as predicates, others express an object-verb relation or a relation of possession, or any other possible relation:

(11)   *maman pati*   (Anouk 2;3,13)
       'mummy left'

(12)   *Anouk poule*   (Anouk 2;4,9)
       'Anouk chicken'

(13)   *lapin ici*   (Anouk 2;3,13)
       'rabbit here'

(14)   *autoi aankleeje*   (Machiel 2;0,6)
       'car dress'

(15)   *Machiel hebben*   (Machiel 2;1,19)
        'Machiel have'

(16)   *deze Machiel*   (Machiel 3;0,29)
        'this one Machiel'

(17)   *deze uit*   (Machiel 2;0,29)
        'this one out'

In her first period, Anouk seems to have no preference as for word order: in her French utterances, there are an equal number of XP_NP orders and of NP_XP orders.

(18)   *aussi pomme*   (Anouk 2;4,17)
        'also apple'

(19)   *pomme aussi*   (Anouk 2;4,17)
        'apple also'

(20)   *Anouk peur*   (Anouk 2;8,3)
        'Anouk fear'

(21)   *peur petit canard*   (Anouk 2;8,3)
        'fear little duck'

Elsewhere (Hulk & van der Linden 1996) we have argued that in this "early syntax" period nothing interesting can yet be said about word order.[4] Variation in early syntax word order has also been mentioned in the literature both for bilingual (Parodi 1990) and for monolingual children (Radford 1990).

Interestingly, however, in this period Anouk also produced some French utterances consisting of three words, which seem to reflect a Dutch SOV word order, where the verb was either finite or infinite. We have not (yet) found such orders in Machiel's data.

(22)   *Anouk papa dessine*   (Anouk 2;4,23)
        'Anouk daddy draws'

(23)   *Anouk maman dessine*   (Anouk 2;4,23)
        'Anouk mummy draws'

(24)   *Anouk riz manger*   (Anouk 2;5,20)
        'Anouk rice eat'

(25)   *maman un aute manger*   (Anouk 2;7,5)
        'mummy another eat'

It might be the case that these utterances are precursors of the next stage in the development of clause structure where children start to adjoin an element to this early binary branching structure, as in:

(B)   [X(P)[YP ZP]]

This adjoined element, which may also occur to the right hand side, is still underspecified as for its syntactic and pragmatic features. It can be an NP, but also a *wh*-word, or just another element, as illustrated in the following utterance by Anouk where the Dutch word *nee* ('no') is right-adjoined to the Small Clause *Anouk chaud*:

(26)   [[*Anouk chaud*] *nee*]
       'Anouk hot no'

However, at this stage, the exact status of such three word utterances with SOV order is not completely clear, we will come back to them below.

The status of the SOV structure in Anouk's French will become clearer during the second period, which starts at age 2;7,5. Her MLU is then above 2.4 and some of her utterances are clearly showing the presence of a functional projection, e.g. the ones with a subject clitic which in French requires the presence of an Infl-type projection:

(27)   *ils sont partis*   (Anouk 2;8,22)
       'they have left'

Utterances in which the finite verb is followed by the negative marker *pas*[5] 'not' also indicate that movement of the verb out of VP to an FP has taken place:

(28)   *mami connait pas*   (Anouk 2;6,11)
       'mummy knows not'

(29)   *veux pas*   (Anouk 3;1,4)
       'want not'

Such structures are characteristic of the next stage in the emergence of the clause structure, where the adjoined position is reanalysed as a functional projection, with a head and a specifier:

(C)   FP[XP F [YP ZP]]

It is generally assumed that in this stage the basic word order is the same as in the adult language: XP_V (Head-Final) in Dutch and V-XP (Head-Initial) in French. In the next section we will, however, see that, for bilingual children, this seems not always to be the case.

3.   Deviant word orders?

In this section we will first present utterances produced by Anouk that show an XP_V word order that seem to be more Dutch-like than French-like. Next we will consider some cases discussed in the literature of utterances with XP_V order in the production of other children acquiring a Head-Initial language. This concerns both bilingual and monolingual children. We will give a brief overview of the type of explanations proposed to account for such word orders. Then we will come back to Anouk and we discuss the plausibility of the different analyses proposed elsewhere, in relation to the XP_V orders produced by Anouk.

3.1 *Anouk*

The most interesting period in Anouk's French data goes from age 2;7,5 until age 3;6,25. In that period there is a predominance of adult like (S)_V_XP orders, but she produces a non-negligible number of utterances showing deviant XP_V orders, both with finite and with non-finite verbs. Utterances with finite verbs take two forms, either they are of the format XP_V_S as in:

(30)	*pour Sophie est le gateau*	(Anouk 2;7,5)
	'for Sophie is the cake'	

(31)	*une autre petite chemise fait mami*	(Anouk 2;11,13)
	'another little blouse makes granny'	

or they do not have a subject and just show XP_V order, as in:

(32)	*petit nounours cherche*	(Anouk 2;8,3)
	'little bear looks for'	

In most utterances with this order the verb is non-finite:

(33)	*un pomme de terre manger*	(Anouk 2;8,3)
	'a potato eat'	

(34)	*ça écouter*	(Anouk 2;8,13)
	'that listen to'	

(35)	*maman écouter*	(Anouk 2;11,13)
	'mummy listen to'	

(36)	*aussi ça jeter*	(Anouk 3;1,4)
	'also that throw away'	

(37) *l'autre mettre*   (Anouk 3;3,17)
      'the other one put'

(38) *beaucoup de papier prendre*   (Anouk 3;4,28)
      'a lot of paper take'

(39) *un tout petit faire*   (Anouk 3;4,28)
      'a very small one make'

In two utterances with deviant word order we find both a finite and an non-finite verb. In (40) there is the finite auxiliary *a* 'has' followed by the past participle *mis* 'put', in (41) there is an impersonal modal auxiliary *faut* 'must' followed by an infinitive *essayer* 'try'.

(40) *beaucoup de pepernoot a mis Zwarte Piet par terre*
      'a lot of sweets has put Zwarte Piet on the floor'

                                                          (Anouk 3;6,25)

(41) *un aute faut essayer*   (Anouk 3;3,29)
      'another must try'

In the last period, until age 3;10,07, Anouk does not produce any French utterances with XP_V word order.

3.2   *Other bilingual children*

Elsewhere in the literature on bilingual acquisition of a Head-Final and a Head-Initial language, utterances with XP_V order in the V_XP language have also been reported. Müller et al (1996), for example, mention the following XP_V utterances in French produced by Ivar, a bilingual French-German child:

(42) *thé thé verse*   (Ivar 2;5,7)
      'tea tea pour'

(43) *et Ferez connais pas*   (Ivar 2;6,27)
      'and F. (I) know not'

They do not discuss the possibility that the appearance of such word orders may be due to the crosslinguistic influence of German on French. They analyse these sentences as a combination of topicalisation of the nominal object with two null clitics: a null subject and a null object clitic. In other words they see these utterances as left dislocations, corresponding to the following adult sentence:

(44) [*le thé$_i$* [*je le$_i$ verse*]]
      'the tea I it pour'

Döpke (1998) has studied crosslinguistic influence in bilingual German-English children and she has also found (some) XP_V structures in their English. She gives the following examples:

(45)   feet hide too   (NS-E2;6)

(46)   me pusher want   (CW-E2;4)

(47)   me it broke   (NS-E2;1)

According to Döpke, a dislocation analysis is not possible here because the object can be preceded by a subject, as shown in (46) and (47). Note that we also found such SOV orders in Anouk's earliest data. Moreover Döpke also found utterances with complex verb structures which clearly can never be dislocations:

(48)   can you that over bring   (CW-E4;0)

(49)   I want look have   (JH-E2;1)

She considers these utterances illustrations of the fact that these children receive an input which offers more contrasts for word order than monolingual children do. Therefore, she argues structural interference is possible: such interference results from the German and English input being processed in relation and in contrast to each other (Döpke 1998).

In the next section we will see however that monolingual English and French children also produce XP_V orders, under certain pragmatic conditions.

3.3 Monolingual children

In the literature on the (monolingual) acquisition of English, a Head-Initial language like French, utterances are discussed which display XP_V word order. Radford (1990) has proposed to analyse these as involving topical information which is left dislocated. This left dislocation, which strictly speaking is adjunction not really dislocation,[6] can take place at the level of VP or IP, according to Radford. Moreover, he sees a parallelism between the syntax of topics and the syntax of wh-phrases: both can be adjoined to VP, with the subject in SpecVP carrying oblique case, as in the following examples:

(50)   where me sleep?   (Adam 2;11)

(51)   a car me got   (Nina 2;5)

At a later stage, wh-phrases and topics adjoin to IP and the nominative subject is in SpecIP:

(52)   *where he can ride in?*

(53)   *my tights I want*   (Nina 2;5)

As for the acquisition data of monolingual French children, Clark (1985) mentions the following three examples with XP_V order:

(54)   *chapeau chercher*
        'hat look for'

(55)   *maman let lit*
        'mummy letter read'

(56)   *cheveux couper papa*
        'hair cut daddy'

Unfortunately, she does not give any information about the age or MLU of the children who produced these utterances.

Ferdinand (1996) also gives a number of examples of utterances showing XP_V word order produced by monolingual French children:

(57)   *puzzle cassé*   (GRE 1;9,14)
        'puzzle broken'

(58)   *couteau met*   (NAT 2;2,2)
        'knife put'

(59)   *cheveux est ça*   (GRE 1;9,28)
        'hair is that'

(60)   *un pomme de terre donne*   (GRE 2;1,25)
        'a potato give'

(61)   *l'eau froide @ montrer*   (DAN 1;8,3)
        'the cold water show'

(62)   *à l'eau veux*   (DAN 1;9,3)
        'in the water want'

Here we find the same patterns we have seen in Anouk's utterances: XP_V orders where the verb is finite or non-finite and one example of XP_V_S (59).

According to Ferdinand, these utterances very often constitute an answer to a question and, therefore, she proposes analysing the XP in first position as a focalised element, which expresses new information.

Moreover, Ferdinand shows that this strategy of putting new information in sentence initial position is also found in a later stage of development in utterances with a subject clitic,[7] as illustrated by the following examples from Philippe:

(63)   *la maison on casse*   (PHI 2;1,26)
       'the house one breaks'

(64)   *celui-là on lève*   (PHI 2;1,26)
       'that-one one lifts'

(65)   *un sucre tu manges*   (PHI 2;6,20)
       'a sugar you eat'

(66)   *sur le lit elle est la dame*   (PHI 2;1,19)
       'on the bed she is the lady'

(67)   *bleu elle est*   (PHI 2;6,13)
       'blue she is'

If one leaves out the subject clitic in these utterances, one obtains the same
XP_V word order we have seen above:

(68)   la maison [on] casse

At this stage of development, children often leave out the subject.[8]

Summarising, we see that XP_V structures are found not only with children
acquiring a Head-Final language, but also, more rarely, in the data of children
acquiring Head-Initial languages. In monolingual children these utterances have
generally been analysed as involving adjunction of an XP to VP or IP, be it for
various pragmatic reasons[9]. For bilingual children an alternative explanation has
been proposed in terms of crosslinguistic influence.

In the next section we'll consider again the XP_V utterances produced by
Anouk, in relation to the analyses proposed in the literature.

3.4   *Back to Anouk*

3.4.1   *XP_V: Adjunction for pragmatic reasons*
The following dialogue shows that in the period when Anouk produces the XP-V
orders, she still is in a stage where subject (clitics) are not obligatory:

(69)   Mother: *le petit oiseau saute?*
                 'the little bird springs'
       Anouk: *non vole*   (Anouk 2;11,27)
                 'no flies'
       Mother: *oui il vole*
                 'yes he flies'

Therefore, it might be possible to analyse these XP_V utterances, at least the ones with a finite verb, as proposed by Ferdinand for monolingual children: involving fronting of a (focalised) XP constituent in the stage of language development where null subject (clitics) are the rule.

Consider in this respect the following dialogue:

(70) ⟨Anouk and her mother are discussing a "petit gateau"⟩
   Mother: *tu veux le manger?*
   　　　　'you want it eat' (Anouk 2;7,5)
   Anouk: *non*
   Mother: *il faut le regarder, il faut pas le manger, non*
   　　　　'one must it look at, one must not it eat, no
   Anouk: *pour Sophie est le gateau*
   　　　　'for Sophie is the cake'
   Mother: *c'est pour Sophie, le petit gateau?*
   　　　　'it is for Sophie, the little cake'

Clearly *pour Sophie* constitutes new information; in adult French one would have used a right dislocation, as does the mother, or adjoin the PP in the following way:

(71) *pour Sophie il est le gateau*

If one leaves out the subject clitic, the utterance used by Anouk arises.

Interestingly, Kail (1989), quoting Bates & MacWhinney (1989), observes in a completely different situation that young children place new information at the beginning of utterances, followed by old or less focal elements of meaning, contrary to adults, who tend to start their sentences with old or topical information. Psycholinguistically speaking, an analysis of the XP_V orders as focalisations is not an implausible one.

Moreover, we have shown elsewhere (Hulk & van der Linden 1996) that Anouk also produces utterances with an XP in initial position followed by a subject clitic and a finite verb, in the same period where she produced the XP_V utterances without subject clitic, just as we have seen above for Philippe ((63)–(67)):

(72) *un aut livre de Babar je connais* (Anouk 2;11,13)
   'another book of Babar I know'

(73) *la carte de mami tu vois* (Anouk 2;11,27)
   'the card of granny you see'

(74) *une maison et une tour Eiffel je fais* (Anouk 3;1,4)
   'a house and a Eiffel tower I make'

(75)   *de l'eau froide je veux*   (Anouk 3;3,17)
       'cold water I want'

(76)   *un bébé caillou j'ai trouvé*   (Anouk 3;4,28)
       'a baby stone I have found'

Do we have to conclude then that there is no difference between Anouk's utterances and the ones of monolingual children? In the next section, we will argue that the answer is yes and no.

4.   What about crosslinguistic influence?

On the one hand, we have seen that XP_V patterns are found in monolingual children acquiring a Head-Initial language, such as French or English; in that respect, Anouk is not different. On the other hand, in Anouk's utterances these patterns are a lot more frequent than in the speech of monolingual French children. Let us consider this difference in frequency in some more detail, first for utterances with a finite verb, and second, for infinitives.

In fact, what is more frequent than in monolingual children, is not the fronting itself, because that is found also in monolingual children. However, in the latter case, generally, a subject clitic is present, as we have seen above, observe the following utterance by Philippe:

(77)   *dans le garage je le porte*   (Philippe 2;2,3)
       'in the garage I it carry'

It is the fronting in combination with a null subject and the use of a finite verb, creating an apparent XP_V order, that is far more frequent in the bilingual data.

Interestingly, we also found other examples of fronting in combination with a null subject in Anouk's data, involving not an object or a PP, but an adverb or a *wh*-phrase. These are very exceptional in monolingual French children (Ferdinand gives only one example):

(78)   *après va dormir*   (Anouk 3;1,4)
       'afterwards go sleep'

(79)   *maintenant vont dormir*   (Anouk 3;1,4)
       'now go sleep'

(80)   *après peux aller à ton travail*   (Anouk 3;3,17)
       'afterwards can go to your work'

(81)   *pourquoi fait la cuisine pour ses copains?*   (Anouk 3;3,25)
        'why cooks for his friends'

Müller et al (1996) also mention such an utterance produced by Ivar, a French-German bilingual child:

(82)   *maintenant sont dans l'armoire*   (Ivar 2;8,15)
        'now are in the cupboard'

Here, clearly the adverbial does not express new information, but serves as the spatial or temporal anchorage of the sentence. We would like to claim however that it is adjoined, just as the XP in the XP_V examples seen above, and that the subject clitic is missing.

Why are such adjoined structures with null subject clitics more frequent in Anouk's French than in the French of monolingual children?

We think that this difference in frequency reflects the *indirect* influence of Dutch. As is well known, in (adult) Dutch we find not only basic OV orders but also, as a consequence of the V2 characteristic, clauses with fronted objects or adjuncts followed by a (finite) verb (and a subject):

(83)   *Zuurkool lust ik niet*
        'sauerkraut I don't like'

(84)   *Nou ga ik weg*
        'Now go I away'

The beginning of such sentences shows OV (or more generally XP_V) word order. On the one hand, in Dutch, especially in the case of a fronted object, this constituent gets a (contrastive) accent and, therefore, will be more salient to the child then the postverbal subject pronoun.

On the other hand, in colloquial adult French a lot of sentences with a subject clitic also contain a left or right dislocated nominal subject, as illustrated in the following sentences:

(85)   *où il est le fil?*
        'where he is the thread'

(86)   *papa il aime pas ça*
        'daddy he loves not that'

As is well known from the literature on the acquisition of French subject clitics, in the beginning children either leave them out, or realise them as a schwa-like sound (cf. Ferdinand 1996; Hulk 1995).

When one leaves out the subject clitic in a sentence with right dislocation such as (85), the resulting order looks very "Dutch like": there seems to be inversion of the subject and the verb (87), just as in a V2 language such as Dutch (88):

(87)   *où est le fil?*
       'where is the thread'

(88)   *waar is de draad?*
       'where is the thread'

Hulk (1995) has shown that French monolingual children do indeed produce such utterances, be it rarely. Now, for the bilingual child getting input both from colloquial French, such as (85) and from Dutch, such as (88), the situation is a lot more complicated then for the monolingual French child. The input may look partially overlapping to him/her. Therefore, it does not come as a surprise that bilingual children have problems with the position and status of subjects in French[10].

This mainly concerns utterances with a finite verb and a missing subject clitic. Now the question can be raised: what about XP_V orders in Anouk's root infinitives in French as in (38) above?

(89) = (38)   *beaucoup de papier prendre*   (Anouk 3;4,28)
              'much paper take'

It is clear that infinitives never take a subject clitic; consequently, it is not very plausible to assume that Anouk's XP_V infinitives involve a null subject clitic. Nevertheless, it is not excluded to analyse these utterances as also involving preposing of the XP and adjunction to VP or to an FP, just as in the case of the finite XP_V utterances. Indeed one of the analyses proposed in the literature for root infinitives is that they involve an empty aspectual or modal auxiliary (see Ferdinand 1996 for such a proposal concerning French). If we adopt such a proposal the XP-V root infinitives could be analysed as involving fronting and adjunction of an XP to the (empty) FP above VP. We have seen in (80) above that Anouk produces utterances such as the following where the adverb is in front of a modal auxiliary, which is repeated here as (90):

(90)   *après peux aller à ton travail*   (Anouk 3;3,17)
       'afterwards can go to your work'

If one leaves out the modal auxiliary in such an utterance, one obtains an XP_V root infinitive. We indeed found examples of such fronted adverbs in Anouk's data:

(91) *maintenant faire autre chose*   (Anouk 2;11,27)
      'now do something else'

(92) *en bas, en bas donner*   (Anouk 3;3,17)
      'downstairs, downstairs give'

(93) *quand-même tout donner*   (Anouk 3;3,17)
      'nevertheless everything eat'

Interestingly, (93) shows a property of adult French infinitives that may also have played a role in confusing Anouk about the possibility of XP_V word order: certain objects, such as bare quantifiers *tout* 'everything' and *rien* 'nothing' and clitic objects may precede infinitives, creating an XP_V order which is similar to the basic XP_V order in Dutch root infinitives:[11]

(94) French: *je vais*   *le*   *manger*
      Dutch: *ik ga*   *het*   *eten*
               'I go'   it   eat'

(95) French: *tu veux*   *tout*   *avoir*
      Dutch: *jij wil*   *alles*   *hebben*
               'you want everything have'

In Dutch, basic XP_V root infinitives are very frequent in acquisition data (see Wijnen & Verrips 1998 for an overview). This phenomenon is sometimes related to the observation (Klein 1974) that Dutch care takers display a preference for SOV-word order in child-addressed speech, often achieved by the use of (modal) auxiliaries. Moreover the last part of the sentence gets the accent and therefore is more salient for the child than the preceding part. Young children imitate their mother's preferred word order but repeat only the accentuated part and leave out the auxiliary.

Anouk also produces a lot of such root infinitives in Dutch: between age 2;7,28 and age 3;04,28, 27% of the total number of Dutch verbs are root infinitives.

(96) *soep eten*   (Anouk 2;9,17)
      'soup eat'

(97) *geen baby maken*   (Anouk 2;10,11)
      'no baby make'

(98) *nog meer kijken*   (Anouk 2;11,27)
      'still more look'

Interestingly, Anouk also produces a high percentage of French root infinitives and these take a long time to disappear. The total percentage of these root infinitives (included the ones with correct and the ones with deviant word order) is much higher than that produced by monolingual French children. We cannot go into this phenomenon here, but we just want to suggest that this high frequency of French root infinitives may be due to the indirect influence of Dutch. Dutch children are known to produce a (very) high percentage of root infinitives in the early stages of acquisition; this has been related to the input Dutch children receive, which often presents a salient XP_Vinf order at the end of the utterance. Now, Anouk also gets such an input in Dutch which in Mac-Whinney's terms has to compete with the French input. Moreover, as we have seen above in certain cases the object may precede the infinitive in French, even in a basic configuration. Therefore, here we have again a situation where the Dutch and the French input partially overlap, creating a difficult situation for the bilingual child to cope with. Just as in the case of the finite XP_V utterances, we can say that the structures Anouk produces are not different from the ones produced by monolingual children, but that she uses them more frequently and much longer. This we assume is due to the indirect influence of Dutch: Anouk receives not only input which clearly gives evidence for the French or the Dutch word order, but she also receives input which to her bilingual ears is ambiguous and may for some time incorrectly be taken to constitute evidence for a Dutch like word order pattern in French.

Summarising, we think that the XP_V orders in bilingual French-Dutch children are not an example of transfer of basic Dutch OV-orders nor of missetting of a parametric value on the basis of the Dutch input. They represent an example of a general tendency in child language to build up the clause structure by adjoining pragmatically salient element to the clause, a phenomenon also present in monolingual French children. Their frequency in the language of our bilingual child may be explained by the indirect influence of the adult Dutch input, which has a lot of OV structures in root infinitives and where fronting of XPs in finite sentences is a general syntactic phenomenon and where subject pronouns appear in unaccented, postverbal position.

5.   Conclusion

In this chapter, we have looked into crosslinguistic influence at the syntactic level in bilingual children. We have seen that just as in the case of acquisition of the lexicon input plays a crucial role. It is on the basis of input that words are learned and that syntactic rules are discovered by the child. Processes of storage, activation and access to the acquired knowledge are probably to a large extent comparable across the two language domains. For bilingual individuals in a monolingual language context, one language is activated while the other is inhibited. However, inhibition is never complete: we have seen that they prefer to stick to the words and the syntactic system of one language, but that influence from the other language cannot be completely suppressed. The input in two languages confronts bilingual children with a sometimes confusing sample of possibilities from which to choose.

For bilingual children, establishing the syntactic rules of each language may be a much harder task than for monolingual children. Not only are there two systems to be acquired instead of one, but the input to which children are exposed may seem ambiguous to them. Disambiguation is harder when the adult input in one language offers cues for an erroneous analysis of the other language. Our French-Dutch bilingual subject is exposed to word orders in French and Dutch which may lead her to the conclusion that XP_V orders or root infinitives may be used in French as they are in Dutch. Some of theses structures are possible but very rare in French; we find them in monolingual French children under the influence of pragmatic strategies. The fact that Anouk produces them more frequently and for a much longer period suggests that this happens under the concomitant influence of the same pragmatic strategies in combination with the possibility to use these structures regularly in Dutch.

Acknowledgments

The investigation reported on in this chapter has been carried out in collaboration with Elisabeth van der Linden of the University of Amsterdam, who wrote the preceding chapter on the access and activation in the lexicon.

Notes

1. Under certain conditions the subject can also follow the verb in interrogative root sentences in literary, written French. In colloquial spoken French, however, questions are formed without subject verb inversion.

2. For a limited number of verbs (such as *connaitre, savoir, aimer, détester, comprendre*) a thematic object may be adjoined clause-initially:
   (i)   *ça elle sait*
          'that she knows'
   (ii)   *les moules je déteste*
          'mussels I hate'

3. Compare to V2 languages such as Dutch where both topicalised and focalised constituents may be fronted to SpecCP:
    (i)   *De appels heeft Jan gegeten*
          'the apples has John eaten'

4. It might be the case that we witness here the last moment before the achievement of syntactic differentiation by Anouk (cf. the preceding chapter).

5. In the first period Anouk only expressed clausal negation by a left or right peripheral *non/nee* or *pas* 'not'. The same holds for Machiel:
    (i)   *mener non*   (Machiel 2;00,05)
          'bring no'
    (ii) *non pas ça va*   (Anouk 2;05,20)
          'no not that goes'

6. In dislocated structures the left (or right) adjoined constituent is repeated in the form of a (clitic) pronoun inside the clause: *Marie$_i$, je l$_i$'ai vue l'autre jour* 'Marie, I her have seen the other day'

7. Interestingly, Blanche-Benveniste (1996) cites examples from spoken (adult) French involving precisely this word order. These utterances have a special intonation and are analysed as focalisations:
    (i)   *un verre de sangria ils donnaient*
          'a glass of sangria they gave'
    (ii) *un pain il nous faut demain*
          'a bread we need tomorrow'
    Moreover, such constructions are reported to be frequent in Belgian French.

8. There is an abundant literature on this topic, which we will not discuss here.

9. We will leave aside the question whether the fronted constituent should be analysed as a topic or a focus. We think that it can express both pragmatic functions, maybe because this position has not yet its fully specified features.

10. Elsewhere Hulk (to appear) shows that Anouk acquires the French subject clitics more or less in the same order as monolingual French children discussed in the literature. She is however quite a bit slower: only at age 3;03,17, 70% of all Anouk's utterances with a finite verb contain a subject clitic, whereas the monolingual child Philippe reaches this percentage at age 2;06 and the (monolingual) child A. studied by Hamann at al (1995), at age 2;09. Moreover, contrary to what has been found in monolingual children, there is no convincing evidence in Anouk's data in favour of an analysis of her subject clitics as agreement markers, rather than weak pronouns. This also suggests that there is an indirect influence of Dutch, which has weak subject pronouns and no real clitics of the agreement-marker type. The position of Dutch subject pronouns partly overlaps with that of the French subject clitics. Consequently Anouk has problems with the status and position of French subject clitics, due to partially overlapping, conflicting input from both her languages.

11. See Hulk (1997, to appear) who shows that Anouk has problems with the correct position of object pronouns in French which may also be related to the partial overlap with Dutch.

References

Bates, Elizabeth & Brian MacWhinney. 1989. "Functionalism and the competition model". In B. MacWhinney & E. Bates (eds), *The Crosslinguistic Study of Sentence Processing*. Cambridge: Cambridge University Press.

Blanche-Benveniste, C. 1996. "Trois remarques sur l'ordre des mots dans la langue parlée". *Langue Française* 111: 108–119.

Clark, Eve. 1985. "The acquisition of Romance with special reference to French". In D. I. Slobin (ed.), *The Crosslinguistic Study of Language Acquisition*. Hillsdale, NJ: Lawrence Erlbaum. Vol. 7: 687–767.

De Houwer, Annick. 1990. *The Acquisition of Two Languages From Birth: A Case Study*. Cambridge: Cambridge University Press.

Döpke, Susanne. 1996. "The weaker language in simultaneous bilingualism: why it is not like L2", unpubl. paper, Monash University.

Döpke, Susanne. 1998. "Competing language structures: the acquisition of verb placement by bilingual German-English children". *Journal of Child Language* 25(3): 555–584.

Ferdinand, Astrid. 1996. *The Development of Functional Categories. The Acquisition of the Subject in French*. PhD HIL Leiden.

Gawlitzek-Maiwald, Ira & Rosemary Tracy. 1996. "Bilingual bootstrapping". *Linguistics* 34: 901–926.

Hamann, Cornelia, Luigi Rizzi & Uli Frauenfelder. 1995. "On the acquisition of the pronominal system in French". *Recherches Linguistiques de Vincennes* 24: 83–103.

Hulk, Aafke C. J. 1995. "L'acquisition du sujet en français". *Recherches Linguistiques de Vincennes* 24: 33–55.

Hulk, Aafke C. J. 1997. "The acquisition of French object pronouns by a Dutch/French bilingual child". In A. Sorace et al. (eds), *Proceedings of GALA'97 conference on Language Acquisition*. Edinburgh, 521–526.

Hulk, Aafke C. J. to appear. "L'acquisition des pronoms clitiques français par un enfant bilingue français-néerlandais".

Hulk, Aafke C. J. & Elisabeth van der Linden. 1996. "Language mixing in a French-Dutch bilingual child". *Toegepaste Taalwetenschap in Artikelen* 55 (EUROSLA 6, A selection of papers): 89–103.

Kail, Michèle. 1989. "Cue validity, cue cost and processing types in sentence comprehension in French and Spanish". In B. MacWhinney & E. Bates (eds), *The Crosslinguistic Study of Sentence Processing*. Cambridge: Cambridge University Press.

Klein, R. M. 1974. *Word Order: Dutch Children and Their Mothers*. Publications of the Institute of General Linguistics 9, University of Amsterdam.

Lanza, Elizabeth. 1992. "Can bilingual two year olds codeswitch?" *Journal of Child Language* 19: 633–658.

Leopold, Werner. 1949–1970. *Speech Development of a Bilingual Child: A Linguist's Record*. Vols. 1–4. New York: AMS Press.

MacWhinney, Brian. 1987. "Applying the competition model to bilingualism". *Applied Psycholinguistics* 8: 315–327.

Meisel, Jürgen M. 1989. "Early differentiation of languages in bilingual children". In K. Hyltenstam & L. Obler (eds), *Bilingualism Across the Life Span. Aspects of Acquisition, Maturity and Loss.* Cambridge: Cambridge University Press: 13–40.

Meisel, Jürgen M. (ed). 1990. *Two First Languages. Early Grammatical Development in Bilingual Children.* Dordrecht: Foris.

Meisel, Jürgen. (ed). 1994. *Bilingual first language acquisition: French and German grammatical development.* Amsterdam and Philadelphia: John Benjamins.

Müller, Natascha, Berthold Crysmann & Georg A. Kaiser. 1996. "Interactions between the acquisition of French object-drop and the Development of the C-system". *Language Acquisition* 5: 35–63.

Paradis, Johanne & Fred Genesee. 1996. "Syntactic acquisition in bilingual children". *Studies in Second Language Acquisition* 18: 1–15.

Parodi, Teresa. 1990. "The acquisition of word order regularities and case morphology". In J. Meisel (ed), *Two First Languages. Early Grammatical Development in Bilingual Children.* Dordrecht: Foris, 157–193.

Radford, Andrew. 1990. *Syntactic Theory and the Acquisition of English Syntax.* Oxford: Basil Blackwell.

Roeper, Tom. 1992. "From the initial state to V2: acquisition principles in action." In J. Meisel (ed), *The Acquisition of Verb Placement, Functional Categories and V2 Phenomena in Language Acquisition.* Dordrecht: Kluwer.

Schlyter, Suzanne & Gisela Håkansson. 1994. "Word order in Swedish as the first language, second language and weaker language in bilinguals". *Scandinavian Working Papers in Bilingualism* 9: 49–66.

Taeschner, Traute. 1983. *The Sun is Feminine. A study of Language Acquisition in Bilingual Children.* Berlin: Springer.

Tracy, Rosemarie. 1995. *Child Languages in Contact: Bilingual Language Acquisition (English–German) in Early Childhood.* Habililitationsschrift, Universität Tübingen.

Vihman, Marilyn. 1985. "Language differentiation in the bilingual child". *Journal of Child Language* 12: 297–325.

Wijnen, Frank. 1995. "Incremental Acquisition of Phrase Structure". *Proceedings of NELS* 25: 105–118.

Wijnen, Frank & Maaike Verrips. 1998. "The acquisition of Dutch syntax". In S. Gillis & A. de Houwer (eds), *The Acquisition of Dutch.* Amsterdam and Philadelphia: John Benjamins.

The Interplay Between Language-Specific Development and Crosslinguistic Influence

Susanne Döpke
Monash University

1. Introduction

Much interest in bilingual first language acquisition during the last two decades has focussed on the question of whether or not very young bilingual children are able to differentiate between their two languages. Controversies have arisen regarding whether language mixing and pragmatically unmotivated codeswitching are evidence of fusion of the two linguistic systems, whether they are features of the weaker language being learned like a second language, or whether they are performance limitations unrelated to the children's ability to develop linguistic knowledge.

In this paper I will explore possible origins of seemingly crosslinguistic structures. For this purpose I will compare the developmental structures of a small group of bilingual German–English youngsters with those of the average monolingual child. I will show that most of the untypical developmental structures found in the speech of bilingual children also occur in monolingual data but that they are more frequent in the bilingual data. I will argue that structural similarities between the two languages affect the strength of particular cues within each of the languages. Thus, there is a situation of cross-language cue competition. The children's strive for contrast between the languages helps them to resolve the structural incompatibilities and once their processing abilities have grown they are able to integrate a wider range of structural cues. This allows them to retract from the non-target overgeneralisations again.

2.   What is the status of untypical structures?

The literature on the subject of untypical structures in the speech of young
bilingual children suggests three possibilities for explaining them: (a) a single
syntactic system made up of structures from both languages, (b) one language
dominating over the other, and (c) cognitive interaction between the languages.

Under the first possibility, it is assumed that, during the early stage of
language development, young children are unaware that they are dealing with
two languages. Therefore, they initially develop a joint syntactic system for both
languages. This position was first put forward by Leopold (1947) and developed
in more detail by Volterra & Taeschner (1978). It has found support in a range
of studies in the early eighties (Redlinger & Park 1980; Saunders 1982;
Taeschner 1983; Vihman 1985). If Possibility 1 is correct, then the syntactic
structures which bilingual children produce should be very similar in form and
frequency, irrespective of the language spoken (Genesee 1989). In addition,
crosslinguistic influences should be bilateral.

Under the second possibility, it is assumed that the two languages of the
bilingual child develop at unequal rates. In other words, the bilingual child makes
use of the syntactic structures of the faster developing, or stronger, language
when generating sentences in her weaker language (Schlyter 1993; Gawlitzek-
Maiwald & Tracy 1996; Lanza 1997). If Possibility 2 is correct, crosslinguistic
influences should be unilateral from the stronger to the weaker language.

As a third possibility, I am suggesting that the children's immature stage of
structure building is affected by cross-language cue competition. In that view,
the children are assumed to be aware that they are dealing with two language
systems, and they intend to express this awareness not only in their lexical but
also in their structural choices. However, they also notice the similarities between
the languages that they learn, and similar structures gain strength crosslinguistically. In addition to my own studies (Döpke 1992, 1998, 1999a, 1999b),
evidence for this possibility can also be found in the work of Hulk & van der
Linden (1996), Paradis (in print) and Müller (1998). If Possibility 3 is correct,
then (a) target structures should be in the majority, (b) crosslinguistic structures
should be bilateral, and (c) it should be possible for the seemingly crosslinguistic
structures to have been generated on the basis of intra-linguistic input, that is,
without reference to the other language.

The aim of this paper is to review the evidence for and against these three
possibilities in my data and to develop the argument in favour of cross-language
cue competition. I will do this through a three-way comparison of bilingual

children's target structures, bilingual children's non-target structures and mono-lingual language development.

3.   Method

The data were drawn from a longitudinal study of four German-English bilingual children, two boys (CW and JH) and two girls (NS and AS). The first three children were first-born, and AS was the younger sister of NS. Each child heard German from the mother and English from the father. English was also the language spoken between the parents and in the society at large. Thus the children had plenty of contact with English, but German was largely limited to interactions with their mothers. To make up for the limited exposure to German, the mothers were very consistent with their own language choice and insisted on the children complying with the 'one person-one language' rule. As a result, all four children were able to use German spontaneously throughout the period of recording.

The span of data collection was constrained by availability, starting between 2;0 and 2;7 and finishing between 3;5 and 5;0. The children were recorded monthly on audio and video equipment in free play and other types of spontane-ous interaction for two sessions of 45 minutes to one hour, one session each with their German-speaking mother and a familiar English speaker. The data were transcribed by research assistants, and the transcriptions were checked for accuracy by me.

The children's developing language abilities were monitored through MLU-word averages of their spontaneous utterances each month. The collation of MLU-word averages into phases as suggested by Clahsen, Penke & Parodi (1993/94) was extended to cover longer utterances and resulted in the following phases: Phase II 1.75–2.74, Phase III 2.75–3.74, Phase IV 3.75–4.75 and Phase V+ 4.75+. The advantage of this procedure lies in reducing the erratic effect which individual recording situations can have on the quantification of data and allows the collation of rare structures to interpretable levels. Table 1 shows the children's entry age into each phase, separately for German and English.

With due caution because of the conceptual problems associated with MLU counts and the added difficulties with comparing them across languages, two things are evident from Table 1: firstly, there is developmental progress in both languages, and secondly, for the most part English utterances are slightly longer than German utterances, except in the case of AS. Where ages are given in brackets, we do not exactly know when the child first entered a particular phase because there are no recordings leading up to it. This is particularly pertinent in

Table 1. *Overview of the children's entry age into phases*

Phase	CW		NS		JH		AS	
	G	E	G	E	G	E	G	E
II	2;4	2;3	(2;2)	(2;2)	(2;0)		(2;7)	(2;7)
III	2;7	2;7	2;5	2;4	2;3	(2;0)	(2;10)	2;11
IV	3;0	2;9	3;1	2;8	2;8	2;3	3;3	3;3
V	(4;8)	3;6	3;6	3;3	3;5	3;0	3;11	3;11

Ages in brackets indicate the first recording or a recording after a break.

the case of CW's entry into Phase V in German because of a gap of eight months since the previous recording. Given the wide range of developmental variability among monolingual children, there is no reason to believe that the bilingual children are significantly different from monolingual children with respect to utterance length at various ages.

Analyses have so far been performed on the base position of the verb in the verb phrase, the position of verbs in relation to negation and modal particles, the development of finiteness, and the use of non-finite verbs in positions reserved for finite verbs in German. For each of these analyses comparative information is available regarding monolingual children's development. The differences in the language systems of German and English with respect to each of these will be briefly explained in the next section together with the target structures produced by the bilingual children. In Section 5, the bilingual children's non-target structures in each of these areas will be compared to similar non-target structures in monolingual children. This will be followed by a discussion of the motivation for these non-target structures in Section 6 and the insights into the production processes afforded to us by the data in Section 7.

4.   Children's target structures

4.1   *The base position of the verb*

The position of the verb in the verb phrase is Head-Initial in English, but Head-Final in German. This difference expresses itself in the very first multiword utterances of young children in that the nonfinite verb precedes the verb complement in English, and vice versa in German. Thus, example (1) is typical of young children's English, and example (2) is a typical developmental utterance in German.

(1)   *Nise do that*   (NS-E2;3)
      (S) V XP
      'Denise does/did that' or 'Denis, do that!'

(2)   *Mama Tennis spielen*   (CW-G2;3)
      Mum tennis play
      (S)   XP   V
      'mum plays/is playing tennis' or 'mum, play tennis!'

Well over 90% of all utterances with simplex verbs feature the V_XP configuration, as in (1), in the children's English. Since (2) is a developmental structure in German, it naturally declines over the four phases from above 40% of all sentences with simplex verbs in Phase II to 10% or less in Phase V. That it never totally disappears is due to adult German allowing elliptical utterances consisting only of a VP as well as the pragmatically softened version of the imperative, which has the nonfinite verb in sentence final position. Thus, utterances with simplex verbs nearly always precede the complements in English, but frequently follow them in German. This tendency is strongest during the early stages of the children's development, but also still happens to some degree during the later stages (Döpke 1998).

In adult German, simplex verbs are required to take on finiteness features and to move to the V2 position. This effectively leads to SVO being an acceptable target structure in German and in English and is therefore an area of pervasive structural overlap between the languages. At the same time, it is the reason for the developmental XP_V structure to gradually diminish.

However, the verb nonfinal-final difference between English and German is preserved in sentences with complex verbs featuring an auxiliary or modal verb plus a nonfinite main verb, as in examples (3) and (4).

(3)   *we can make it   tall*   (NS-E3;3)
      S   Aux V   XP XP

(4)   *ich kann Essen machen*   (CW-G2;3)
      I   can   food   prepare
      S   Aux XP   V
      'I can prepare food'

In the children's English, in sentences with complex verb forms the verb precedes the complement, as in (3), in nearly 100% of cases. In the children's German, the target structure with the verb following the complement, as in (4), is well represented with levels between 60% and 90% in Phases II and V. However, it dips to levels between 26% and 42% in Phases III and IV (Döpke

1998). While this is unexpected in German, the children's structures are nevertheless very different from their English structures in quantitative terms, due to the coexistence of the verb-final option. We will come back to the non-target word order in Section 5.

4.2 *Finiteness*

While SVO is a syntactic surface structure that can be found in English as well as in German, the languages differ in that finiteness is always marked on verbs in this position in German, but not so in English. In both languages, the children increase finiteness marking in obligatory contexts from Phase II through to V. Because finiteness is more pervasive in German than in English, absolute numbers of finite verbs are always higher in German than in English (Döpke 1999b).

In order to compare the rate with which finiteness develops across the two languages, two measures were employed which were chosen for their comparability between German and English: (a) person suffixes on simplex verbs in third person singular contexts, and (b) finiteness in all contexts requiring overt finiteness marking. The latter includes all auxiliary and modal contexts, past tense in both languages, and simplex verbs in all singular person contexts in German but in English only in the 3rd person singular. For both measures, utterances with finite forms are calculated as a percentage of all utterances requiring the relevant finiteness features.

For all except CW, the percentage of finiteness marking is higher in the children's German than in their English on both measures. This difference is more pronounced for the 3rd person singular measure, ranging between 14% to 70% difference, than for the comprehensive finiteness measure where the difference ranges between 11% and 57% (Döpke 1999b). The fact that finiteness develops faster in the bilingual children's German than in their English is in keeping with German monolingual children attaining finiteness marking more quickly than English monolingual children (Phillips 1995; Lindner & Johnston 1992).

In the case of CW, the finiteness rate in English exceeds the finiteness rate in German by between 3% to 30% for the 3rd person singular measure and 3% to 10% for the comprehensive finiteness measure. I will propose an explanation for the disparity between CW and the other children in Section 7.

4.3 *Verb raising*

While the movement of the German Head-Final verb to the V2 position can lead to word order similarities in German and English utterances, further modification with negation or modal particles makes it evident that the structural similarity of SVO is merely superficial. In example (5a) and the developmental utterance in (5b) we see that the pre-complement verb in English remains in its base position at the head of the VP and that modal particles and negation precede it. This contrasts with German simplex verbs being moved out of the verb phrase to the V2 position. As a consequence, mid-sentence modifications like modal particles and negation follow the verb, as in (6a) and (6b), or are scrambled further into the verb phrase as in (6c).

(5) a. *we just play this*   (JH-E2;11)
         Prt V   XP

     b. *that not   come downs* (sic!)   (AS-E3;5)
         Neg V   XP
         'that doesn't come down'

(6) a. *die haben auch Schuhe*   (JH-G2;4)
         they have also shoes
              V   Prt XP
         'they have shoes too'

     b. *ich mache nicht den Kaffee so*   (AS-G2;11)
         I   make not   the coffee like that
             V   Neg XP   XP
         'I don't make the coffee like that'

     c. *ich weiß es   nicht*   (NS-G3;6)
         I   know it   not
             V   XP Neg
         'I don't know that'

In Döpke (1999a) I show that, in each language environment and each phase of their development, all four bilingual children produce more mid-sentence modification structures which are language-specific than mid-sentence modification structures taken from the other language. In other words, verbs are mostly moved past the negation or modal particle when the children speak German, but stay in their base position when they speak English. Moreover, the acquisition of target structures passes through the same steps of development as have respectively been identified for the monolingual acquisition of English and German.

The rate of language-specific versus cross-language structures varies from child to child and from phase to phase. In German, phase tallies range from a low of 2:1 in Phase II of JH and NS, and Phase III of CW to a high of 40:1 language-specific to cross-language structures in Phase V of NS and AS. In English the range is between 4:1 in Phase II of AS and 55:1 in Phase V of CW. For NS and AS, the rate of language-specific to cross-language structures is higher in their German than in their English, whereas for CW and JH the trend is reversed. Thus, the difference between German and English increases as the children's language becomes more complex.

It needs to be noted, though, that many utterances with mid-sentence modification exhibit the same structure in German and English. These are of the type S_Aux_Neg/Prt_V or S_Aux_Neg/Prt. They, too, are target structures, but because they are shared between the two languages they are excluded here. The relative proportions of target versus non-target structures are, therefore, much more favourable than those cited for language-specific structures versus non-target structures. This will be explored in more detail in Section 5.

4.4 *Conclusions regarding Possibility 1*

The evidence presented so far clearly supports the position that the grammatical structures of the bilingual children's output are not identical in the two languages. In quantitative terms, the children differentiate English and German. When they speak English, they almost always use English target structures, either of the adult type or developmental structures typical of monolingual English-speaking children.

When they speak German, they also predominantly use adult or child target structures and follow similar developmental routes to monolingual German-speaking children. The greatest differences to monolingual children is found with respect to the word order in the verb phrase in Phases III and IV. But even here, it is clear that the children are not producing identical syntactic structures in the two languages.

Thus, by and large, the development of each of the two languages is oriented towards the relevant language-specific input, although this is much clearer in the children's English than in their German. Possibility 1, according to which the bilingual child originally assumes that her two languages share the same syntactic systems, is therefore untenable.

At the same time, the evidence presented with respect to target structures indicates that there is a component of the output which does not conform with target expectations. I will turn to this in the next section.

5.   Children's non-target structures

In what follows I will describe the non-target structures that occur in each of the structural areas discussed in Section 4. This will allow us to consider Possibility 2, namely that unequal dominance of the languages causes the children to use the structures of their stronger language in their weaker language.

5.1   *The base position of the verb*

The placement of verbs in Head-Initial position in the verb phrase is one of the two areas which are strongest with respect to non-target structures in the children's German (Döpke 1998). This structure is exemplified in (9).

(9)   *ich möchte tragen   dich*   (CW-G3;2)
        I   want   to carry you
        S   Aux   V   XP

Such structures have been said to be unattested in monolingual children's German (Penner 1994) or have been argued to be due to right-adjoinment of the verb complement (Köhler & Bruyere 1995–96). For the bilingual children, they are modest in numbers during Phases II and V (n < 8), but equalled or out-numbered the target structures of Aux_XP_V in Phases III (22 < n < 34) and IV (34 < n < 148). Their sheer frequency as well as the fact that they commonly involve direct objects make right-adjoinment an unlikely explanation. The effect is illustrated in Figure 1 for three of the children.[1]

Though errors in the head direction of the verb in English are rare, they do occur. They can comprise simplex verbs in Head-Final position as in (10) or complex verbs as in (11).

(10)   *me pusher want*   (CW-E2;4)
        S XP   V

(11)   *I want look have*   (JH-E2;1)
        S V   XP V

Errors in the order of verbs and verb complements are very rare in the data from monolingual English-speaking children. The few examples that have been reported in the literature involve two-word utterances, which can convincingly be interpreted as topicalisation structures (Radford 1990: 79f.). Utterances like those in (10) and (11), which involve subjects or complex verbs, have not been reported. The fact that each of the four bilingual children occasionally produces

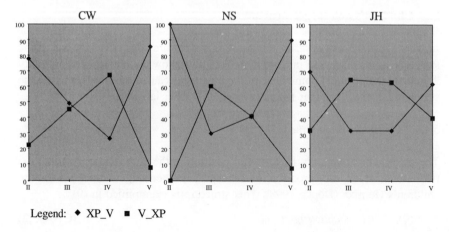

Legend: ◆ XP_V ■ V_XP

Figure 1. *Relative order of verbs and their complements in complex verb constructions in the children's German*

utterances of this type has to be considered a difference to monolingual populations in spite of its lack of systematicity.

To sum this up, we need to acknowledge that there is systematic variation of the order of verbs and verb complements in the German verb phrases of the bilingual children and occasional variation of this type in their English. Neither of these variations can be found in monolingual children of the respective languages.

5.2 *Finiteness*

The German matrix clause requirement for nonfinite verbs to be in final position and finite verbs to be in the V2 position find expression in the bilingual data in the fact that finite verbs are rarely found in final position[2] and pre-complement verbs are mostly finite. Interestingly, this also translates to the Aux_V_XP structure, as in (12).

> (12)   *ich kann seh   dein Pferd*   (JH-G3;0)
>   I   can   see   your horse
>   S   Aux V+1SG XP

This tendency for marking pre-complement verbs in complex verb structures as finite is strongest in JH, who marks 40% (n=16) and 44% (n=84) of them in this way in Phases III and IV, respectively. For the other children this is a phenomenon of Phases III and IV as well, with 28% (n=16) and 15% (n=11) in the NS corpus and 8% (n=3) and 12% (n=19) in the CW corpus. It is weakest for AS with only 6% (n=6) and 3% (n=3) in Phases III and IV, respectively (Döpke 1998, 1999b). This suggests that finiteness is associated with the verb being in pre-complement position, but not necessarily in V2.

Agreement errors on simplex verbs come to between 10% and 20% in one phase or another in German. This makes it difficult to dismiss them as "rare" as is usually done for monolingual German-speaking children (Clahsen, Eisenbein & Penke 1996). In English, agreement errors remain at 5% or less. Comparisons with the rate of finiteness development in monolingual children suggest that the bilingual children persist with nonfinite forms longer than expected (Lahey et al. 1992; Döpke 1999b).

As is typical of bilingual children, lexical gaps are filled with the help of words from the other language. Structurally, the morphological marking of cross-language verbs is of interest. There are a total of 257 English verbs in the four children's German. Not surprisingly 72% (n=186) of them contain no ending, which is equal to the -Ø ending for 1SG in German and presents an overlap in the affixation of German and English verbs. 19% (n=49) of English verbs in the German context contain other German verb affixes and only 9% (n=22) are imported with their English verb morphology attached. These include -s as well as -ing.

In contrast, there are only 35 German verbs in the children's English. Of these, 43% (n=15) are bare stems and therefore morphologically either English or German. 48% (n=17) of the German verbs are imported with their German verb morphology intact. Only three German verbs (9%) take on English verb morphology in the English context, all of them produced by AS. Thus, in relation to the number of imported verbs, English verbs are more likely to be integrated into the German morphological system than German verbs are morphologically integrated into English.

The greater strength of German verb morphology is also evident from the transfer of verb affixes on their own. There were 14 German verbs marked with -s or -ing in the children's German and 13 English verbs marked with a German verb affix in the children's English. In relation to the total cross-language verb influence this constitutes a much higher percentage of German verb morphology in English (13/48=27%) than English verb morphology in German (14/271=5%).

In sum, there are several areas in which the bilingual children exhibit differences to monolingual children of either language. This includes the association of finiteness marking with the pre-complement position of the verb rather than the V2 position in German, the level of agreement errors and, of course, cross-language verb morphology.

5.3 *Verb raising*

As we have just seen, the bilingual children's German lacks the obligatory connection between finiteness and V2. This is further evident in nonfinite verbs preceding the verb complements as in (13), the negation or modal particle as in (14) or even the subject as in (15).

(13) *ich finden* *Pflaster*   (NS-G2;6)
   I find   band-aid
   S V+nonfinite XP

(14) *du tanzen* *auch da*   (AS-G2;11)
   you dance   also there
   S V+nonfinite Prt XP

(15) *wo gehen* *deine Auto*   (CW-G2;9)
   where go   your car
   WH V+nonfinite S

In monolingual children, examples like (13) are rare and limited to the early stages of development, and those in (14) and (15) are all but non-existent (Poeppel & Wexler 1993; Clahsen & Penke 1992; Clahsen, Penke & Parodi 1993/94; Rohrbacher & Vainikka 1995). In the bilingual data, they appear commonly at rates of 30% to 50% of all simplex verbs in V2 position during one phase or another (Döpke 1999b). A similar tendency can be found occasionally in monolingual children (Köhler & Bruyère 1995/96). The regularity with which nonfinite verbs appear in each of the bilingual children's corpora sets them apart from monolingual German children. Thus, it is not only that finite verbs appear in positions other than V2, as we have seen in the previous section, but that nonfinite verbs appear in the V2 position.

 Another facet of verb raising in the bilingual data is that the children do not treat it as obligatory, but instead, merely as a possible structure. This can be seen from utterances like those in (16) and (17).

(16) *ich nicht weiß das*   (AS-G3;1)
   I not know that
   S Neg V+1sG XP

(17) *Katze nicht gehen* *zu Bett*   (JH-G2;11)
   I not go   to bed
   S Neg V+nonfinite XP

Structures like those in (16) and (17) are not frequent. This is partly due to negated utterances being relatively infrequent in naturally occurring data anyway, and partly due to the fact that the children also use the full range of possible target structures at the same time that they produce the non-target structures. However, there are some examples of this type from each of the four bilingual children (CW:35, JH:11, NS:17, AS:6). They are of interest for two reasons: firstly, they add to the picture we gained from $Aux\_V_{nonfin}\_XP$ and $Aux\_V_{fin}\_XP$ above, namely that the bilingual children in this study do not necessarily associate verb movement with movement to V2 and that it is the pre-complement position rather than V2 which motivates them to mark verbs as finite; and secondly, monolingual German-speaking children do not produce structures like those in (16) or (17). So far the only exception to this has been reported for an Austrian child by Schaner-Wolles (1995/96).[3] Thus, there is once again a difference between the bilingual children and monolingual children in that the unusual structures can be found predictably, though infrequently, in the bilingual data, but only exceptionally in monolingual children.

Parallel to the lack of verb raising in German, there is evidence for verb raising in English. Mostly these are V_Neg/Prt structures as in (18), but they can also involve scrambling as (19). In addition, there are a few isolated examples of subject-verb inversion from each child, as in (20).

(18)   *you go not to bed*   (JH-E2;9)
          S   V Neg XP
          'you don't go to bed'

(19)   *let him not out*   (CW-E3;7)
          V XP Neg XP
          'don't let him out!'

(20)   *got your baby teeth*   (NS-E3;7)
          V S   XP
          'has your baby got teeth?'

Verbs preceding the negation as in (18) and (19) are said to be non-existent in monolingual English-speaking children (Déprez & Pierce 1993). Subject-verb inversion has only been reported in a handful of cases and was limited to those verbs that can be involved in residual V2 structures such as the copula and the verbs *go* and *come*. Extended V2 is commonly seen as mis-identification of the particular verb as an auxiliary instead of a main verb (Radford 1992; Roeper 1996; but see Schelletter, this volume, for an alternative view). In the present data, verb raising is more frequent (CW:15; JH:5; NS:33; AS:29) and a much wider range of verbs and verb forms is involved including *want, got, fits, ride, hurt, let, making, have to* and *coming*. The fact that each of the four bilingual children studied produce some examples of this type makes them not only more frequent than in monolingual data but also predictable to some degree (Döpke 1999a).

There is one more unusual structure worth mentioning, which interestingly enough also appears in both languages. This involves both elements of complex verbs preceding the negation or modal particle.

> (21) *ich kann tragen   nicht das*   (NS-G2;6)
>   I   can   carry   not   that
>   S   Aux V+nonfinite Neg   XP
>   'I can't carry that'

> (22) *das kann mach   auch eine Kopfstand*   (JH-G3;0)
>   this can make   also a headstand
>   S   Aux V+1SG Prt XP
>   'that can make a headstand too'

> (23) *you going to make not   that house*   (CW-E3;3)
>   S   V   V   Neg XP
>   'you are not going to make that house'

While each child only produces a few examples of this type, the fact that they at all occur is significant and contributes to our picture of children's acquisition of verb morphology. Unusual structures such as these, however infrequent, suggest that verbs may not necessarily move to V2 and verb raising may not be causally dependent on finiteness.

In sum, verb movement is haphazard in German, presenting itself more as an option to the bilingual children than as an obligation and without its intrinsic connection to finiteness or the V2 position. In English verb movement is extended beyond the residual V2 structures to include a wider range of verbs and involves movement past the negation and modal particles. Both of these features, lack of verb raising in German and verb raising in English, have occasionally been found in monolingual children, but the fact that four out of four bilingual children produce such structures constitutes a notable difference between monolingual and bilingual children.

5.4 *Conclusions regarding Possibility 2*

We have seen from the various areas of analyses in this section that there are more non-target structures in the children's German than in their English.

Together with the children's progression in terms of MLU-words in the two languages we can conclude that, by and large, their English is stronger than their German. Given the children's sociolinguistic situation, this is not surprising.

In contrast to the expectations expressed for Possibility 2, however, cross-language influences are not unilateral from English to German. Dominance does not express itself in the absence of cross-language influences from the weaker to the stronger language, but only in the generally weaker effect of German on English than vice versa. Moreover, in the development of finiteness the effect of German on English exceeds that of English on German. This suggests that the direction of crosslinguistic influences is at least partly related to the strength of a structural phenomenon within its donor language, rather than to sociolinguisticly based dominance alone. The principal bilateral aspect of crosslinguistic influences in spite of one-language dominance makes Possibility 2 untenable.

6.   Motivation for non-target structures

The data reviewed in Sections 3 and 4 show that the bilingual children predominantly produce expected target structures in both languages. Nevertheless, we have also seen varying degrees of evidence for non-target structures. The comparison of their non-target structures with exceptional findings from monolingual children indicates that the bilingual children's non-target structures are not impossible in the respective monolingual acquisition contexts. Thus, the untypical structures do not contradict the conclusions reached on the basis of the predominance of target structures, namely that the children are sensitive to the fact that they are hearing two languages and that they orient themselves on the language-specific input respectively in German and English

The main difference between the bilingual and monolingual data lies in the frequency with which the two populations follow exceptional routes. While these untypical structures have only been reported occasionally for monolingual children, they are evident for each of the four bilingual children. The bilingual children in the present study have much in common with the monolingual children we compared them with in terms of age, developmental stage and the fact that they learn language in close interaction with their parents. Therefore, the differences to monolingual data need to be attributed to the bilingual children acquiring two languages concurrently. The question is *why* the bilingual children produce untypical developmental structures so predictably in spite of their obvious orientation towards target language norms.

In what follows, I will conceptualise the interplay between target structures and untypical developmental structures as due to cross-language cue competition. For that, I will draw on the Competition Model developed by MacWhinney (1987; Bates & MacWhinney 1989).

The Competition Model purports that grammar is learned through establishing connections between meaning and form on the basis of structural cues and through the competition of cues for related functions. The successful resolution of such competition leads to robust structural schemata. Cues which are frequently available, reliable and perceptually salient win over cues of lesser strength. In other words, strong cues are assigned to their appropriate grammatical functions more quickly than weak cues. If there is competition between several cues for the same function or if the same cue represents several functions, the acquisition of a particular structural phenomenon will be delayed. Thus, it is the tension between similarities and contrasts which drives language acquisition. Within the context of multiple language acquisition, a basic contention of the Competition Model is that forms which bear similarities in two or more languages compete across languages (MacWhinney 1997).

There is evidence for the tension between the contrasts and similarities of German and English in the data of the bilingual children. As far as contrast is concerned, the children realised and actively instantiated the structural differences of German and English. The first type of evidence is indirect: many of the target structures which the children produced were language-specific. A particularly good example is the contrast in the verb phrase between XP_V in German and V_XP in English during the early phase of their structural development and the corresponding contrast between Aux_XP_V in German and Aux_V_XP in English in the later phase. The second type of evidence is very direct: we find German verb endings on English verbs in the German language context, as in examples (26) and (27). This appears to be an active effort on the part of the children to mark transferred verbs as German.

(26)   *und du kann pat-en mich*   (AS-G3;11)
        'and you can pat+NONFINITE me'

(27)   *ich kann dive-e unter*   (CW-G3;7)
        'I can dive+1SG under'

In looking more widely at the non-target use of verb affixes in the children's German in general, we find (a) that the bilingual children are more likely to make person errors than monolingual German-speaking children (Döpke 1999b), and (b) that those verb affixes which instantiate contrast between the languages, namely -n, -t, -e and -st, are more frequently over-applied than the -Ø affix, which represents morphological overlap between the languages. The frequencies for erroneously used contrasting verb affixes versus the erroneously used overlapping verb affix are displayed in Table 2.

Table 2. *Contrast versus similarity on pre-complement simplex verbs*

		Phase II		Phase III		Phase IV		Phase V	
JH	contrast	26	.81	33	.77	75	.65	7	.64
	similarity:	6	.19	10	.23	40	.35	4	.36
CW	contrast	33	.83	115	.96	99	.86	13	1.
	similarity	7	.17	5	.04	16	.14	0	.00
NS	contrast	36	.97	147	.93	58	.88	16	.70
	similarity	1	.03	11	.07	8	.12	7	.30
AS	contrast	5	.71	72	.91	41	.89	5	.83
	similarity	2	.29	7	.09	5	.11	1	.17

Table 2 supports the argument that the bilingual children actively pay attention to the contrasts between their languages. However, it should also be noted that the overuse of the -Ø affix is not necessarily due to the similarities with English. Its multifaceted and therefore oblique function within German is an equally likely cause. If similarities between the languages and interference from English are the main reason for the overuse of verb affixes, one should expect -Ø to be over-applied much more widely.

At the same time, there is evidence that the children notice similarities between the two languages and that these similarities threaten the contrasts between the languages during Phases III and IV. In particular, the V_XP structure, which occurs in both languages, although for different structural reasons, is more strongly represented in the bilingual children's German than is common in the data from monolingual German-speaking children. That the V_XP structure had developed into a more robust schema than the XP_V structure became apparent when the children started to combine Aux and Neg with V_XP to form Neg_V_XP, as in (16) and (17) above, and Aux_V_XP, as in (9). This contrasts starkly with monolingual German-speaking children whose combinations of Aux and Neg with VP always result in Aux_XP_V and Neg_XP_V. Given the systematic group differences between monolingual and bilingual children in this respect, we need to assume that the strength of the V_XP schema in the bilingual children's German is significantly increased through the corresponding V_XP schema in English. In other words, the bilingual children are obviously aware that XP_V is a structure specific to German and that V_XP is possible in both languages. At the same time, they are obviously unaware of the restrictions under which V_XP can appear in German, as we can see from finite main verbs in Aux_V$_{fin}$_XP in examples (12) and (27), and from nonfinite verbs in unequivocal V2 position in examples (14) and (15).

Direct proof that the bilingual children are concurrently aware of the corresponding structures in German and English comes from occasional utterances in which the structural slots typical of German as well as those typical of English are filled in the same utterance, as in the following three examples from the children's German corpora.

(28)   *du kann **sitzen** vorn hier   **sitzen***   (NS-G3;8)
        you can sit   in front here sit
        S   Aux **V**   XP   **V**
        'you can sit up here'

(29)   *ich hab **dieser** festhalte   **BALL***   (JH-G2;11)
        I   have this   on-hold+1SG ball
        S Aux **O**   V   **O**
        'I have held on to this ball'

(30)   *ich **nicht** weiß **nicht***   (CW-G3;0)
        I   not   know not
        S **Neg** V   **Neg**
        'I don't know'

A similar phenomenon can also be observed in English, although not quite to the same extent. Here it is only AS and NS who display outward signs of cross-language cue competition.

(31)   *man **goes** not **going***   (AS-E3;3)
        S   **V**   Neg **V**

Examples (28) to (31) are not unlike the concurrent filling of the verb final position and the V2 position, of which there are a few reported examples from monolingual German-speaking children. These have been argued to indicate that the children are aware of the structural relationship between the underlying and the derived positions (Clahsen 1991; Tracy 1991; Meisel & Müller 1992; Roeper 1996). The bilingual data show that the children are concurrently aware of the German and English positions in much the same way as monolingual children are aware of the various verb positions within German.

To sum this up, there are very direct signs of cross-language cue competition. This supports the contention expressed earlier in this section that intra-language cues gain strength through cross-language similarities. This affects the robustness of the syntactic schemata. As a result, some structures are used more or less frequently than is common for monolingual children of the respective languages. This is most notable with respect to V_XP and XP_V in German during Phases III and IV. At the same time, the children strive towards actively expressing the contrasts between their two languages as much as their still immature understanding of the syntactic structures of their languages allow them to do.

7.   Generating and retracting from non-target structures

The previous section was concerned with *why* the bilingual children show evidence of cross-language influences in spite of their general orientation towards the language-specific structures of German and English. I have argued that the untypical structures are not the result of direct interference from the other language but are potentially possible on the basis of language-specific input alone. I will now consider *how* the untypical structures are generated from within the structural possibilities of German and English, respectively, and how the children are able to eventually retract from them.

I have argued above that, for the bilingual children, the V_XP schema is more robust than XP_V and that this motivates them to combine Neg or Aux with V_XP rather than with XP_V as monolingual German-speaking children do. In fact, all of the children's non-target utterances in German can be generated from the following perfectly well-formed two-word schemata.

V_XP	or	XP_V
S_Aux	or	S_V
Aux_S	or	V_S
Aux_Neg	or	V_Neg

Longer utterances can be generated by first constructing the sub-parts along the lines of familiar schemata and then chunking them together with others. This way we get perfectly inconspicuous target structures as in (32), as well as the non-target structure in (33).

(32)=(4)   *ich kann Essen machen*   (CW-G2;3)
             I can   food make
             S_Aux   XP_V
             'I can make food'

(33)=(12)   *ich kann seh dein Pferd*   (JH-G3;0)
             I can   see+1SG your horse
             S_Aux   V_XP

We can ascertain the adequacy of this model of conjoining chunks of pre-constructed sub-parts from finiteness markers on pre-complement verbs in (33) above and (34) below or from the placement of the negation in (35).

(34)=(16)   *ich nicht weiß das*   (AS-G3;1)
            I   not   know that
            S   Neg V+1SG XP
            'I don't know that'

(35)   *ich kann drück nicht*   (NS-G2;9)
            I can   press not
            S Aux   V+1SG Neg
            'I can't press'

The frequency with which various possible conjoinments are chosen needs to be seen as related to the robustness of particular schemata: frequent conjoinments indicate robust schemata, less frequent ones indicate weaker schemata. The robustness of syntactic schemata, in turn, is due to the strength of the available structural cues. The relative strength might be affected by corresponding cues in a second language or by individual children's attention patterns. In this way, we can explain why different populations, like monolingual and bilingual children, generate the same non-target structures but at vastly different frequencies.

Differences in individual attention patterns can further explain within-group variation and reconcile effects that occur systematically in some children but only occasionally in others. For the bilingual data presented here, the effect of individual attention patterns on the path of development is most visible with respect to verb morphology. While all four children appear to use verb morphology as a means of instantiating differences between German and English, JH orients himself towards finiteness markers early on. For CW this purpose is served by the nonfinite -en affix, which severely delays the acquisition of subject-verb agreement for him, as we have seen in Section 4.6 above. Neverthe-less, example (27) shows that structures as in (33), which are very frequent in the middle phases in the JH corpus, are also evident in the CW corpus. The most likely explanation is that they are generated by the same cognitive forces, but that their frequencies were mediated by differences in individual attention patterns.

The argument that non-target structures can principally have been generated on the basis of language-specific input alone can be proposed for English as well. If one contends that copulas are instantiations of verbs and that the cue competition between copulas and the residual V2 structures in English can make the child believe that main verbs may move to the position of auxiliaries, as we have done in Section 5, then all of the sub-structures above, except for XP_V, are also well-formed in English. From the fact that the evidence for V_Neg and V_S patterns remain marginal in the bilingual children's English, we can conclude that the strength of these patterns is very weak with respect to lexical verbs. The extent of their appearance in bilingual English as opposed to monolingual English, however, suggests that they are more general than in monolingual populations. In light of the sparsity of cross-language effects from German to English it is unfortunately difficult to say any more about their origins. Data from German-English bilingual children living in a German-speaking country and who present more systematic evidence of cross-language influences from German to English will probably be able to contribute more insights, in particular with respect to utterances with verb-final patterns in bilingual children's English. Unfortunately, the two subjects studied by Tracy (1995) did not do that, but such structures have frequently been reported to me by parents of other English-German bilingual children in Germany.

Thus, the relationship between the target-specific constructions of sub-parts of utterances and the non-target nature of more complex structural configurations suggests that the bilingual children pay attention to the language-specific order of lexical items on the surface of utterances and are initially not aware of the hierarchical organisation of the corresponding structures in the adult language. Explicit evidence for this comes from $Aux\_V_{fin}\_XP$ and V_{nonfin}_Neg as well as $Aux\_V\_Neg\_XP$ in the children's German. It is likely that the $Neg\_V_{fin}\_XP$ structure in their English originates in this way as well.

This is not unlike arguing that the functional category Neg is initially adjoined to the verb phrase and does not yet invoke the selection restrictions typical of its use in adult language (Hoekstra & Jordens 1994), or that, at first, Neg instantiates a "special projection" (Tracy 1995), whose functional properties are not yet connected to the wider structure of the utterance. Like mine, these accounts see the early structures as stepping stones to their full functional identification. However, my account differs from the others in that I am suggesting that longer pre-constructed structural chunks are being conjoined. These are based on well-established schemata from the two-word stage. Similar operations have also been suggested by Ellis (1996) for second language acquisition and by Peters (1977) for first language acquisition. In contrast to Peters, however, I have evidence that the sub-parts of the utterances are the children's own productions and are not imitations from the adult input.

As the children's phonological memory increases, they become aware of the structural co-occurrences across the sub-parts of utterances. This allows them to resolve the incompatibilities between Aux_XP_V and Aux_V_XP and leads to the retraction from the non-target utterances in German. At the same time, it resolves the superficial overlap of V_XP in German and English and excludes the doubling of finiteness through Aux and V_{fin} in the same utterance. The contrast between V_Neg in German and Neg_V in English appears to play a pivotal role in this development. It is through the identification of the structural incompatibilities of the chunked sub-parts that the functional hierarchies are established. Once they are in place, contrasts between the two languages are re-established, although at a more abstract level, and 'interference' structures all but disappear.

8. Conclusions

The quantitative analysis of the bilingual children's syntactic structures supports the conclusions reached for other language combinations with respect to the independent development of the two languages. However, non-target structures are also evident. These call into question the strictness with which the separate development hypothesis has been formulated.

The qualitative analysis of the non-target structures indicates that cross-linguistic influences are principally bilateral. They can therefore not have been caused by the dominance of one language, but need to be seen as due to the cognitive challenges posed by the simultaneous exposure to two languages. This is not to say that the frequency with which crosslinguistically influenced structures appear is not affected by environmental factors.

In order to reconcile the somewhat conflicting evidence for language separation as well as crosslinguistic influences, I have drawn on the concept of cross-language cue competition. Superficially, the cross-language structures could have been produced on the basis of language specific cues. I have argued that cross-language similarities affect intra-linguistic cue strength. This was evident from the greater frequency with which bilingual children choose possible intra-linguistic structures which are not commonly attended to by monolingual children. Therefore, the bilingual evidence presented here strongly supports Possibility 3.

An important component of the Competition Model is the tension between contrasts and similarities of structural cues. This dichotomy goes some way towards explaining the coexistence of evidence for language separation as well as crosslinguistic influences. It also removes the need to exclude lesser frequencies as irrelevant. The Competition Model can potentially account for the full spectrum of variation in the acquisition paths of bilingual children of various language combinations and, therefore, various structural complexities, as well as for monolingual children's path of development.

Acknowledgments

The project has been funded by ARC Small Grants in 1992, 1994 (Melbourne University) and 1995 (Monash University). Since mid-1994 I have been an ARC Fellow. I gratefully acknowledge this support. My thanks go to the families who participated in the study, and my research assistants Angelika Roethgen, Irmi Gürtler, Katja Goodall and Fiona Salmon.

Notes

1. For AS, this analysis is still outstanding.

2. Finite verbs in final position in matrix clauses are rare in monolingual German-speaking children as well but commonly taken as prove of the highly language-specific final position of Infl (Clahsen 1991; Meisel & Müller 1992; Weissenborn 1994; Roeper 1996).

3. The child studied by Schaner-Wolles (1995/96) is the same as the one in the Köhler & Bruyère (1995/96) study.

References

Bates, Elizabeth & Brian MacWhinney. 1989. "Functionalism and the Competition Model". In B. MacWhinney & E. Bates (eds), *The Crosslinguistic Study of Sentence Processing*. Cambridge: C.U.P.

Clahsen, Harald. 1991. *Child Language and Developmental Dysphasia*. Amsterdam and Philadelphia: John Benjamins.

Clahsen, Harald & Martina Penke. 1992. "The acquisition of agreement morphology and its syntactic consequences: new evidence on German child language from the Simone-corpus". In J. Meisel (ed), *The Acquisition of Verb Placement*. Dordrecht: Kluwer.

Clahsen, Harald, Martina Penke, & Teresa, Parodi. 1993/94. "Functional categories in early child German". *Language Acquisition* 3: 395–429.

Clahsen, Harald, Sonja Eisenbein & Martina Penke. 1996. "Lexical learning in early syntactic development". In H. Clahsen (ed), *Generative Perspectives on Language Acquisition*. Amsterdam and Philadelphia: John Benjamins.

Déprez, Viviane & Amy Pierce. 1993. "Negation and functional projections in early grammar". *Linguistic Inquiry* 24: 25–647.

Döpke, Susanne. 1992. "Approaches to first language acquisition: evidence from simultaneous bilingualism". *Australian Review in Applied Linguistics* 15: 137–150.

Döpke, Susanne. 1998. "Competing language structures: the acquisition of verb placement by bilingual German-English children". *Journal of Child Language* 25(3): 555–584.

Döpke, Susanne. 1999a. "Crosslinguistic influences on the placement of negation and modal particles in simultaneous bilingualism". *Language Sciences* 21: 143–175.

Döpke, Susanne. 1999b. "The development of verb morphology and the placement of finite verbs in young bilingual German-English-speaking children." ms.

Ellis, Nick C. 1996. "Sequencing in SLA. Phonological memory, chunking and points of order". *Studies in Second Language Acquisition* 18: 91–126.

Gawlitzek-Maiwald, Ira, & Rosemarie Tracy. 1996. "Bilingual bootstrapping". *Linguistics* 34: 901–926.

Genesee, Fred. 1989. "Early bilingual development: one language or two?" *Journal of Child Language* 16: 161–179.

Köhler, Katharina & Sabine Bruyère. 1995–96. "Finiteness and verb placement in the L1 acquisition of German". *Wiener Linguistische Gazette* 53–54: 63–86.

Hoekstra, Teun & Peter Jordens. 1994. "From adjunct to head". In T. Hoekstra & B. Schwartz (eds), *Language Acquisition Studies in Generative Grammar.* Amsterdam and Philadelphia: John Benjamins.

Hulk, Aafke C. J. & Elisabeth van der Linden. 1996. "Language mixing in a French-Dutch bilingual child". *Toegepaste Taalwetenschap in Artikelen* 55 (EUROSLA 6, A selection of papers): 89–103.

Lahey, Margaret, Jacqueline Liebergott, Marie Chesnick, Paula Menyuk & Janet Adams 1992. "Variability in children's use of grammatical morphemes". *Applied Psycholinguistics* 13: 373–398.

Lanza, Elizabeth. 1997. *Language Mixing in Infant Bilingualism.* Oxford: Clarendon.

Leopold, Werner. 1947. *Speech Development of a Bilingual Child.* New York: AMS Press.

Lindner, Katrin & Judith Johnston. 1992. "Grammatical morphology in language-impaired children acquiring English or German as their first language: a functional perspective". *Applied Psycholinguistics* 13: 115–129.

MacWhinney, Brian. 1987. "The Competition Model". In B. MacWhinney (ed), *Mechanisms of Language Acquisition.* (The 20th Annual Carnegie Symposium on Cognition. Carnegie-Mellon University). Hillsdale, NJ: Lawrence Erlbaum.

MacWhinney, Brian. 1997. "Second language acquisition and the Competition Model". In A. De Groot & J. Kroll (eds), *Tutorials in Bilingualism. Psychological Perspectives.* Hillsdale, NJ: Erlbaum.

Meisel, Jürgen M. & Natascha Müller. 1992. "Finiteness and verb placement in early child grammars, evidence from simultaneous acquisition of French and German in bilinguals". In J. Meisel (ed), *The Acquisition of Verb Placement.* Dordrecht: Kluwer.

Müller, Natascha. 1998. "Transfer in bilingual first language acquisition", *Bilingualism* 1(3): 151–171.

Paradis, Johanne. in print. "Do bilingual two year olds have separate phonological systems?" *International Journal of Bilingualism.*

Penner, Zvi. 1994. "Possible domains for individual variation in early developmental stages". In R. Tracy & E. Lattey (eds), *How Tolerant is Universal Grammar?* Tübingen: Niemeyer.

Peters, Ann. 1977. "Language learning strategies". *Language* 53: 560–563.

Phillips, Colin. 1995. "Syntax at age two: crosslinguistic differences". *MIT Working Papers in Linguistics* 26: 325–382.

Poeppel, David & Kenneth Wexler. 1993. "The full competence hypothesis of clause structure in German". *Language* 69: 1–33.

Radford, Andrew. 1990. *Syntactic Theory and the Acquisition of English Syntax.* Oxford: Blackwell.

Radford, Andrew. 1992. "The acquisition of the morphosyntax of finite verbs in English". In J. Meisel (ed), *The Acquisition of Verb Placement.* Dordrecht: Kluwer.

Redlinger, Wendy & Tschang-Zin Park. 1980. "Language mixing in young bilinguals". *Journal of Child Language* 7: 337–352.

Roeper, Tom. 1996. "Is bi-lingualism universal? A view from first language acquisition". ms.

Rohrbacher, Bernhard & Anne Vainikka. 1995. "On German verb syntax under age two". *Proceedings of the 19th Annual Boston University Conference on Language Development,* Vol. 2: 487–498.

Saunders, George. 1982. *Bilingual Children: Guidance for the Family.* Clevedon: Multilingual Matters.

Schaner-Wolles, Chris. 1995–96. "The acquisition of negation in a verb second language: from 'anything goes' to 'rien ne va plus'". *Wiener Linguistische Gazette* 53–54: 87–119.

Schlyter, Suzanne. 1993. "The weaker language in bilingual Swedish-French children". In K. Hyltenstam & A. Viberg (eds), *Progression and Regression in Language,* C.U.P., Cambridge.

Taeschner, Traute. 1983. *The Sun is Feminine: A Study on Language Acquisition in Bilingual Children.* Berlin: Springer.

Tracy, Rosemarie. 1991. *Sprachliche Strukturentwicklung.* Tübingen: Narr.

Tracy, Rosemarie. 1995. *Child Languages in Contact: Bilingual Language Acquisition (English-German) in Early Childhood.* Habililitationsschrift, Universität Tübingen.

Volterra, Virginia & Traute Taeschner. 1978. "The acquisition and development of language by bilingual children". *Journal of Child Language* 5: 311–326.

Vihman, Marilyn M. 1985. "Language differentiation by the bilingual infant". *Journal of Child Language* 12: 297–324.

Weissenborn, Jürgen. 1994. "Constraining the child's grammar: local well-formedness in the development of verb movement in German and French". In B. Lust, J. Whitman & J. Kornfilt (eds), *Syntactic Theory and Language Acquisition: Crosslinguistic Perspectives.* Vol. 1. Hillsdale, NJ: Lawrence Erlbaum.

Negation as a Crosslinguistic Structure in a German-English Bilingual Child

Christina Schelletter
University of Hertfordshire

1. Introduction

The present study looks at a particular type of crosslinguistic structures in bilingual children, namely those that conform to one language with regard to the application of grammar rules but contain lexical items mainly from the other language. In a broader context, these structures constitute a particular type of contact between the two languages of a bilingual, which has been described as language mixing (Lanza 1997).

Language mixing has been taken as evidence that the child initially has only one system (Volterra & Taeschner 1978, Taeschner 1983). More recently, it has been argued that mixing at a lexical level can be interpreted as borrowing a lexical item from one language where there is no equivalent in the other (Paradis & Genesee 1996). Gawlitzek-Maiwald & Tracy (1996) suggest that a similar strategy is adopted for grammatical structures. The latter suggestions are compatible with an approach that assumes two separate systems from the outset (Separate Development Hypothesis, De Houwer 1990). Further evidence that the two languages are analysed separately comes from a study by Sinka and Schelletter (1998) on the morphosyntactic development of two bilingual children.

The most likely candidates for crosslinguistic structures of the kind described above are those where the two language systems clearly differ. For English and German, one such area is word order. German is a verb-second language which has been analysed as verb-final in the underlying structure, English on the other hand is an SVO language.

The word order differences also affect the placement of negative elements in the case of sentential negation, giving rise to the possibility of crosslinguistic structures. These potential structures are the focus of the present study. In particular, the aim is to look more closely at possible reasons for the occurrence of crosslinguistic structures in this particular area as well as the language direction. In order to make more specific predictions, negation in English and German will be reviewed below.

1.1 *Negation in English*

English has three overt negative forms: the minor form *no*, and the major forms *not* and *n't*. The element *no* can either occur alone as an utterance or it may precede a negated sentence. In addition, *no* can be used as a negative quantifier. Other, lexical forms of negation, such as the prefix *un-* are not considered here.

According to Brown & Bellugi (1964) and Klima & Bellugi (1966), English children's early negative sentences are structures with the negative element *no* in initial position signalling sentential negation. The negative elements *not* and *n't* occur after the first finite auxiliary in a sentence with both main verb and auxiliary present. If there is only one finite lexical verb, the auxiliary *do* is generated and the negative element is attached to the auxiliary.

This difference between auxiliaries and modals on the one hand and main verbs on the other is accounted for within the Universal Grammar (UG) framework (Chomsky 1995; Pollock 1989) in terms of thematic role assignment and a weak Agreement feature in English (Cook & Newson 1996).

The framework assumes that there are lexical projections such as NP, VP and PP and also a number of functional projections, such as Complementiser (CP), Tense (TP), Agreement (AgrP) and Determiner (DP). Negation is assumed to be an independent syntactic category, Neg (Ouhalla 1991) which is situated between Tense and Agreement but its position and status can vary according to different languages.

Verbs are generated under the VP. All finite verbs and auxiliaries need to move to Agreement in order to have their agreement features checked. Since auxiliaries and modals do not assign a thematic role to their complements, they are able to move beyond Agreement and can occupy a position to the left of the subject, as in yes/no questions or *wh*-questions. They can pick up the negative element *n't* which gets cliticised onto the modal or auxiliary.

Main verbs are not able to move further because Agreement is assumed to be weak in English. If they moved further, they would not be able to assign a thematic role to their complements and violate the Head Movement constraint. In order to form a yes/no question or express sentential negation, the dummy auxiliary *do* is generated under Agreement which can move further and has the negative element cliticised on it.

Radford (1992) argues that children's medial negation structures lacking *do* as well as agreement marking on the main verb show that the functional category Agreement has not yet been acquired. On the other hand, Harris & Wexler (1996) present evidence to show that children's sentential negation often varies between the full finite form of the auxiliary or modal with the negative element cliticised on it, as in (1), or they produce a structure where no movement has taken place and the verb is not marked for tense or agreement, as in (2).

(1)   she doesn't go

(2)   she not go

(3)   *she not goes

Harris & Wexler suggest that forms like (1) and (2) together show that at this particular stage children regard Tense marking as optional (optional infinitive stage). Structures like (3), on the other hand, are not compatible with the optional infinitive grammar because the verb would have to rise over negation to have its features checked.

Radford cites an example by Erreich et al. (1980: 163) where a child produced an inverted use of the verb *go* in a yes/no question.

(4)   goes paci in mouth?

Examples like (3) and (4), however, are rare in English monolingual children.

1.2 *Negation in German*

German has three negative forms: the minor form *nein*, and the major forms *nicht* and *kein*. The element *nein* corresponds to the English *no* and is used in a similar way, either as single-word negation, or in conjunction with a negated sentence. The element *kein* corresponds to *no* used as a quantifier, except that *kein* is marked for the gender and case of the noun that it modifies.

Déprez and Pierce (1993) cite evidence to show that German children, similar to their English counterparts, also use the negative element *nein* or *nicht* in sentence-initial position to signal sentential negation. At a slightly later stage, this is followed by structures where *nicht* occurs after the finite verb.

Unlike English, there is no restriction on the movement of main lexical verbs in German. Agreement is assumed to be a strong feature. This means that no insertion of a dummy auxiliary like *do* is necessary and *nicht* is not cliticised.

There seems to be a difference in the literature with regard to the status of negation in German. One possibility is to analyse it as an independent syntactic category, as in English, which is also situated between Tense and Agreement. This analysis is assumed by Déprez & Pierce (1993). Children's structures containing postverbal negation can then be interpreted as evidence that the child has moved the finite verb over negation, as in (5), which is the German equivalent of the English sentence (1).

(5)   *sie geht   nicht*
       she go+3SG not
       'she doesn't go'

A different analysis is suggested by Zanuttini (1996). Rather than taking Negation to be an independent syntactic category, she assumes that the negative marker in some Germanic languages has the status of an adverbial. This analysis implies that (5) has the same status as (6).

(6)   *sie kommt   niemals*
       she come+3SG never
       'she never comes'

1.3 *Predictions for German-English acquisition*

In the previous sections, two important differences between English and German have been identified that might be the source of crosslinguistic structures: firstly, the two languages differ in terms of Agreement being either a strong or a weak feature, and secondly, negation might have a different status in the two languages. At the same time, there is a similarity in the position of the negative element after finite auxiliaries and modals.

One possibility for crosslinguistic overgeneralisation would be that the child sets the Agreement parameter equally for both languages. The strong evidence for verb movement in German and the evidence for movement of some verbs in English might lead the child to set Agreement as a strong feature in both languages. This would result in movement of main finite verbs over Negation as in (7) but also give rise to ungrammatical question forms, as in (8).

(7)   *he goes not

(8)   *comes he today?

The other possibility relates to the status of negation. If this is different in the two languages, this would open up the possibility that the bilingual child might transfer the analysis of negation of one language to the other. If lexical category acquisition does indeed precede that of functional categories (Radford 1990), it would be expected that the child treats negation as adverbial in both languages.

2. Methodology

The study of negation is based on the author's second German–English bilingual daughter, Sonja. Her mother is a German native speaker and her father a native English speaker. The parents followed the 'one person-one language' principle (Ronjat 1913) from the birth of the first child. Conversations between parents were in English. Although the mother was the primary caretaker, the child regularly spent two hours a week with an English child minder from the age of 4 months. This time was increased to 3 days from the age of 10 months. On the basis of these contacts, the input of the respective two languages at the time of the data collection was judged to be fairly equal.

Recordings were made about fortnightly in both languages, up to 45 minutes per language, during free play sessions. Sonja started speaking later than her older sister and reached the two-word stage by about two years. Her English data were recorded mainly with just her father present as interlocutor, from the age of 2;2 onwards. However, there were no recording sessions at 2;4 to 2;5. The German data were recorded with Sonja's mother and, on occasions, her sister was also present. Recording started at the age of 1;11. The present study presents longitudinal data from Sonja between 1;11 and 2;9.

For the purpose of the present study, two periods of observation were established: for German, the first period ranged from 1;11 to 2;3 and the second

Table 1. *German–English subject, number of utterances*

Age	With English interlocutor			With German interlocutor		
	English	Ge*	Mx*	German	En*	Mx*
1;11				75	9	3
2;0				226	13	18
2;1				177	0	13
2;2	113	17	13	191	3	11
2;3	150	8	6	207	0	16
2;4				264	10	2
2;5				275	0	4
2;6	231	7	5	180	0	3
2;7	252	4	15	196	0	2
2;8	112	0	2	82	0	1
2;9	109	0	1			
Total	967	36	42	1873	35	73

*Non-target language utterances or utterances with lexical items from both languages

period from 2;4 to 2;8. For English, the first observation period was from 2;2 to 2;3 and the second period from 2;6 to 2;9. Table 1 provides the ages and sizes of the data samples in terms of complete and intelligible utterances at monthly intervals.

The utterances in the table that represent mixes between the languages are restricted to the lexical insertions from the other language and do not include crosslinguistic structures.

All data were transcribed, using the Salt transcription format (Miller & Chapman 1996). Codes were inserted for specific features of the data, such as negation, and lists of the codes accessed via the Salt programmes.

3. Results

3.1 *Negation in German*

Negation is an optional feature in free speech samples. Not surprisingly, negated structures were not found to be very frequent in the data. In the first period of observation between 1;11 and 2;3, there were 50 utterances containing negative elements, out of a total of 962 complete and intelligible utterances during this period. This is the equivalent of 5%. Table 2 gives an overview of the negative elements that were employed during this time and the context in which the elements occurred.

Table 2. *Negative elements in Sonja's German from 1;11 to 2;3*

Context/Neg form	nein	nicht	kein	nein+kein	Total
Minor	34	0	0	0	34
Phrasal	0	2	4	1	7
Clausal	0	7	0	0	7
Other	0	2	0	0	2
Total (%)	34	11	4	1	50
	(68)	(22)	(8)	(2)	(100)

As can be seen from Table 2, all three types of negative elements occurred in the first period of observation, however, the most frequent form was *nein* as a minor utterance, either on its own or before a phrase or clause. Examples are given in (9).

(9)   a.   M: *willst du Milch haben?*   (SO-G2;1)
                   'do you want some milk?'
             C: *nein, Creme*
                   'no, cream' ⟨refers to skin cream⟩
       b.   M: *willst du schlafen gehn?*   (SO-G2;3)
                   'do you want to go to sleep?'
             C: *nein, (na) schlaf-en (na) Junge.*
                   no, sleep+INF boy
                   'no, the boy is sleeping'
       c.   M: *is das die Wippe?*   (SO-G2;3)
                   'is that the seesaw?'
             C: *nein, is seesaw.*
                   'no, is seesaw'.

The contexts in which the utterances (9a to c) occurred, show that they are all instances of anaphoric negation (Wode 1977). This is the case where the negative relationship does not hold between the initial negative element and the rest of the utterance. Non-anaphoric negation involves the negative element *nicht* in final position in (10a) and immediately follows the verb in (10b).

(10)   ⟨Mother and child are playing with playmobil figures⟩
        a.   M: *der is zu klein für den.*   (SO-G2;3)
                    'that is too small for him'
              C: *kann das nich.*
                    can that not
                    'can't do it'
        b.   C: *des pass nich*   (SO-G2;3)
                    that fit not
                    'that doesn't fit'
              M: *nein, das passt dem nich*
                    'no, that doesn't fit him'

In the second period of observation between 2;4 and 2;8, the percentage of utterances with negative elements rose to 7.5%. There were 76 instances out of 1019 complete and intelligible utterances. Table 3 gives the equivalent overview of the types of negative elements used and the context for the later period of observation.

Table 3 shows that while the percentage of utterances with the negative element *nein* decreased from 68% to 41%, the deployment of *nicht* rose from 22% to 45%. The negative element *nein* occurred as a minor utterance, either on

Table 3. *Negative elements in Sonja's German between 2;4 and 2;8*

Context/Neg form	nein	nicht	Kein	nein+kein	Total
Minor	31	0	0	0	31
Phrasal	0	3	6	0	9
Clausal	0	28	0	3	31
Other	0	3	0	2	5
Total (%)	31	34	6	5	76
	(41)	(45)	(8)	(6)	(100)

its own or in conjunction with a noun phrase or clause. Sentential negation was frequently expressed by the pattern nich+VP where the sentence contained a verb in the infinitive form, as in (11).

(11)   a.   ⟨the child wants to draw with pens⟩
      M: *nicht mit dem Stift auf den Teppich malen*
         'don't draw on the carpet with the pen'
      C: *nich der Stift Teppich mal-en*   (SO-G2;5)
         not the pen carpet draw+INF
         'not draw (with) the pen (on the) carpet'
  b.   M: *wer muss sich denn hinlegen?*
         'who has to lie down then?'
      C: *nich da hinleg-en, Mama*   (SO-G2;6)
         not there lie+INF down, mummy
         'don't lie down there, mummy'

The first example in (11a) shows that the child models the pattern on the mother's utterance. In German, commands can be expressed by impersonal imperatives which contain only a nonfinite verb in final position and no subject, as in

(12)   *bitte die Fenster schliess-en*
     please the windows shut+INF
     'Please shut the windows'

If these clauses are negated (negative indirect commands), the negative element occurs in first position, as in (13). This command can be found as a notice underneath train windows.

(13)   *Nicht hinauslehnen*
     not out-lean
     'Do not lean out of the window'

This pattern predominantly occurs in Sonja's language between 2;4 and 2;6. From 2;7 onwards, sentential negation increases where the negative element is placed after the finite verb. Examples are given in (14).

(14)　a.　⟨Child and her sister look at a picture book⟩
　　　　　S:　*was macht der Junge denn?*
　　　　　　　'what is the boy doing?'
　　　　　C:　*und der schwimm-t nich.*　　　　　　　(SO-G2;7)
　　　　　　　and he　swim+3SG not.
　　　　　　　'and he's not swimming'

　　　　b.　⟨Mother and Child look at a picture book⟩
　　　　　M:　*was is denn da noch?*
　　　　　　　'what else is there?'
　　　　　C:　*wir schau-en das　nich*　　　　　　　(SO-G2;7)
　　　　　　　we　see+3PL　that not
　　　　　　　'we don't see that'.

　　　　c.　⟨Child does not want Mother to put her nappy on⟩
　　　　　M:　*dann musst du dir die Windel eben selber anziehn.*
　　　　　　　'then you have to put the nappy on yourself'
　　　　　C:　*ich kann die Windel nich an-zieh-en*　　　(SO-G2;8)
　　　　　　　I　can　the nappy　not　on-put+INF
　　　　　　　'I can't put the nappy on'

All three examples in (14) are fully grammatical structures. In (14a) the negative element occurs immediately after a finite lexical verb. In (14b) it is placed in final position after the object of a finite lexical verb and in (14c) it occurs after the object of a finite modal and before the participle. In all cases, the finite verb is marked for tense and agreement and must therefore have moved out of the VP to Agreement and Tense to have its features checked. As the verbs in (a) and (b) are lexical verbs, their position and marking implies that the child has correctly set the Agreement parameter in German to be a strong feature. Further evidence for this assumption comes from yes/no questions in the child's data.

(15)　C:　*komm-t　　Heike?*　　　　　　　　　　(SO-G2;1)
　　　　　come+3SG Heike?
　　　　　'is Heike coming?'

(16)　C:　*steh-t　　Giraffe?*　　　　　　　　　　(SO-G2;5)
　　　　　stand+3SG giraffe?
　　　　　'is (the) giraffe standing?'

(17)   C: *schläf-t   *der beiden?*   (SO-G2;5)
              sleep+3SG the   two?
              'is (are) the two sleeping?'

In examples (15) to (17), the child has moved a finite lexical verb to sentence-
initial position for the purpose of the yes/no question, whereas in English the
auxiliary *be* is required for the same purpose. Example (17) contains an agreement error since the subject is plural, whereas the marking on the verb is 3rd
person singular.

    In order to investigate the possibility that *nicht* has the status of an adverbi-
al, the child's adverbial structures in general were also examined. The data
included no other adverbials expressing negation in the period of observation. In
cases where adverbials occurred in conjunction with finite verbs, these were
correctly placed either initially, or after the finite verb, as in (18). Where there
was a finite and a non-finite verb, adverbials frequently occurred with the non-
finite verb, similar to *nicht*, as in (19).

(18)   C: *und iss-t   schon.*   (SO-G2;6)
              and eat+3SG already
              'and is already eating'

(19)   C: *das hab ich von*   Nikolaus   gekriegt* (SO-G2;8)
              that have I   from+ACC Father Christmas got
              'I got this from Father Christmas'

It seems that structurally, the negative element *nicht* and adverbials are quite
similar, yet their functions differ. While adverbials are often optional in the
sentence, sentential negation affects the meaning of the whole clause.

    Crediting the child with only as much structure as is necessary for the
analyst to propose (structure-building hypothesis, Radford 1995) would mean to
assume adverbial status for the negative element. This would be generated under
the VP, similar to other types of adverbials in German.

    On the other hand, the child's negative structures from 2;7 onwards are
correct and appropriately used. The verb is correctly inflected for tense and
agreement for the singular person forms. From a full competence view (Poeppel
& Wexler 1993) the child can be assumed to have as much structure as the adult
grammar has, certainly as far as negation as well as tense and agreement is
concerned.

3.2 *Negation in English*

For negation in English, two observation periods are considered; the first, from 2;2 to 2;3 and the second from 2;6 to 2;9. In the first period there were 5 utterances containing negative elements out of a total of 307 utterances (1.5 %). Four of these were single word utterances containing the negative element *no*. The remaining utterance is mixed in that it contains the first person form of the German verb *sein* 'to be'.

(20)   <u>bin</u> a kiss not   (SO-E2;2)

The order of the negative element in (20) seems to be closer to German than English; however, given that there is a German verb inserted in the utterance, it is difficult to know what structure the child was aiming for.

Table 4 summarises the frequency of negative elements in the second observation period from 2;6 to 2;9 as well as the context in which these elements occur.

In the second observation period, there was a total of 49 utterances containing negative elements, out of a total of 738 complete and intelligible utterances. This corresponds to about 6.5%. The element *no* occurs as a single word utterance, but also in conjunction with a clause. The examples are listed in (21).

Table 4. *Negative elements in Sonja's English between 2;4 and 2;8*

Context/Neg form	no	n't	not	no+not	Total
Minor	15	0	0	0	15
Phrasal	0	0	2	0	2
Clausal	0	1	21	4	26
Other	0	0	6	0	6
Total (%)	15	1	29	4	49
	(31)	(2)	(59)	(8)	(100)

(21) a. ⟨Father and Child are looking at baby   (SO-E2;6)
              pictures of the child⟩
          F: that's baby Sonja
          C: no, baby sleeping
      b. F: there's a Hannababy
          C: no, the other one Hannababy   (SO-E2;6)
      c. F: do you think they were going to bed now?
          C: no, that one go to bed   (SO-E2;7)

As the examples show, there is no indication that the child uses the pattern 'no+Clause' as non-anaphoric negation. Table 4 shows that there is only one case in the observation period where the child uses *n't*. This example is given in (22).

(22)   C: no, they won't go in   (SO-E2;7)

It seems likely that the child used *n't* as a non-productive form in (22) and has therefore not acquired this element. Instead, the majority of negated utterances in the child's English data includes the element *not*. This element is placed either after an auxiliary or copula as in (23), but it also occurs after main verbs, as in (24).

(23)   a.   C: there Papa car.   (SO-E2;6)
             C: it's not too hot.
        b.   F: what's baby doing now?
             C: it's not baby.   (SO-E2;6)
        c.   F: is that John?
             C: that's not finished.

(24)   a.   F: pussycat belongs in the box
             C: *no, pussycat want-s not box   (SO-E2;6)
        b.   F: yeah, Papa's doing it
             C: mummy do-s it not this   (SO-E2;7)
        c.   ⟨the child has hurt herself⟩
             F: how did it happen?
             C: *I climb not   (SO-E2;7)
        d.   C: *mummy want-s not breakfast, yeah?   (SO-E2;9)

As was said before, the placement of the negative element *not* after auxiliaries in English is similar to that in German. Not surprisingly, all the examples in (23) are grammatical. However, the placement of the negative element in the examples in (24) are not. In all cases, the verb occurs to the left of *not* and the resulting structure is therefore like a German negative structure with English lexical items. This is exactly the type of crosslinguistic structure that was expected to occur in the data.

The question is what could be the source of this type of structure. Out of the ten occurrences of crosslinguistic structures in the second observation period, there are three clear examples where 3rd person marking is missing and one case where it is present. In the remaining six utterances, the presence or absence of tense and agreement marking is not visible because the subject is first person singular or third person plural.

The structures above present conflicting evidence regarding the status of negation and the setting of the agreement parameter. If the child had analysed negation as a functional category and set the agreement parameter the same way as in German, there should be evidence of the movement of lexical verbs in structures like *wh*-questions or yes/no questions.

In the second period of observation there were 107 questions, the majority of them *wh*-questions with a contracted copula verb. Only 18 questions include a lexical verb and there are two main patterns; in 6 utterances, the child correctly inserts the dummy auxiliary *do*, as in (25), in 8 utterances there is no subject and no dummy auxiliary, as in (26).

(25) a. C: do you want this one?   (SO-E2;7)
        b. C: Ellen, do you want some milk, ok?   (SO-E2;8)

(26) a. C: want that one?   (SO-E2;8)
        b. C: want to sit *in my lap?   (SO-E2;8)

While the examples in (25) conform to the correct adult marking, those in (26) do not seem to involve any verb movement out of the VP. The different question types can be seen as the result of optional tense marking (Harris & Wexler 1996). There is no evidence from the above examples that the child treats the verb *want* in English like an auxiliary, and yet this verb is marked for agreement and occurs to the left of the negative element *not* in (24d). Furthermore, the child occasionally produces sentences where the negative element occurs to the left of an untensed verb, as in the language of English monolingual children.

(27)   mummy (wants) not want a cassette   (SO-E2;6)

It is unlikely that the child's treatment of verbs changes according to different structural demands. The evidence above suggests that the child is treating the verb *want* as a main verb in English which cannot move beyond agreement. This is in line with the correct setting of the agreement parameter for English, although this cannot be verified for any other examples.

The second possible explanation for the crosslinguistic negation structures is that they are analysed as adverbials in both languages. If this is the case, the negative element should be generated under VP and occur to the right of the verb in English, but to the left of the verb in German in the underlying structure.

This difference can affect adverbial placement in structures where a finite and a non-finite verb is present. In German, this is typically before the non-finite verb, in English it is after. The evidence from the child's data in (28) and (29) suggest that the respective orders are followed in the majority of cases.

(28) a. C: want to go to Palmer Park today?   (SO-E2;8)
        b. C: the mummy can do not   (SO-E2;7)
        c. C: boy want to go in there   (SO-E2;8)

(29) a. C: *da   kann man nich anschnallen*   (SO-G2;6)
              there can one not strap+INF in
              'one can't strap oneself in there'

      b. C: *und der muss hier setzen*   (SO-G2;7)
              and that must here sit+INF
              'and that must sit here'

      c. C: *der Junge muss da   rutschen*   (SO-G2;7)
              the boy   must there slide+INF
              'the boy must slide there'

The data suggest that the placement of adverbials is compatible with the word order requirements for each language. Hence the child does not simply adopt German word order for the placement of the negative element *not* in English. The examples involving *want* also show that misclassification of main verbs as auxiliaries is not generally supported by the data either.

The data are compatible with an analysis whereby negative elements in both languages are analysed as adverbial elements rather than functional categories. This analysis accounts for their occurrence after finite (and non-finite) verbs without assuming a wrong setting of the Agreement parameter or an auxiliary analysis of certain main verbs in English.

Further support for this analysis is given by the almost complete absence of structures involving the contracted negative element *n't*. This element is assumed to be generated as the head of the functional category Neg. Analysing the negative element as an adverbial implies that no functional category is required.

4.   Discussion

The present study looked at the crosslinguistic negation structures of one bilingual child, Sonja, between the ages of 1;11 and 2;9. While the placement of the negative element in German sentential negation in relation to the verb generally conform to that of adult grammar, sentential negation in English structures with a lexical verb does not. Similar English crosslinguistic negation structures are also reported by Döpke (1999) in a study of four German-English bilingual children.

One possible explanation for the occurrence of such structures is an overgeneralisation of the setting of the agreement parameter from German to English. This would allow lexical verbs to be raised over negation. Similarly, Radford (1992) suggests that some monolingual children might treat certain lexical verbs like auxiliaries.

This analysis is not confirmed here because there is no evidence for verb raising in other structures, such as question formation in the child's English. German yes/no questions with lexical verbs, on the other hand, do show correct fronting of lexical verbs.

An alternative explanation for the occurrence of crosslinguistic negation structures in the child's English is that negation is analysed as a lexical category that has the status of an adverbial, rather than a functional category. This is in line with the proposal by Zanuttini (1996) regarding the status of the negative element in some Germanic languages, including German.

In addition, Zanuttini also suggests that the English negative elements *n't* and *not* each have a different status. While the former is the head of a functional category, the latter can be analysed as an adverbial element. This suggestion would account for the absence of contracted negation in the child's English negation structures in the period of observation.

The analysis of the child's negation structures has highlighted that the crosslinguistic structures found are not simply the application of one rule to both language systems. Since the different word order patterns of both languages are observed in the placement of negative elements and adverbials, the child clearly separates the two language systems.

The data also clearly show that this type of crosslinguistic structure only becomes apparent at the point where the child starts using more lexical verbs, yet the underlying representation of negation does not change during the period of observation. This is due to the similarities of the two languages regarding the placement of negation in structures with just a copula or modal.

Gawlitzek-Maiwald & Tracy (1996) define cases where a syntactic structure in one language fulfils a booster function in the other language as 'bilingual bootstrapping'. It is not clear whether the term can be applied in this case. If the analysis suggested here is correct, the child analyses negative elements in terms of adverbials rather than functional categories. Since adverbials occur in both languages, there is no booster function involved as such. On the other hand, the child's choice of negation structure in English facilitates the expression of this particular language function without the need of another functional projection.

The prediction was that crosslinguistic structures can be found in the child's English, since German main verbs and English auxiliaries together provide more evidence in favour of strong agreement. While the direction of the language contact is in line with the predictions, the setting of the parameter for both languages is not confirmed. In contrast to the present study, the direction of crosslinguistic influence in Döpke's data is more prevalent in the children's

German than in their English. Such differences highlight the role of input as an important factor in the use of crosslinguistic structures.

5. Conclusion

The present study has investigated a particular type of language mixing at the syntactic level. It is suggested that the child analyses negative elements in both languages as adverbial elements. In doing so, the child observes particular language-specific word order patterns, even if the placement of the negative element after lexical verbs in English does not conform to English grammar. This result is compatible with the assumption that the child has separate language systems from early on. Overall, the child's crosslinguistic structures seem to facilitate the expression of negation without the use of a functional projection. Yet other factors, such as input might play an important role in the direction of such language contacts.

Acknowledgments

Thanks to Professor Michael Garman for his comments on an earlier version of this chapter and the support of the project research team, ESRC-grant no. R000222072, awarded to Michael Garman, Christina Schelletter and Indra Sinka.

References

Brown, Roger & Ursula Bellugi. 1964. "Three processes in the child's acquisition of syntax". *Harvard Educational Review* 34: 133–151.

Chomsky, Noam. 1995. *The Minimalist Programme*. Cambridge, Mass: MIT press.

Cook, Vivien J. & M. Newson. 1996. *Chomsky's Universal Grammar. An Introduction*. Oxford: Blackwell.

De Houwer, Annick. 1990. *The Acquisition of Two Languages from Birth: A Case Study*. Cambridge: Cambridge University Press.

Déprez, Viviane & Amy Pierce. 1993. "Negation and functional projections in early grammar". *Linguistic Inquiry* 24(1): 25–67.

Döpke, Susanne. 1999. "Crosslinguistic influences on the placement of negation and modal particles in simultaneous bilingualism". *Language Sciences* 21: 143–175.

Erreich, Anne, Viginia Valian & Judith Winzemer. 1980. "Aspects of a theory of language acquisition". *Journal of Child Language* 7: 157–179.

Gawlitzek-Maiwald, Ira & Rosemarie Tracy. 1996. "Bilingual bootstrapping". *Linguistics*, 34: 901–926.

Harris, Tony & Kenneth Wexler. 1996. "The optional-infinitive stage in child English. Evidence from negation". In H. Clahsen (ed), *Generative Perspectives on Language Acquisition*. Amsterdam/Philadelphia: John Benjamins, 1–43.

Klima, Edward & Ursula Bellugi. 1966. "Syntactic regularities in the speech of children". In J. Lyons & R. Wales (eds), *Psycholinguistic Papers*. Edinburgh: Edinburgh University Press, 183–208.

Lanza, Elizabeth. 1997. *Language Mixing in Infant Blingualism*. Oxford: Clarendon.

Miller, Jon & Robin Chapman. 1996. *Systematic Analysis of Language Transcripts*. University of Madison-Wisconsin.

Ouhalla, Jamal. 1991. *Functional Categories and Parametric Variation*. London: Routledge.

Paradis, Johanne & Fred Genesee. 1996. "Syntactic acquisition in bilingual children". *Studies in Second Language Acquisition*, 18: 1–25.

Poeppel, David & Kenneth Wexler. 1993. "The full competence hypothesis of clause structure in early German". *Language* 69: 1–33.

Pollock, Jean-Yves. 1989. "Verb movement, Universal Grammar, and the structure of IP". *Linguistic Inquiry* 20: 365–424.

Radford, Andrew. 1990. *Syntactic Theory and the Acquisition of English Syntax*. Oxford: Blackwell.

Radford, Andrew. 1992. "The acquisition of the morphosyntax of finite verbs in English". In J. Meisel (ed), *The Acquisition of Verb Placement*. Dordrecht: Kluwer.

Radford, Andrew. 1995. "Towards a structure-building model of acquisition". In H. Clahsen (ed), *Generative Perspectives on Language Acquisition*. Amsterdam and Philadelphia: John Benjamins, 43–89.

Ronjat, Jules. 1913. *Le dévelopment du langage observé chez un enfant bilingue*. Paris: Champion.

Sinka, Indra & Christina Schelletter. 1998. "Morphosyntactic development in bilingual children". *International Journal of Bilingualism*. 2(3): 301–326.

Taeschner, Traute. 1983. *The Sun is Feminine: A Study on Language Acquisition in Bilingual Children*. Berlin and Heidelberg: Springer.

Volterra, Virginia & Traute Taeschner. 1978. "The acquisition and development of language by bilingual children". *Journal of Child Language* 5: 311–326.

Wode, Hennig. 1977. "Four early stages in the development of L1 negation". *Journal of Child Language* 4: 87–102.

Zanuttini, R. 1996. "On the relevance of tense for sentential negation". In A. Belletti & L. Rizzi (eds), *Parameters and Functional Heads*. New York: Oxford University Press, 181–207.

'I Want A Chimney Builden'

The Acquisition of Infinitival Constructions in Bilingual Children

Ira Gawlitzek-Maiwald
University of Mannheim

1. Introduction

It is generally assumed that embedded infinitival constructions (ICs)[1] such as (1) and (2) appear early in the acquisition of English (Hyams 1984, 1988; Limber 1973; Menyuk 1969; Pierce 1992), whereas German ICs such as (3)–(5) show up rather late in the acquisition sequence (Mills 1985).[2]

(1)   I wanna do that   (early)[3]

(2)   I like to eat spaghetti   (early)

(3)   ⟨Hilde makes a pen walk on the table⟩
            laufen machen lassen!   (2;0)
            walk   make   let
            'let (it) walk'

(4)   *der Bär will   was   zu fressen haben*   (3;1,23)
            the bear wants something to eat   have
            'the bear wants to have something to eat'

(5)   *du   kannst ja   versuchen, noch ein bebi   zu finden*   (N2;10)
            you can   PRT try   an-other baby to find
            'you can try to find another baby'

The emergence of ICs and other constructions suggests the following implicational sequences, (6) and (7), for the acquisition of English and German respectively.

(6)   English:
       main clauses ⇒ embedded non-finite ⇒ subordinate
                         constructions   clauses$_{(+finite)}$

(7)   German:
       main clauses ⇒ subordinate clauses$_{(+finite)}$ ⇒ embedded non-finite
                                                              constructions

Why should that be so? At least two possibilities seem plausible: either there are systematic differences between German and English syntax which cause the difference in acquisitional sequence or the current perception of the implicational sequence is wrong. In this paper I am going to argue for both possibilities. The first English ICs, usually *want to* infinitives, appear around a child's second birthday. I will analyse these as precursors of ICs instead of as genuine representatives of adult-like ICs. This is because at that age we find no other evidence for the existence of adult-like functional projections in English. Rather, the first ICs — which are usually analysed as ICs in the literature — are first indicators for the beginning development of functional projections above VP in English. The whole set of ICs is acquired later, just as in German. Thus the current perception of the implicational sequence will have to be modified.

Nevertheless, there are real asynchronies in the acquisition of functional projections between the development of English and German in the bilingual children and I will argue that these are due to systematic differences between the two languages.

Bilingual data are particularly relevant in this kind of argumentation, as different and asynchronic development of two languages in one child must be due to differences either in the languages concerned or in the kind of exposure the child has to the two languages, but they are not due to different stages of cognitive development in one child.

After a brief overview of the method applied (Section 2), I will present data relevant to the acquisition of ICs. Mixed utterances will be discussed first and then compared to the non-mixed utterances of the same children (Section 3). Section 4 then presents a brief description of English and German adult sentence structure. This is followed by a discussion of the findings.

2.   Method

2.1 *Data*

This investigation is based on the analysis of approximately 32,200 spontaneous utterances produced by three bilingual English-German speaking children.[4] All these utterances have been checked for the emergence of ICs and structures which might be related to their acquisition. The children were audio and video taped at regular intervals, ie. every two to four weeks for at least two and a half years. The utterances were transcribed right after each recording, typed, and cross checked (Gawlitzek-Maiwald 1997, chapter 5). Table (1) gives a quantitative overview of the data used.

Table 1. *Quantitative overview of data*

Child	Utterances	
	Total	Coded in Data Bank
Adam	13,403	6,167
Hannah	6,420	5,637
Laura	12,413	5,178
Total	32,236	16,982

2.2 *The children*

Table (2) summarises some background information about the children involved in this study.

Table 2. *Background of the children*

	Hannah	Adam	Laura[5]
Lg of Mother	English	German	
Lg of Father	German	English	
First Recording	2;1.13	3;6.28	2;5.10
Last Recording	5;8.10	5;9.13	4;7.24
# of Recordings	25[6]	46 in each language	

Initially all families opted for the one-parent-one-language strategy but Hannah's parents switched to a familiy language (English) vs. language of the society (German) when Hannah was 1;7. Thus, although the terminology of "dominant" or "balanced" bilingualism is problematical (Romaine 1989; Hakuta 1986), by the end of the data collection Hannah could be called a balanced bilingual while Laura and Adam remained German dominant throughout.

3. Results

3.1 *Bilingual acquisition of ICs*

The following table shows that the overall number of mixed utterances produced by Adam, Hannah, and Laura is not very large.[7]

Only a very small percentage of these mixed utterances is related to ICs, but these examples will prove to be interesting and relevant to the overall path of acquisition.

Table 3. *German, English, and mixed Utterances*

Child	# of coded utterances	all German	all English	Mixed
Hannah	5,637	3,883 (68.9%)	1,009 (17.9%)	352 (6.2%)
Adam	6,167	3,110 (50.4%)	2,327 (37.7%)	363 (5.9%)
Laura	5,178	3,769 (72.8%)	614 (11.9%)	405 (7.8%)

What do we know about the acquisition of ICs by bilingual English–German children? From Leopold's diary study we know that his daughter Hildegard produces precursors to English ICs *before* she uses auxiliary and modal verbs (Leopold 1949: §666, §683, §689), ie. from 1;11 onwards. In German, Hildegard seems to start with *bare* Infinitives after verbs of perception. First precursors to ICs are documented from 3;7 onwards. The first examples are ICs which modify pronouns such as *"Bitte, ich wills was zu essen haben!"* ('Please I'd like to have something to eat') (Leopold 1949: §792); only after the age of 4;10 is a range of structures documented. However, in Hildegard's case this delay in the acquisition of German could be due to the dominance of her English.

Leopold did not record any ICs in mixed utterances produced by Hildegard, while all three children of the present study produce a few of them.[8]

(8) ⟨trying to put doll into buggy⟩   (H2;3,17)
     die mama helf mir — strap it in
     the mum help me   strap it in
     'mum should help me to strap it in'

Hannah utters (8) at a time when she is about to acquire the German main clause, which is six months before she productively uses adult-like main clauses in English. This example reflects the status of the two language systems at the time. The matrix structure with the finite verb is German while the [bare]Infinitives, a VP-structure, is English, with the order of the verb and its complement being target-like, cf. (8'). In a German VP it would be different, cf. (8").

(8')   English: $[_{XP}$ help me $[_{VP}$ strap it in]]
(8")   German: $[_{XP}$ hilf mir $[_{VP}$ sie anschnallen]]

At first sight the following examples all look like precursors to [for-to]Infinitives. However, apart from *for* and a few other English lexical items these utterances consist of German words and the embedded structures show the German V2-effect. When we take a closer look it is in fact hard to decide whether these are precursors to ICs or to finite structures.

(9)   *warte doch for* [*ich bin fertig mit diesem puzzle*]   (H2;7,11)
      wait PRT for I   am ready with this   puzzle
      'wait for me to be ready with this puzzle'

(10) *ich warte for* [*es ist faschingsfest*] *dann kann ich*   (H2;7,20)
      I   wait for it is carneval   then can I
      mein clown suit wearen
      my   clown suit wear+INF
      'I wait for it to be carneval then I can wear my clown suit'

(11)   *papa du muβt warten for* [*me to dressed*]   (H2;6,14)
        'papa you must wait   for me to (get) dressed'

Perhaps it is not even necessary to decide whether they are precursors to finite
or non-finite structures as the smallest common denominator of these utterances
is that they appear as complements of *for,* which seems to open up a new phrasal
level on top of the available one. In examples such as (9) and (10) *for* clearly
governs a German main clause; but in (11) it governs an English phrase which
deviates from the target as the infinitival particle *to* is combined with a past
participle. We cannot decide whether the reason for this deviation is that Hannah
does not yet know the combinatorial restrictions of *to* — which seems rather
unlikely — or whether she has dropped the verb *get.*

The following examples again consist mainly of German lexical items, but
this time the syntax, at least of the ICs, is English.

(12)   *simone is zu klein zu gehen in die kita*   (H2;7,14)
        'simone is too little to go   to the day care centre'

(13)   *willst du auch eins zu look at?*   (H2;9,11)
        want you too   one to look at
        'do you also want one to look at?'

(14)   ⟨building a town with cardboard pieces⟩   (H4;3,9)
        ich weiβ wo   sie   hinstellen
        I   know where them there-put
        'I know where to put them.'

Examples (12) and (13) were produced at a time when Hannah did not have
command over the equivalent German structures, ie. she could not produce
simone ist zu klein, um in die kita zu gehen or *willst du auch eins zum Anschauen?*
(14) is the only example where Hannah overgenerates an English *wh*-infinitive
structure in German. *wh*-infinitives in German are only possible with *bare*
Infinitives and they have two intonation contours (e.g. *Ich frage mich, woher sie
nehmen?* 'I wonder where to get them from'); however, Hannah's utterance has
only one and it mirrors an English structure which she productively uses at that
time. Thus the example has been classified as mixed.

Hannah's last example of a mixed IC to be discussed is special. It looks like
a perfect English control infinitive;[9] however, the context makes it clear that
something has gone wrong with case marking.

(15)   ⟨H pushing her naked teddy in a buggy⟩   (H2;9,2)
        why — he wants to push him NACKT

The target utterance might be the control IC *I want to push him naked* or the ECM structure *he wants me to push him naked* or the passive construction *he wants to be pushed naked*. Whatever the target is: Hannah does not use any of these structures productively yet at the time.

Adam produces fewer mixed utterances than Hannah and there are only five examples documented which are directly related to the acquisition of ICs:

(16) ⟨building a town with Duplo bricks⟩ (A3;10,27)
  now I want a chimney builden\ (2x)

(17) ⟨talking about an octopus, A has drawn⟩ (A4;4,3)
  a. *they didn't got — they didn't got hands zu drawing*
  b. *and they didn't got feets zu zu — soll mir AUCH ma malen*
  '... feet to to — should we draw too?'

(16) is a fairly complex example: The verb *want* receives the subcategorisation frame of the German modal verb *wollen*, thus it combines with a VP and not with a finite subordinate clause or an IC as required by *want*.[10] In addition to this, the structure of the VP is German although the lexical items are English: The main verb follows its complement and it carries the German infinitival ending *-en*. In example (17a) Adam not only borrows the German infinitival marker *zu* but also combines it with the present participle form of the verb, which is a deviant combination in both languages. In (17b) the infinitive particle is the point where the switch occurs, then Adam hesitates and carries on in German.

The next example was produced under very special circumstances and must thus be considered with caution.

(18) ⟨A is asked to translate I's utterances into German⟩
  I: Does Ute know how to feed a horse? (A5;7,29)
  A: *is die is die Ute weiß — ah I forgot it*
   is the is the Ute knows — ah I forgot it
  I: Does Ute know how to feed a horse?
  A: *is die Ute weiß wie man PFERD füttern*
   is the Ute knows how one horse feed

Adam's translation falls short of what he is able to produce in German at that time, ie. perfect target-like questions and subordinate clauses. This is most likely provoked by his attempt at "mimicking" English *do*-support. In the IC this is interesting because Adam keeps the non-finite form of the verb, although the German construction requires a finite verb. Although this calque leads to deviant structures, it illustrates that he knows about equivalences on the level of finiteness in the two languages.

Of course, on the basis of just a few examples, one cannot draw any far-reaching conclusions. But the production of these utterances coincides with the appearance of distinct developmental milestones (cf. Tracy 1995; Gawlitzek-Maiwald 1997). (16) occurs at a time when Adam begins to produce precursors to the German subordinate clauses, (17) after they are acquired and the English main clause is about to be established.

When Laura talks to an English-speaking interlocutor, she produces many mixed utterances; however, most of them are not related to the development of ICs. In one corpus she produces five variants of an aspectual verbal combination (cf. Jaeggli & Hyams 1993). These can be assigned to a cline from German, (19), to English (even though not target-like), (22), and mixed variants (20)–(21) in between.

(19)	we gehen einkaufen (2x)	(L3;1,3)
(20)	we gehen shopping	(L3;1,3)
(21)	we goen shopping	(L3;1,3)
(22)	we going shopping	(L3;1,3)

They occur after she has already acquired the finite German subordinate clause but only occasionally produces English structures which are more complex than a VP. They illustrate that Laura does not yet use auxiliaries or agreement marking on main verbs in English; if inflections occur, they are borrowed from German, as in (21), or the clause is non-finite, as in (22).

A year later we again find a few mixed structures which are related to the acquisition of ICs, (23)–(25). At that time a subset of German ICs has been acquired and the English main and subordinate clause are about to become target-like.

(23) *for [dass des nich runterfällt]*   (L3;10,2)
      for   that this not down-falls
      'so that it does not fall down'

(24) *I want to do it out*   (L4;2,22)

(25) ⟨L wants to listen to recorded utterances⟩   (L4;2,22)
      [*I want to sleep*] *will ich hören*
      'I'd like to hear: I want to sleep.'

(23) is Laura's only precursor to a *for-to* Infinitive. She takes up the *for* from the input but then changes to a finite German structure, which is semantically adequate. Examples (24)–(25) illustrate that even in mixed ICs *want* is the most prominent matrix verb for ICs. The bracketed ICs are adult-like English, only

other parts of the utterances are influenced by German.

So far it has become clear that the children observed do not produce many mixed utterances which are IC-related. Those which we find show different degrees of mixing, and different parts of the utterances are affected. However, one feature is common to most of the utterances discussed so far: If signs of agreement and/or tense marking occur, they are German, while English parts of the utterances are restricted to VPs or ICs. In order to obtain a clearer sense of what is going on in bilingual acquisition with respect to mixing and ICs, it is necessary to look at the monolingual structures produced by the very same children and to relate the mixed utterances to the overall development of the two languages. The following sections provide a brief overview of how ICs emerge in English and German.

3.2 The monolingual acquisition of ICs

3.2.1 English
We know (cf. de Villiers & de Villiers 1985; Limber 1973, 1976) that at the time when first English ICs — mainly with *wanna* — are attested, sentences consist of verbs and one or two arguments, (26); obligatory arguments may be missing, e.g. the subject (27) and (29), or the object (28).

(26) *I need it*

(27) *push car*

(28) *doggie bite*

(29) *wanna swim*   (de Villiers & de Villiers 1985: 44)

These utterances can be described as simple VPs, especially since inflected auxiliary and main verbs, modals, and the copula are not yet documented. Later on, *to* Infinitives in combination with *have* appear roughly at the same time as the first modal verbs, and shortly after that we also find *to* Infinitives with *go* (Fletcher 1979: 266).

The same holds for the English data from Adam, Hannah, and Laura: When the first examples of *have* and *want to* infinitives are documented, only rudimentary precursors to *wh*-questions (without inversion or else formulaic) are attested; there is no evidence for modal or auxiliary verbs.

At the age of 2;3,17 Hannah produces several precursors to ICs, cf. (30). A little later we find examples of modal and auxiliary verbs, (31)–(32); these, however, are singular examples.

(30)   I want to look at the puppets (3x)   (H2;3,17)

(31) I can't walk   (H2;4,17)

(32) I'm wiping it all up   (H2;6,15)

A few months later modals and auxiliaries are productive and we also find yes-no-questions, thus we can assume that at least one functional projection above VP has been acquired. However, *wh*-questions are still formulaic or they do not contain obligatory modals and auxiliaries and finite subordinate structures are not documented. This suggests that the full range of adult-like projections has yet to be acquired, thus Hannah's ICs cannot be adult-like either.

In Adam's data we find a first *have to* infinitive in the first recording, (33), but even a few weeks later there are no examples of auxiliary or modal verbs or target-like inflected full verbs, (34). Months later *wh*-questions still appear without the obligatory auxiliary, (35).

(33) we've to build a flag on it   (A3;6,28)

(34) the train go that way   (A3;7,14)

(35) what you build[11]   (A3;10,27)

It takes another eight months until we find evidence for the productive use of an adult-like main clause and also perhaps subordinate clause. However, during all these months, many examples occur which are related to the acquisition of ICs.

Laura received less English input than Adam did, thus we observe an example of slow-motion acquisition of English. There is no evidence for functional projections in her English up until the age of 3;10,2. However, we do find precursors to ICs. These are an early single example of a *going to* infinitive, (36), aspectual verbal combinations as in (37), and from 3;3 onwards examples of *to* Infinitives after *want* and *like*, (38)–(39).

(36) we're going to walk   (L2;2,29)

(37) n no we go shopping   (L3;1,3)

(38) I want to play pirates   (L3;10,28)

(39) I don't like to play pirates   (L3;10,28)

From 3;10,2 on Laura's English develops considerably and then we also find *wh*-questions, yes-no questions with inversion, modal verbs, and finite embedded structures.

This brief overview shows that at the time when first ICs appear, none of the three children shows signs of the acquisition of agreement or tense marking in English. Structures are still best analysed as VPs or as special projections of individual lexical items which embed a VP (cf. Tracy 1995). If there is no independent evidence for the existence of functional levels above VP in the children's English, we can conclude that the first ICs cannot really be analysed as they would be in the adult system, ie. as clauses of some higher functional level.

As soon as we find evidence that the children have acquired a first functional projection above VP, more matrix verbs which embed ICs emerge. Apart from *want*, the following verbs are documented: *have, going, try, know, let, make*, and *help*. Occasionally we also find precursors to *for-to* Infinitives. At the end of the period observed, the following range of structures is attested:[12]

> (40) and he wants me to tell you another story   (H3;3,17)

> (41) they want to press that button on that   (H4;0,3)

> (42) why are some people quick to eat   (H3;2,12)
>   and some people slow?

> (43) that's one to eat the mosasaurus   (A4;0,17)

> (44) I don't know how to speak   (A5;5,0)

> (45) let's go in a restaurant   (L4;3,12)

By the time our data collection comes to an end, the children use only a relatively small range of matrix verbs for ICs and the range of ICs is limited: Raising structures are not attested at all, ECM structures appear very rarely and usually in set phrases. Only control structures occur with a slightly higher frequency and variation.

3.2.2 *German*

In Gawlitzek-Maiwald (1997), a systematic longitudinal study of the acquisition of German ICs,[13] the following acquisitional sequence is documented: When first precursors to ICs appear in German, the German main clause is already established. Precursors to ICs in German vary more than they do in English. First subcategorised ICs follow the verbs *lassen, brauchen, probieren* ('let', 'need', 'try'). At roughly the same time first aspectual ICs, nominalised ICs, and for some children *um-zu* Infinitives emerge. All these structures are rare in the children's utterances, and it takes quite some time until a larger number of ICs is recorded. The first subcategorised ICs to be acquired are control structures, e.g. *wir versuchen, die Tür zu öffnen* ('we are trying to open the door'). They are followed by ECMs, *sie läßt den Klotz liegen* ('she lets the block lie' meaning 'she's leaving the block where it is'). Raising ICs, e.g. *sie scheint wieder früh zu kommen* ('she seems to be arriving early again') are acquired rather late; the children in this study do not produce them.

For Hannah the first documented German ICs are aspectuals such as (46).

From age 2;3 on she produces them regularly. (47)–(49) illustrate typical main clause structures of this time. From age 2;5 onwards we find enough evidence to assume that Hannah has acquired the German main clause.

(46)   *mama komm mit spazieren*   (H2;3,17)
       mum come with go-for-a-walk
       'mum, let's go for a walk'

(47)   *nein, ich bin eine hannah*   (H2;2,27)
       no I   am a   Hannah
       'no, I'm called Hannah'

(48)   *ich hab so viele sachen da*   (H2;4,17)
       'I   have so many things there'

(49)   *du hast du den mund aufgemacht?*   (H2;4,17)
       you have you the mouth open-made
       'have you opened your mouth?'

Adam starts producing ICs rather late. Apart from one doubtful example, the first structures are documented at age 3;10,0: (50) is an object control structure with deviation in case and number marking of the subject and (51) is an aspectual verbal combination.

(50)   ⟨A pointing to a crane and a wagon on the shelf⟩
       und den   kann helfen mitbauen (A3;10,0)
       and this (Kran and wagon) can help   with-build
       'and this one can help us building'

(51)   *und sie kommt dadurch   gefahren*   (A3;10,0)
       and she comes here-through driven
       'and she comes driving through here'

At this time the German main clause is well established in Adam's system; however, subordinate clauses take another six months to become productive. Nominalised ICs such as (52) are the next type of IC to emerge. These and the aspectuals are from now on well represented in the data.

(52)   *hey ich komm mit zum   schwimmen*   (A3;10,27)
       hey I   come with to-the swim
       'hey I'll come swimming with you'

For Laura the first documented ICs are also aspectuals, (53), followed by [bare]Infinitives after *brauchen*, (54).

(53)   *de mann bleib   stehen*   (L2;6,26)
        the man remains stand
        'the man remains standing'

(54)   *ich brauch- brau noch probieren*   (L2;8,10)
        I   need-   need still try
        'I still have to try'

At the time these precursors are documented, Laura has acquired the German main clause. Around her third birthday finite German subordinate clauses are target-like. This is more than a year before we can assume that Laura has acquired some of the ICs.

In sum, what we find in the acquisition of German is that children have acquired at least the main clause structure, and some of them are on their way to tackling finite subordination as well, when first precursors to ICs appear. This contrasts with the findings for English, where we find no evidence of functional levels above VP when first ICs appear.

In German the range of structures acquired during the time of data collection is somewhat wider than in English. As already mentioned, all three children regularly produce aspectual ICs and nominalisations. As in English the few attested ECM structures are rather formulaic, such as (55), while control structures, (56)-(57), eventually become productive. This is particularly obvious with respect to (56), which deviates from the target in case marking. Matrix verbs used are *anfangen, brauchen*[14], *helfen, lassen* ('begin', 'need', 'help', 'let').

(55)   *des mußte   halt liegen lassen*   (A5;2,26)
        this must-you PRT lie   let
        'you have to leave it where it is'

(56)   ⟨H wants to unwrap present but can't get paper off⟩
        M: Why don't you ask Ira to help you?   (H4;0,3)
        H: *helf mich mal*
            'help me'
        I: Mhm. Komm gleich. Was soll ich denn machen?
        H: *mich helfen des aufzumachen*
            me   help   this open-to-make
            'help me to unwrap this'

(57)   *du   brauchst keine mehr zu holen*   (L4;2,22)
        you need   no   more to get
        'you don't need to get any more'

Figure 1, which is displayed at the end of this paper, summarizes the acquisitional paths of English (upper part) and German (lower part) in the bilingual children discussed above. Grey areas represent times when mixing increases in the children's utterances; this usually happens before functional categories are acquired. Thin lines around constructions and categories indicate precursor structures while bold lines highlight adult-like structures and usage.

4.   English and German ICs: A brief look at the target systems

I have argued that children's early ICs — especially in English — cannot be analysed as they would be in the adult systems. To support this argument we have to take a look at the way sentences and ICs are analysed in the adult grammars. First consider the English examples in (58).

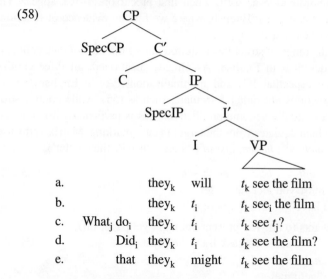

(58)

CP

SpecCP   C′

C   IP

SpecIP   I′

I   VP

a.		they$_k$ will	t_k see the film
b.		they$_k$ t_i	t_k see$_i$ the film
c.	What$_j$ do$_i$	they$_k$ t_i	t_k see t_j?
d.	Did$_i$	they$_k$ t_i	t_k see the film?
e.	that	they$_k$ might	t_k see the film

In line with suggestions in linguistic theory (cf. Chomsky & Lasnik 1991; Radford 1997), I assume that subjects originate in SpecVP, ie. the VP of examples (58a) — (e) at d-structure is [$_{VP}$ *they see the film*]. For main clauses such as (58a) and (58b) at least one phrasal level above VP is needed, here labelled as IP for inflectional phrase. In order to provide positions for complementisers and moved elements, questions and subordinate clauses need one more functional level, the complementiser phrase.

Now compare (59) for the structure of ICs in adult English.

(59)

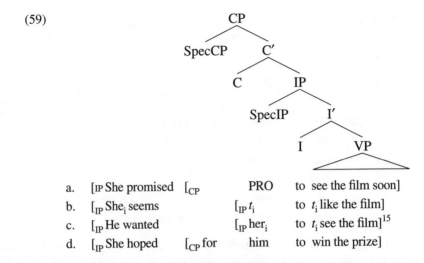

a.	[IP She promised [CP		PRO	to see the film soon]
b.	[IP She_i seems		[IP t_i	to t_i like the film]
c.	[IP He wanted		[IP her_i	to t_i see the film][15]
d.	[IP She hoped [CP for		him	to win the prize]

The infinitival particle *to* is generated in the inflectional node I. This means that ICs containing *to* need at least one level above VP. But how can we then explain those first *to* Infinitives which emerge before other representatives of IP in children's English? I will come back to this question in the next section.

For the analysis of German sentences the situation is slightly more complicated. There are several suggestions as to how the German V2–effect and asymmetrical behaviours of main and subordinate clauses in German could be coped with. I follow Brandt et al. (1992), who suggest different formats for main and subordinate clauses. The authors analyse subordinate clauses with the finite verb in final position as CP/IPs, (60), while sentences with the finite verb in second position are analysed as IPs, (61).

(60)

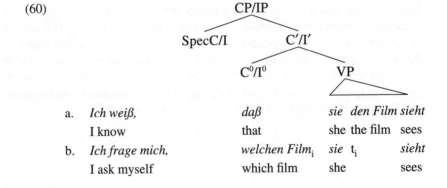

a.	*Ich weiß,*	*daß*	*sie den Film sieht*	
	I know	that	she the film sees	
b.	*Ich frage mich,*	*welchen Film_i*	*sie t_i*	*sieht*
	I ask myself	which film	she	sees

(61)

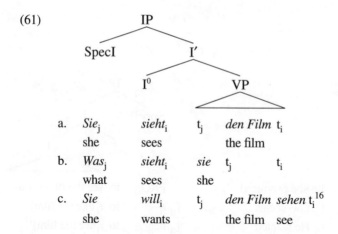

a.	*Sie*ⱼ	*sieht*ᵢ	tⱼ	*den Film* tᵢ
	she	sees		the film
b.	*Was*ⱼ	*sieht*ᵢ	*sie* tⱼ	tᵢ
	what	sees	she	
c.	*Sie*	*will*ᵢ	tⱼ	*den Film sehen* tᵢ[16]
	she	wants		the film see

There is no general agreement as to how German ICs are to be analysed. I assume that control structures are CP/IPs, (62), while raising ICs, (63), and ECMs, (64), are VPs.

(62) *Sie verspricht,* [$_{CP/IP}$ *PRO die Zeitung   zu kaufen*]
      she promises   the newspaper to buy

(63) *Er*ᵢ *scheint* [$_{VP}$ tᵢ *müde zu sein*]
      he seems   tired to be

(64) *Sie hört* [$_{VP}$ *ihn spielen*]
      she hears   him play

This short description of the English and the German target systems shows three points: First, children need functional levels to produce adult-like ICs and second, despite superficial similarities between English and German ICs — in both languages we find a triplet of construction types and a triplet of introducing particles — there are differences. For example ECM and Raising ICs seem to differ with respect to their category in the two languages. And *to* Infinitives can be either of the three major ICs, while *zu* Infinitives can only be control or raising ICs. And the third observation is that there are open questions concerning the projection level of ICs, the precise analysis of ECM structures in both languages, and the internal structure and analysis of German Raising ICs.

5.   Discussion

I have described how three bilingual German–English-speaking children acquire ICs. For each of these three children three acquisition stories can be told: one for English, one for German, and one for the mixed utterances. The sequence of acquisition in English and German is parallel to what we find in monolingual children speaking only one of these languages. Mixed utterances are systematic in two respects; the children pool their resources from both languages (cf. Gawlitzek-Maiwald & Tracy 1996) and increased mixing occurs when one or both language system(s) is/are about to be restructured.

Table (4) gives an overview of when the IP and CP are acquired and compares this to the occurrence of first precursors to ICs and first adult-like ICs.[17]

Table 4. *Overview of acquisition of IP, CP, and ICs*

	First Precursors to ICs	IP acquired	CP acquired		adult-like ICs & matrix verbs
English					
Hannah	2;8	2;9	2;11	3;0	*want, have, go*
Adam	3;6	4;6	5;0	4;6	*need, let, help,*
Laura	3;3	3;10	—	—	*want, go, have*
German					
Hannah	3;1	2;4	3;1	4;0	*helfen, vergessen, brauchen*
Adam	3;10	3;6	4;4	4;7	*brauchen, helfen*
				5;4	*anfangen, probieren*
Laura	2;6	2;8	3;1	3;2	*brauchen*
				3;7	*helfen*

Despite the long periods of observation, not all types of ICs are acquired either in English or in German. The table highlights again that in English precursors of ICs appear before the IP is acquired, while in German they are documented only after the IP is established. In both languages adult-like ICs, ie. those which are clearly subcategorised and non-deviant, appear after or around the time when the CP is acquired. Adam is an exception here, as he produces target-like ICs before he has acquired the English CP. Although his ICs already look target-like, in his finite structures we do not find enough evidence for two functional projections above VP before age 5;0; only then does it seem justified to assume that the CP has been acquired.

We find two types of asynchronies in the systems: The German functional projections are acquired before the English ones, while first structures resembling ICs appear in English before they appear in German.[18] Or to say it differently: By just looking at first occurrences of ICs we could be tempted to argue that the implicational sequence given in (6) and (7) at the beginning is correct. However, as soon as we take the following two aspects into account (which I have been stressing time and again), it cannot:

(a)   In the English target *to* Infinitives are IPs and CPs, thus children need to have these functional projections for the respective ICs to assign adult-like structures to them. But when first ICs emerge, we do not find any other evidence for the existence of an IP than infinitival *to*, thus these first ICs cannot have adult-like structure.

(b)   Only after these first ICs are documented do we find deviant structures related to other constructions which can be analysed as precursors of an emerging IP.

As the asynchrony between the languages cannot be due to different stages of cognitive development in the same child, the reason for the asynchrony must lie in systematic differences between English and German. German is a V2-language and children have to figure out which of the verb positions they come across is the basic one. In English the position of the main verb is (superficially) always the same.[19] Although this might look like the easier acquisition task at first sight, the fact that children acquiring English require more time to figure out that there are functional projections above VP suggests that this is in fact a disadvantage. In addition to this, German children find more morphological cues in the input for functional levels above VP. Taking into account that *to* is often the first element of those which are base generated in I^0 in adult English to appear in child speech, it might be *the* element signalling to the children that there is more structure above the English VP.

This view is supported by the mixed utterances of Hannah and Laura, who combine what they know of the *structure* of the two languages while the development of German is ahead of English, cf. the following examples repeated here as (65)–(66).

(65)   [$_?$ *simone is zu   klein* [$_{Engl}$ *zu gehen in die kita*]]   (H2;7,14)
         simone is too small   to go   in the day care centre

(66)   [$_{Engl}$ we go-[$_{Germ}$ en] SHOPping]   (L3;1,3)

Adam's mixed ICs occur when he is about to restructure his systems. So again mixed language is a sign not of a language deficit but of combining what is available to the child in each language at the time.

We also find parallels in the two languages with respect to the types of ICs acquired first and the sequence of acquisition: Control structures[20] and aspectual ICs emerge first, then occasional ECM structures are produced,[21] while raising ICs are not documented in my data. In both languages children use only a relatively small number of matrix verbs that embed ICs.

How can the sequence of acquisition be explained? Of course, frequency in the input could play a role, but there might also be construction-specific reasons — which go across languages — for the observed acquisition sequence. Let us first consider how ICs differ from finite clauses and sentences. The major differences probably lie in the verb form and the realisation of the subject. In English and German, verbs in ICs are not marked for tense and agreement. The difference in verb forms is probably easier for German children as they are confronted with morphologically different forms, whereas English children find only minimal contrasts in verb morphology. With respect to subject realisation there is not much difference between the two languages: The subject in control structures is the non-lexical pronoun PRO. The subject in ECM structures is a lexical DP exceptionally case-marked as objective. The subject of a raising IC is a trace, ie. a lexical DP which surfaces in a dislocated position. Thus I would argue that the subject in control structures could be called a prototypical IC subject, as it is maximally different from subjects in finite clauses. The subject in ECM ICs is more difficult to acquire, because it is lexical and receives case under special conditions. Subjects in raising ICs are complex for two reasons: Ultimately they are lexical DPs and thus not sufficiently different from subjects in finite constructions and in addition their generation involves movement (at least in English), which also makes the structure more complex.

Pulling the different lines of argumentation together, we find considerable asynchronies in the development of English and German, while the acquisition of different IC types takes place in the same order in both languages. I have argued above that language-specific differences are responsible for the asynchronic development of English and German, while construction-specific features produce the particular order in which different ICs are acquired. As this holds true across languages, it might serve as support for a UG-oriented analysis. Of course, to make this argument stronger one would have to look at the acquisition of ICs in other languages.

6.   Summary

I started off with the question of whether the suggested implicational sequences for English and German in (6) and (7) are correct and, if so, why there are differences between English and German.

Longitudinal data from three bilingual English-German speaking children showed characteristic asynchronies in the acquisition of IP and CP in the two languages. Despite these asynchronies we observed a certain order of acquisition for different ICs across children and across languages. This sort of parallelism and asynchrony in one individual made it possible to trace language- and construction-specific factors of language acquisition which facilitate or hinder the acquisition of a specific construction.

The English and German of the bilingual children observed develop parallel to what we know about the monolingual acquisition of the respective languages while the mixed utterances are predominantly produced at times when one or both language system(s) is/are being restructured or when one language is developmentally ahead of the other.

But what about the original question concerning the different implicational sequences? If we disregard the overall language system(s) of these children, we could indeed argue that English ICs are acquired before finite subordinate clauses, but as soon as we take into account that there are no other constructions and/or elements documented which provide evidence for the existence of a projection level above VP, ie. to IP, while we already find first *want to* ICs this is not really plausible. If IP is not available, these first ICs cannot be adult-like ICs. Thus the implicational sequence mentioned at the beginning has to be modified for English as in (67) below. It then matches the one for German.

(6)   English:
       main clauses $\Rightarrow$ subordinate clauses$_{(+\text{finite})}$ $\Rightarrow$ embedded non-finite
                                                              constructions

The investigation of the acquisition of ICs in bilingual children is interesting and relevant in two respects: First, bilingual data help us to reconsider preconceptions about monolingual acquisition and thus, second, they provide us with an argument in favor of systems thinking as Capra (1996: 29f) describes it in the following quote:

> The great shock of twentieth-century science has been that systems cannot be understood by analysis. The properties of the parts are not intrinsic properties, but can be understood only within the context of the larger whole. Thus the relationship between the parts and the whole has been reversed. In the systems approach, the properties of the parts can be understood only from the organisation of the whole. Accordingly, systems thinking does not concentrate on basic building-blocks but rather on basic principles of organisation. Systems thinking is 'contextual', which is the opposite of analytical thinking. Analysis

means taking something apart in order to understand it; systems thinking means putting it into the context of a larger whole.

In short, the aim of this study has been to look at the emergence of ICs in the context of a child's complete language system and to relate that emergence to changes in the system rather than looking at phenomena in isolation.

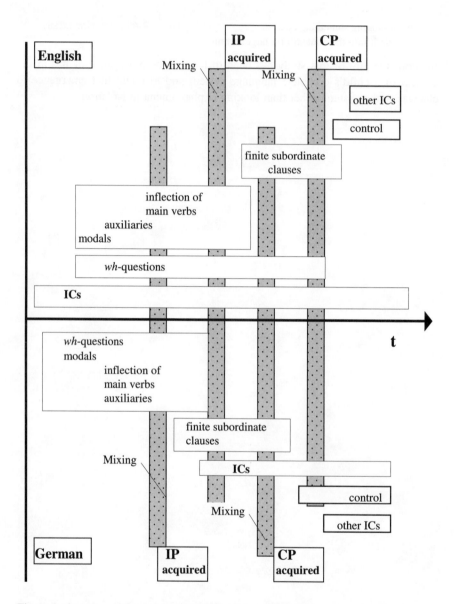

Figure 1. *Overview of the development of English and Grammar*

Acknowledgments

I would like to thank friends and colleagues who read earlier versions of this paper and made valuable suggestions: Susanne Döpke, Stefanie Ebert, Ulrike Gut, Anja Guttropf, Elsa Lattey, Kristel Proost, and Rosemarie Tracy.

Notes

1. Participial constructions will not be part of the discussion.
2. Examples (1) and (2) are taken from Menyuk (1971: 142), (3) from Stern & Stern (1928: 47), (4) from Scupin & Scupin (1910: 14), and (5) from Cron-Böngeler (1985: 169).
3. Unfortunately Menyuk does not give a more precise age.
4. This is part of the data of a Tübingen project on the acquisition of complex sentences directed by Rosemarie Tracy and financed by the German Research Foundation (DFG). All told, the project collected approximately 100,000 utterances from 12 children.
5. Laura is Adam's younger sister.
6. Nine of these recordings were made by Hannah's mother (who studied English linguistics). These were later transcribed by me and cross-checked.
7. Note that the figures for English, German, and mixed utterances do not necessarily add up to the number of utterances in total, as a fourth category „both" is not included in this table. This category contains (mainly short) utterances for which it cannot be decided to which language they belong, e.g. vocatives.
8. For a more detailed discussion of mixing in all three children cf. Gawlitzek-Maiwald (1997), for Hannah and Adam cf. Tracy (1995) and for Hannah cf. also Gawlitzek-Maiwald & Tracy (1996). Occasionally all the children produce ICs where only a lexical item is borrowed from the other language, cf. *Er braucht nich einzustrappen* ('he needs not in-to-strap' Hannah 2;9). I am not going to discuss these here.
9. Control infinitives are structures such as (i), where an NP outside the infinitive (usually in the main clause) determines the interpretation of the non-lexical subject PRO of the infinitive. ECMs (=exceptional case marking or accusative cum infinitive in traditional terminology) are structures such as (ii), where an NP in objective case functions as the subject of the infinitive. In raising infinitives such as (iii), the main verb does not assign a thematic role to its subject, thus allowing expletives as subject or NPs raised from an embedded infinitive.
   (i) $Susan_i$ promised Maggie [PRO_i to buy the latest edition]
   (ii) Susan expected [him to prepare dinner]
   (iii) $Susan_i$ happened [t_i to like pizza a lot]
10. The German modal verbs *wollen/möchte(n)* behave like control verbs while the others (*dürfen/ können/mögen/müssen/sollen*) pattern with raising verbs. I assume that all modal verbs embed VP structures (cf. also Rosengren 1992). However, Öhlschläger (1989) assumes that *wollen* and *möchte(n)* embed CPs while the other modals embed IPs.
11. Here even the question *what do you build?* would be deviant as the context calls for a progressive form of the verb. Adam occasionally produces deviant aspect forms like this, which is probably due to influence from German.

12. For the sake of brevity and clarity I quote only some illustrative examples from all the children; for a detailed description of the development of each child cf. Gawlitzek-Maiwald (1997).

13. A few experiments have been conducted on the acquisition of German ICs, cf. Grimm & Schöler (1975), Rothweiler & Siebert-Ott (1988), Schaner-Wolles & Haider (1987), and Schulz (1995).

14. In adult German *anfangen* (begin) as well as *brauchen* (need) are used as raising and control verbs. In the children's utterances, however, it is more likely that they function as control verbs only, as the children always use them with agentive and never with expletive subjects. Unambiguous raising verbs such as *scheinen* (seem) are not attested.

15. How exactly ECM constructions should be analysed is discussed controversially. One suggestion is that subject to object raising takes place, i.e. the subject of the IC is raised to the object position of the matrix verb and case marked (cf. Postal 1974). Another possibility is that ECM verbs embed IPs and that the matrix verb assigns case across the IP (cf. Chomsky & Lasnik 1991).

16. Usually it is assumed that modal verbs in German are base generated in V^0, which subcategorises another VP, and then moved to I^0. For adult German, modal verbs are analysed as raising or control verbs (Öhlschläger 1989); however, for child German this analysis is highly problematical, cf. Gawlitzek-Maiwald (1997: Ch. 8).

17. It will have become clear by now that I work under the assumption of weak continuity. The idea of different projections being acquired at different times would not be compatible with strong continuity.

18. Here Laura is an exception; however, this is hardly surprising if we take into account how long it takes for her English to show any structure above VP at all.

19. Of course there are some residual cases of V2 in English, but they are rare in the spoken input. Children's books present a higher percentage of inversion structures, cf. Tracy (1995: Ch. 4.3.3).

20. It has been claimed that subject control is acquired before object control (Goodluck 1978; Tavakolian 1977). However, this cannot be completely true as we find the object control verbs *helfen* and *help* among the first productive matrix verbs.

21. In my data and in the literature (cf. Pinker 1984; Radford 1990) a few cases of deviant case-marking such as *I want [she to get it]* (H 3;1) are documented. These lend support to the assumption that children indeed analyse the intervening DP as the subject of the infinitive and not as the object of the matrix clause.

References

Brandt, Margarete, Marga Reis, Inger Rosengren, & Ilse Zimmermann. 1992. "Satztyp, Satzmodus und Illokution." In Rosengren, Inger (ed), *Satz und Illokution.* Vol. 1 Tübingen: Niemeyer, 1–90.

Capra, Fritjof. 1996. *The Web of Life: A New Synthesis of Mind and Matter.* London and Hammersmith: Flamingo.

Chomsky, Noam & Howard Lasnik. 1991. "Principles and parameters theory." In A. von Stechow, W. Sternefeld & T. Vennemann (eds), *Syntax: An International Handbook of Continuing Research.* Berlin: Mouton de Gruyter.

Cron-Böngeler, Ute. 1985. "Die Analyse kindlicher Satzstrukturen in den ersten drei Lebensjahren." In H. Gripper (ed), *Kinder unterwegs zur Sprache: Zum Prozeß der Spracherlernung in den ersten drei Lebensjahren.* Düsseldorf: Schwamm, 148–170.

de Villiers, Jill & Peter A. de Villiers. 1985. "The acquisition of English." In D. I. Slobin (ed), *The Crosslinguistic Study of Language Acquisition. Vol. 1.* Hillsdale, NJ: Lawrence Erlbaum, 27–140.

Fletcher, Paul. 1979. "The development of the verb phrase." In P. Fletcher & M. Garman (eds), *Language Acquisition: Studies in First Language Development.* Cambridge: Cambridge University Press, 261–284.

Gawlitzek-Maiwald, Ira. 1997. *Der monolinguale und bilinguale Erwerb von Infinitivkonstruktionen: Ein Vergleich von Deutsch und Englisch.* Tübingen: Niemeyer.

Gawlitzek-Maiwald, Ira & Tracy, Rosemarie 1996. "Bilingual Bootstrapping." In N. Müller (Ed). *Two Languages. Studies in Bilingual First and Second Language Development.* (Linguistics 34) Berlin and New York: Mouton de Gruyter, 901–926.

Goodluck, Helen. 1978. *Linguistic Principles in Children's Grammar of Complement Subject Interpretation* University of Massachusetts: Amherst: PhD. thesis.

Grimm, Hannelore & Hermann Schöler. 1975. "Erlauben — Befehlen — Lassen: Wie gut verstehen kleine Kinder kausativierende Beziehungen?" In H. Grimm, H. Schöler & M. Wintermantel (eds), *Zur Entwicklung sprachlicher Strukturformen bei Kindern: Forschungsberichte der Sprachentwicklung I: Empirische Untersuchungen zum Erwerb und zur Erfassung sprachlicher Wahrnehmungs- & Produktionsstrategien bei Drei- bis Achtjährigen.* Weinheim and Basel: Beltz, 100–120.

Hakuta, Kenji. 1986. *Mirror of Language: The Debate on Bilingualism.* New York: Basic Books.

Hyams, Nina. 1984. "The acquisition of infinitival complements. 'A Reply to Bloom, Tackeff & Lahey.'" *Journal of Child Language* 11: 679–683.

Hyams, Nina. 1988. "The effects of core and peripheral grammar on grammatical development in children." (Ms. UCLA).

Jaeggli, Osvaldo & Nina Hyames. 1993. "On the independence and interdependence of syntactic and morphological properties: English aspectual *come* and *go*". *Natural Language and Linguistic Theory* 11: 313–346.

Leopold, Werner F. 1949. *Speech Development of a Bilingual Child: A Linguist's Record. Vol. 4: Diary from Age 2.* Evanston: Northwestern University Press.

Limber, John. 1973. "The genesis of complex sentences." In T. E. Moore (ed), *Cognitive Development and the Acquisition of Language.* New York: Academic Press, 169–186.

Limber, John. 1976. "Unravelling competence, performance and pragmatics in the speech of young children." *Journal of Child Language* 3: 309–318.

Menyuk, Paula. 1969. *Sentences Children Use.* Cambridge, MA: MIT Press.

Menyuk, Paula. 1971. *The Acquisition and Development of Language.* Englewood Cliffs: Prentice Hall.

Mills, Anne. 1985. "The acquisition of German." In D. I. Slobin (ed), *The Crosslinguistic Study of Language Acquisition. Vol. 1.* Hillsdale, NJ: Lawrence Erlbaum, 141–254.

Öhlschläger, Günther. 1989. *Zur Syntax und Semantik der Modalverben des Deutschen.* Tübingen: Niemeyer.

Pierce, Amy E. 1992. *Language Acquisition and Syntactic Theory: A Comparative Analysis of French and English Child Grammars.* Dordrecht: Kluwer.

Pinker, Steven. 1984. *Language Learnability and Language Development.* Cambridge, MA: Harvard University Press.

Postal, Paul M. 1974. *On Raising: One Rule of English Grammar and Its Theoretical Implications.* Cambridge, MA: MIT Press.

Radford, Andrew. 1990. *Syntactic Theory and the Acquisition of English Syntax.* Oxford: Basil Blackwell.

Radford, Andrew. 1997. *Syntax: A Minimalist Introduction.* Cambridge: Cambridge University Press.

Romaine, Suzanne. 1989. *Bilingualism.* Oxford: Basil Blackwell.

Rosengren, Inger. 1992. "Zum Problem der kohärenten Verben im Deutschen." In P.Suchsland (ed), *Biologische und soziale Grundlagen der Sprache. Interdiziplinäres Symposium 1989.* Tübingen: Niemeyer, 265–297.

Rothweiler, Monika & Gesa M. Siebert-Ott. 1988. "Der Erweb von Infinitkonstruktionen." (Paper presented at the annual conference of the DGfS).

Schaner-Wolles, Chris & Hubert Haider. 1987. "Spracherwerb und Kognition — Eine Studie über interpretative Relationen." In J. Bayer (ed), *Grammatik und Kognition: Psycholinguistische Untersuchungen.* (Linguistische Berichte Sonderheft 1/87). Opladen: Westdeutscher Verlag, 41–80.

Schulz, Petra. 1995. "Finitheit und Faktivität — Wie Kinder Komplementsätze verstehen." University of Tübingen: Ms.

Scupin, Ernst & Gertrud Scupin. 1910. *Bubi im vierten bis sechsten Lebensjahr: Ein Tagebuch über die geistige Entwicklung eines Knaben in den ersten sechs Lebensjahren.* Vol. 2 Leipzig: Th. Grieben's.

Stern, Clara & Stern, William 1975. *Die Kindersprache: Eine psychologische und sprachtheoretische Untersuchung.* Darmstadt: Wissenschaftliche Buchgesellschaft. Reprint of the fourth edition Leipzig 1928.

Tavakolian, Susan L. 1977. *Structured Principles in the Acquisition of Complex Sentences.* University of Massachusetts, Amherst: PhD thesis.

Tracy, Rosemarie. 1995. "Child Languages in Contact: Bilingual Language Acquisition (German-English) in Early Childhood." University of Tübingen: Habilitation.

The Search for Cross-Linguistic Influences in the Language of Young Latvian-English Bilinguals

Indra Sinka

University of Hertfordshire, UK

1. Introduction

The language of children bilingual from birth provides us with an abundance of data that are essential for the study of language acquisition. The bilingual child offers the researcher the opportunity to explore the development of two languages *within the same child* and thus control for chronological and mental age, as well as personality. Data from simultaneous bilinguals also enable us to gain insight into the relationship *between* the two languages concerned and whether this relationship differs from one pair of languages to another.

Much debate has centred on whether bilingual children differentiate between their languages from early on. Evidence of language 'mixing', particularly at the level of grammatical competence, has been seen as supporting the single system hypothesis (Volterra & Taeschner 1978; Redlinger & Park 1980; Taeschner 1983; Vihman 1985; Arnberg 1987), whilst more recent literature (Meisel 1989; De Houwer 1990; Gawlitzek-Maiwald & Tracy 1996; Paradis & Genesee 1996; Sinka & Schelletter 1998) has focused on morphosyntactic development and the bilingual child's ability to differentiate languages from the earliest stages, thus providing support for a separate development hypothesis (cf De Houwer 1995 and Lanza 1997a for overviews of studies contributing to the one- versus two-system argument).

In-depth research into language mixing patterns has also established that such mixing in both adults and children is governed by pragmatic and grammatical constraints; in fact, proponents of both sides of the one- versus two-system debate have argued that the use of mixed utterances falls dramatically when bilingual children acquire sufficient knowledge of inflectional grammar. Vihman (1985) argues that the child's developing awareness of the language choices expected of him or her leads to a pragmatic basis for this change in language behaviour, whereas Meisel (1994) offers the emergence of the functional category INFL as the trigger for decreased mixing. Köppe & Meisel (1995: 278–282) provide a good review of the literature.

Linked to the notion of syntactic constraints, is the question whether the nature of the languages involved affects the output: if cross-linguistic structures are more likely in the language of children where the two languages have similar structural realisations (Döpke, this volume), then does the reverse hold true when a child is presented with languages with different underlying syntactic rules? In the following, I present data on bilingual first language acquisition from languages with differing morpho-syntactic complexity: Latvian and English.

2. Evidence from two young Latvian-English bilinguals

The data come from the longitudinal study of two (unrelated) children of Latvian-English parentage: Māra, the eldest child in her family, and Maija, the youngest of three. Māra's English mother was the primary caretaker, although her Latvian father was very much involved in Māra's care on his return from work each day; the family live in the south of England. In Maija's family, her English father was the primary caretaker, with Maija's Latvian mother also very much involved in her daughter's care on return from work; Maija's family live in the north of England. Latvian grandparents, other relatives and strong local Latvian communities provided both children with additional Latvian input. Both girls were addressed according to the 'one person — one language' principle from birth and through observation and interviews with family members, the input of Latvian and English was judged to be fairly equal for both girls. Audio-recordings of 45 minutes per language were made every fortnight and transcription and analysis of the data were carried out using the SALT programs developed by Miller & Chapman (1996). In this chapter, monthly samples of the first 12 months of the children's language are analysed. Thus for Māra the data presented cover the age range 1;6 to 2;5 and for Maija 1;3 to 2;2.

2.1 Latvian

It is important here to consider briefly the main differences between Latvian and English. Latvian is morphologically more complex: 1st and 2nd person singular and plural and 3rd person forms (common to both singular and plural) of all verbs are marked distinctly for tense (past, present and future) and agreement. All nouns, pronouns, adjectives and determiners have seven cases and are marked for gender (masculine and feminine) and number (singular and plural). There are no definite or indefinite articles in Latvian and nouns can appear without determiners. In addition, Latvian has a freer word order than English. The Latvian-English bilingual child is therefore drawing on two very different systems.

2.2   *The distribution of complete and intelligible utterances*

Tables 1 to 4 provide overviews of the children's language choices when talking with their parents mainly in one-to-one situations. On some occasions a third person was present in the room; where it is felt this may have affected the language choice of the child concerned, the relevant utterances are highlighted and addressed in the discussion that follows. Utterances with unintelligible elements are discounted from the analysis, as are those which are incomplete (the child having voluntarily stopped in mid-utterance or been interrupted before completing the utterance). The remaining complete and intelligible (C&I) utterances have been divided into three types: those which contain elements from only Latvian (Latvian utterances), those which contain elements from only English (English utterances) and those which contain elements from both languages (mixed utterances). Mixing occurs at lexical, syntactic, morphological, phonological and semantic levels (Döpke 1992: 7); the utterances here are categorised according to Lanza's use of 'mixing' as "... a cover term for any type of linguistic interaction between two (and potentially more) languages" (Lanza 1997a: 3). A more detailed discussion of the particular nature of Māra's and Maija's mixed utterances follows later in the chapter. Figures 1 to 4 show the percentage of turns with each of the three types of utterance.

   Tables 1 and 2 illustrate the distribution of Māra's complete and intelligible utterances across the two languages; mean length of utterance in both words (for Latvian and English) and morphemes (for English only) is also included as additional information. The C&I columns give the total number of complete and intelligible utterances in each sample. As can be seen from the utterance totals and the percentages presented in Figures 1 and 2, Māra distinguishes appropriately between the languages from the very first sample, speaking chiefly English with her mother and Latvian with her father or other Latvian interlocutor.

   At first glance, Figures 1 and 2 seem to present fairly straightforward pictures of Māra's language choice. However, it is interesting to note the slight increase in the number and percentage of Latvian utterances, and the mirrored decrease in

Table 1. *Distribution of Māra's C&I utterances: English sessions*

CA	MLU*	MLU**	C&I	English	Latvian	Mixed
1;6,14	1.27	1.37	213	206	6	1
1;7,10	1.40	1.60	263	259	3	1
1;8,14	1.39	1.65	218	209	7	2
1;9,12	1.68	2.04	289	281	5	3
1;10,9	1.71	2.00	220	218	2	0
1;11,8	1.83	2.18	198	186	9	3
2;0,4	2.87	3.28	94	94	0	0
2;1,0	2.93	3.27	238	208	20	10
2;1,30	2.31	2.72	224	221	2	1
2;3,1	3.34	3.90	238	232	1	5
2;3,29	3.43	3.86	306	303	1	2
2;5,4	2.61	2.97	360	359	1	0
Total	–	–	2861	2776	57	28

Mean length of utterance: *in words, **in morphemes

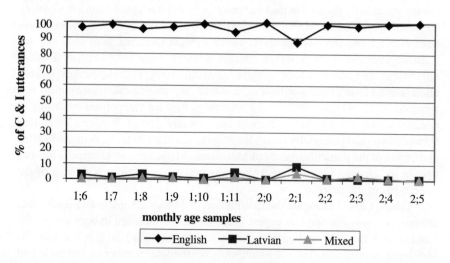

Figure 1. *Percentages of Māra's C&I utterances: English sessions*

English ones, at 2;1 in the English sessions (cf Table 1 and Figure 1); this is also evident in the Latvian sessions; indeed, in Figure 2, after the age of 2;0, a steadier language pattern is established, with an increase depicted in the percentage of Latvian utterances and a decrease in English ones. The counts in Table 2 underline

Table 2. *Distribution of Māra's C&I utterances: Latvian sessions*

CA	MLU*	C&I	Latvian	English	Mixed
1;6,14	1.30	201	148	43	10
1;7,10	1.28	207	199	5	3
1;8,13	1.14	146	141	4	1
1;9,12	1.25	174	154	20	0
1;10,6	1.27	307	292	15	0
1;11,8	1.54	81	59	20	2
2;0,5	1.56	131	95	30	6
2;1,5	1.56	229	196	28	5
2;2,1	1.67	215	193	18	4
2;3,1	1.96	239	223	12	4
2;4,3	2.01	255	243	9	3
2;5,4	1.59	296	293	2	1
Total	–	2481	2236	206	39

* Mean length of utterance in words

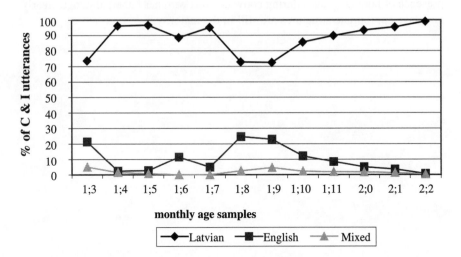

Figure 2. *Percentages of Māra's C&I utterances: Latvian sessions*

this trend by showing a general increase in the number of Latvian utterances and a decrease in English ones. Interestingly, one week after her second birthday, Māra attended a Latvian summer camp for the first time and spent two weeks in an almost totally Latvian environment, with other Latvian-speaking children. She would therefore have experienced increased input in Latvian and a decrease in English. The patterns in Figures 1 and 2 also reveal a very slight dominance in Māra's English at the earliest stages — there is a greater percentage of English utterances in the Latvian sessions than there is of Latvian utterances in her conversations with her mother.

In Tables 3 and 4 below, data are presented for the other bilingual subject, Maija. Although the patterns revealed are similar, there are some interesting differences, as well as similarities, between the two children. Figures 3 and 4 show the percentage of turns with each of the three utterance types.

The utterance counts in Tables 3 and 4 tell a similar story to those presented in Tables 1 and 2: Maija discriminates between the languages from the first recordings and uses the appropriate language with her interlocutors in the majority of cases. Figures 3 and 4 do, however, suggest slight dominance in Latvian at the earliest stages. The situation regarding the use of the two languages is almost a reverse image to that presented by Māra; in Maija's data we have very little evidence of English use during Latvian recordings but there is a much stronger presence of both languages during conversations with her father, although clearly language appropriate structures are still in the majority.

Table 3. *Distribution of Maija's C&I utterances: English sessions*

CA	MLU*	MLU**	C&I	English	Latvian	Mixed
1;2,30	1.26	1.32	144	132	11	1
1;4,21	1.11	1.14	188	131	53	4
1;5,16	1.13	1.21	141	96	40	5
1;6,2	1.16	1.25	251	167	81	3
1;7,0	1.46	1.56	174	150	19	5
1;8,11	1.43	1.55	219	180	39	0
1;9,8	1.51	1.64	212	153	52	7
1;10.6	1.50	1.64	245	221	17	7
1;11,4	1.59	1.82	257	251	3	3
2;0,1	2.02	2.25	287	277	4	6
2;0,29	1.88	2.11	419	381	16	22
2;2,9	1.91	2.09	253	240	1	12
Total	–	–	2790	2379	336	75

Mean length of utterance: *in words, **in morphemes

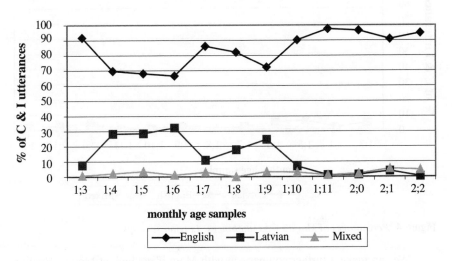

Figure 3. *Percentages of Maija's C&I utterances: English sessions*

Table 4. *Distribution of Maija's C&I utterances: Latvian sessions*

CA	MLU*	C&I	Latvian	English	Mixed
1;2,30	1.05	129	123	6	0
1;4,18	1.07	130	128	2	0
1;5,17	1.31	215	199	13	3
1;6,1	1.22	338	314	16	8
1;6,29	1.25	207	201	4	2
1;8,12	1.48	204	202	2	0
1;9,7	1.66	214	207	5	2
1;10,5	1.53	255	252	2	1
1;11,3	1.89	209	205	0	4
2;0,0	2.08	243	227	11	5
2;0,28	2.00	322	309	8	5
2;2,8	1.69	394	379	7	8
Total	–	2860	2746	76	38

*Mean length of utterance in words

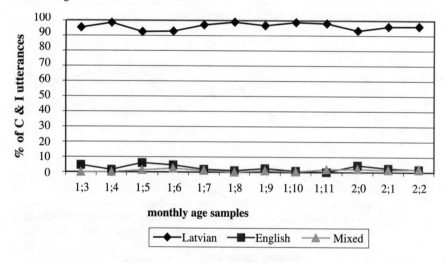

Figure 4. *Percentages of Maija's C&I utterances: Latvian sessions*

We can make a further comparison with Māra if we look at Maija's English session data at 1;9. Following a period from 1;4 to 1;6 in which a fairly steady pattern is established (approximately 70% of English utterances to 30% of Latvian), there is a marked increase in English use, together with a decrease in Latvian.

After 1;7, and culminating at 1;9, there is evidence once again of a marked increase in Maija's use of Latvian in conversations with her father. By 1;10, more appropriate language use has reasserted itself and a steadier pattern is established for the remainder of the data collection. Coincidentally, Maija attended the same Latvian summer camp as Māra, which would have taken place immediately after the recording at 1;8; her data at 1;9 may therefore show the result of increased Latvian and decreased English input during that period.

Tables 5 and 6 provide a summary of the distribution of complete and intelligible utterances across the whole corpus and the language choices made by Māra and Maija. The overall picture highlights the ability of both children to differentiate the languages appropriately in interactions with parents and other interlocutors.

Table 5. *Māra's C&I utterances: overall totals*

Corpus	C&I	English	Latvian	Mixed
English sessions	2861	2776(97.0%)	57 (2.0%)	28 (1.0%)
Latvian sessions	2481	206 (8.3%)	2236 (90.1%)	39 (1.6%)
Total utterances	5342	2982 (55.8%)	2293 (42.9%)	67 (1.3%)

Table 6. *Maija's C&I utterances: overall totals*

Corpus	C&I	English	Latvian	Mixed
English sessions	2790	2379 (85.3%)	336 (12.0%)	75 (2.7%)
Latvian sessions	2860	76 (2.7%)	2746 (96.0%)	38 (1.3%)
Total utterances	5650	2455 (43.5%)	3082 (54.5%)	113 (2.0%)

2.3 *Mixed utterances*

The data from the Latvian-English children reveal a very low percentage of utterances with elements from both languages. Nevertheless, mixed utterances do form a part of these children's linguistic development and as such should not be ignored. The remainder of this chapter is dedicated to exploring these utterances.

2.3.1 *Lexical, morphological and syntactic mixing*

In the discussion that follows, the types of mixing will be categorised into *lexical, morphological and syntactic* mixing. The *lexical* or *morphological* division is based on the traditional distinction between *open class* or *closed class* items or *content words* and *function words* (Bolinger & Sears 1981: 69); see also Muysken (1995: 183), who distinguishes between content and function morphemes by identifying different sub-classes on the basis of four different criteria.

For the research being reported on here, the term *lexical* is used for categories such as nouns, verbs, adjectives, adverbs and prepositions, whose members are content words and have descriptive content (Radford 1997) and *morphological* is used for categories whose members have a grammatical function and carry information about grammatical properties such as tense, agreement and case. The third division, that of *syntactic* mixing, is introduced to highlight influences in syntactic structure from one language to the other. In the case of any cross-category mixing, the mixed utterances are categorised at the highest level: if, for example, an utterance shows evidence of both syntactic and lexical mixing, then the utterance is assigned to the syntactic category only. Utterances in which the children used the non-target language in a 'false start' or reformulation are still classified as mixed utterances (cf Tables 1 to 4 above for the number of mixed utterances per sample).

2.3.2 *Māra*

Lexical mixing. The vast majority of Māra's mixes are lexical.There are 63 utterances in total containing lexical mixing in Māra's data. 25 of these examples are to be found across her English sessions and 38 in her Latvian sessions. Lexical mixing occurs through the use of non-target language content words in otherwise English or Latvian utterances; six of the mixes occur in reformulations.

Focusing first on interactions with her mother, here are some examples of Māra's lexical mixing (M – mother, C – child); the first is a typical example of a Latvian noun inserted in an otherwise English utterance:

(1)   M: what's that?   (MS-E1;7)
       C: *it's a suns*
           it's a dog-MASC-NOM
           'it's a dog'
       M: it's a dog

The following two examples show Māra's understanding of appropriate target language use and the two language systems she is working with. In example (2), mother and child are looking at a rather strange wrist-watch belonging to the investigator, who is also in the room, observing; the investigator is a native Latvian speaker with whom Māra speaks Latvian. In example (3), mother and child are discussing a recent family walk past some sheep in a field:

(2)   M: that's a funny thing, isn't it?   (MS-E1;11)
       C: they're sausages
       M: sausages, inside the watch
       C: *sausages ir   desas*
           sausages be-PRES-3 sausages-FEM-NOM-PLU
           'sausages are sausages'

(3)   M: d'you remember what we said?   (MS-E2;1)
       C: *papa said baabaa aitiṇa!*
           papa said baabaa sheep-FEM-NOM-SING
           'papa said baabaa sheep!'
       M: That's right!

In both instances, Māra shows pragmatic competence: in (2), she is translating for the benefit of both adults in the room; in (3), she selects the language according to the topic of conversation *and* the first language of her father, whose utterance she quotes (cf Fantini (1985), who reports on his son, aged 3;5, quoting other people's utterances). This metalinguistic awareness also underlines the separateness of the two language systems.

At 2;1, Māra has ten mixed utterances, nine of which are classified as containing lexical mixing. Four of these refer to items of Latvian national dress, which are difficult to translate into English and can therefore be considered *cultural forms* (as in Myers-Scotton 1997) or *cultural borrowings* (as in Vihman 1998); in this example, Māra has dressed a toy ladybird — note that her mother also uses the Latvian terminology:

(4)   C: *ladybird's got (um ums um) vainadziņš*
              ladybird's got (um ums um) coronet-MASC-NOM-SING-DIM
                                                                    (MS-E2;1)
              'ladybird's got (um ums um) a coronet'
        M: *she's got a vainadziņš*   *as well?*
              she's got a coronet-MASC-NOM-SING-DIM as well?
              'she's got a coronet as well?'

Māra uses Latvian verbs on seven occasions in her lexical mixes. For four of these
tokens Māra employs the correct Latvian tense and person inflections, as in (5) below:

(5)   C: *Mummy, dejo!*   (MS-E2;1)
              Mummy, dance-2SG-IMPERATIVE
              'Mummy, dance!'

On three successive occasions, however, as in example (6), Māra uses unmarked
forms of the verb *mest* (to throw). The phonological form of the vowel in *met* is
appropriate for the past tense (this differs from the vowel required in the present)
but the 3rd person marker *met-a* is missing.

(6)   M: what did Anna do then?   (MS-E2;3)
        C: *met*   *some buttons*
              throw-PAST-UNMARKED some buttons
              'threw some buttons'
        M: pardon?
        C: *(er) Anna met some buttons*
              '(er) Anna threw some buttons'
        M: she what?
        C: *Anna met some buttons*
              'Anna threw some buttons'

An unmarked verb form, in the place of an inflected verb, where this is required,
is a rare occurrence in Māra's Latvian data. Although precise figures are not yet
available, the vast majority of her verbs in Latvian are marked appropriately for
tense and person; by age 1;8, she shows contrastive use of present and past tenses,
1st and 2nd person singular and 3rd person inflections.

Given the rarity of an unmarked verb form in Latvian, there is almost the
suggestion here that Māra is trying in some way to adopt the main language of the
conversation, by creating an English-like verb form. A similar case is found in
Meisel's (1994: 434) account of the German-French bilingual subject Annika, who
inserts an unmarked German verb into a French utterance. Clearly, however, the

number of such mixed utterances in Māra's data is too small for any firm conclusions to be drawn.

The lexical mixing in her Latvian recording sessions is similar to that shown above. The following two mixed utterances are typical examples taken from conversations between Māra and her father. The first is a reformulation; note the correct use of the determiner — necessary with the English noun, but not the Latvian; in the second, the object (bread) is appropriately marked as feminine accusative singular and diminutive — the English element is a single noun:

(7)   F: *kas   tur   ir?*   (MS-L1;6)
             what-NOM there be-PRES-3
             'what's there?'

       C: *(a eye) acs*
             (a eye) eye-FEM-NOM-SING
             '(a eye) eye'

(8)   F: *kad tu ēdi pusdienas, (kas te) ko tu ēdi?*   (MS-L2;0)
             when you-NOM-SING eat-PAST-2-SING lunch-FEM-NOM-PLU,
             (what-NOM here) what-ACC you-NOM-SING eat-PAST-2-SING?
             'when you had lunch, (what here) what did you eat?'

       C: *maizīti   ar   bacon*
             bread-FEM-ACC-SING-DIM with bacon
             'bread with bacon'

At 1;8, 2;2 and 2;3, Māra employs the correct Latvian bound morphemes on three English lexical items inserted into the Latvian conversation. In the first instance, she is being dressed by her father and in (10) and (11) the two are looking at a picture book:

(9)   F: *kas   tas   ir?*   (MS-L1;8)
             what that-MASC-NOM-SING be-PRES-3?
             'what is that?'

       C: *veste*
             'vest'+FEM-NOM-SING

       F: *nē, tā   nav   veste*
             no, that-FEM-NOM-SING be-PRES-3-NEG vest-FEM-NOM-SING
             'no, that's not a vest/waistcoat'

(10)   C: *(sads) sads*   (MS-L2;2)
             'sad'+MASC-NOM-SING

       F: *nu,   tas   ir   bēdīgs*
             well, that-MASC-NOM-SING be-PRES-3 sad-MASC-NOM-SING
             'well, that one's sad'

F: *viņš ir bēdīgs jo viņš raud, nabadziņš!*
      he-MASC-NOM be-PRES-3 sad-MASC-NOM-SING because
      he-MASC-NOM cry-PRES-3 poorthing-MASC-NOM-SING-DIM
      'he's sad because he's crying, poor thing!'
C: *bēdīgs*
      sad-MASC-NOM-SING
      'sad'

(11) C: <u>*paddlingpools*</u>   (MS-L2;3)
            'paddlingpool'+MASC-NOM-SING
      F: *tas nav baseiniņš kur plunčāties*
            that-MASC-NOM-SING be-PRES-3-NEG pool-MASC-NOM-SING-DIM
            where splash-INF
            'that isn't a paddlingpool to splash around in'
      F: *tā ir liela bļoda*
            that-FEM-NOM-SING be-PRES-3 big-FEM-NOM-SING
            bowl-FEM-NOM-SING
            'that's a big bowl'

Example (9) above poses a slight problem, in that there is a feminine Latvian noun
'*veste*', meaning 'waistcoat'. However, it is far more likely, given the context, that
in this instance Māra is using the English 'vest'. The '*s*' inflection on 'paddling-
pool' in example (11) is voiceless, as required by the Latvian masculine nominative singular marking, and not voiced — as would be the case if this were an
example of English plural marking. These three examples can be compared with
similar ones cited by Lanza (1997a), Myers-Scotton (1997) and Vihman (1998). The
utterances are categorised as *lexical* mixes here and not *morphological* mixes because
the grammatical bound morphemes derive from the language in which the conversation
is taking place (ie Latvian) and are attached to 'borrowed' lexical items from the
other language (English). Although there are only three examples in the data
reported here, this kind of mixing is well-documented in adult codeswitching.

The final example given here shows the use of an English preposition and
adjective in an otherwise Latvian utterance. On this occasion, Māra is chatting
with another family member about the following day's activities:

(12) I: *kur   tu   iesi   rītā?*   (MS-L2;5)
            where you-NOM-SING go-FUT-2-SING tomorrow-MASC-LOC-SING?
            'where are you going tomorrow?'
      C: *iesim (em)   <u>to Latvian</u> *skola*
            go-FUT-1-PLU to Latvian *school-FEM-NOM-SING
            'we're going to Latvian school'

In the utterance above, Māra uses the nominative case for 'school' instead of the accusative (gender and number are correct); the future 1st person plural is the correct form.

Morphological mixing. There are two examples of morphological mixing in Māra's data — one during an English recording session and one during a Latvian session. In the following, whilst talking to her mother, Māra looks at the tape recorder; the mix is an interesting one:

(13)   C: *tas   ir   recording*   (MS-E2;1)
            that-MASC-NOM-SING be-PRES-3 recording
            'that is recording'
       M: Well, don't touch the recording, otherwise it won't work!

There is a coding dilemma here: with 'recording', is Māra producing a present participle, with the Latvian *ir* carrying a grammatical function by providing the obligatory auxiliary and tense marker, or is 'recording' a noun with a missing determiner? The only clue is the mother's treating of it as a noun — but the mother's utterance comes after the child's and there are no other contextual clues.

Māra's *unmixed* utterances during the same recording session do show, however, that she has a firm grasp of determiner use in English. In the recording sample at 2;1, she makes appropriate use of 86 determiners. Here are just four examples, as Māra plays with a toy ladybird, firstly bathing it and then 'taking it to the park':

(14)   C: pop it in the bath   (MS-E2;1)

(15)   C: wash her face   (MS-E2;1)

(16)   C: we're going on that big slide   (MS-E2;1)

(17)   C: the ladybird's big enough for that!   (MS-E2;1)

In example (18), we see Māra trying to make sense of a complex tense. The input she receives from her father gives her firstly the 3rd person form of the auxiliary, *ir* (which is the same for singular and plural); at this point her father starts to translate Māra's initial English statement before abandoning the utterance. Māra's father then addresses her directly in the 2nd person singular form *esi*. However, at her turn, Māra correctly chooses the first person subject and 1st person singular form of the auxiliary in Latvian and then completes the utterance with the English past participle and pronoun.

(18)   C: Māra's done it   (MS-L2;2)
       F: *Māra kas?*
            Māra what-NOM?
            'Māra what?'
       C: Māra's done it
       F: *Māra ir* (abandons the utterance)
            Māra be-PRES-3
            'Māra has'
       F: *ko   tu   esi   darījusi?*
            what-ACC you-NOM-SING be-PRES-2-SING do-PAST PARTICIPLE?
            'what have you done?'
       C: *es   esmu   <u>done it</u>*
            I-NOM be-PRES-1-SING done it
            'I have done it'

Syntactic mixing. There are just two examples of syntactic mixing and both occur
in interactions between Māra and her mother:

(19)   C: she flowers got   (MS-E1;9)
       M: who's got flowers?

(20)   C: Papa's banging the tap now   (MS-E2;2)
       M: so what are we doing this morning?
       C: BigEars and Noddy see

In both cases, Māra imposes Latvian word order on otherwise English utterances.
She flowers got at 1;9 corresponds to the freer Latvian word order that allows SOV
here as well as SVO. In example (20), Māra's father is carrying on with DIY work
in the kitchen, whilst her mother asks her about the children's show they are going
to see that morning. Māra's first utterance in (20) is well-formed but in her reply
to her mother's question, the verb form is unmarked and the word order is OV as
in (19).

All other instances of subject, verb and object use have appropriate SVO
structure, as in the following three examples:

(21)   C: I want a puzzle   (MS-E1;6)

(22)   C: Oh it's a sheep   (MS-E1;7)

(23)   C: He's holding biscuits   (MS-E1;9)

Table 7 summarises the distribution of the three types of mixed utterances in
Māra's corpus, presenting them as percentages (to the nearest 0.05% where

Table 7. *Māra's mixed utterances*

Utterance focus	L	M	S	Corpus
No. mixed	25	1	2	English sessions
% mixed	89.3%	3.6%	7.1%	
% C&I	0.9%	0.03%	0.07%	
No. mixed	38	1	0	Latvian sessions
% mixed	97.4%	2.6%	0%	
% C&I	1.55%	0.05%		
Total mixed	63	2	2	Whole corpus
% mixed	94.0%	3.0%	3.0%	
% C&I	1.2%	0.05%	0.05%	

L – lexical, M – morphological, S – syntactic

possible) of both the total number of mixed utterances and the total number of complete and intelligible utterances (cf Table 5 for overall percentages).

2.3.3 *Maija*

Lexical mixing. In total (cf Table 6), there are 113 mixed utterances in Maija's data. Of these, 98 are classified as lexical mixes: 61 appearing in her English sessions and 37 in her Latvian. The picture is much the same as that presented in Māra's data above, with the majority of non-target language content words being single nouns.

The following three examples, showing the use of a Latvian noun, verb and adjective, come from conversations between Maija and her English father. In the first example, Maija and her father are looking at a book telling the story of two cats, George and Ginger. In the second, Maija is referring to her toy pig, known in English as Piglet (from 'Winnie the Pooh') and in Latvian as *Cūciņa*. In the third, Maija is putting pieces of a jigsaw together:

(24) F: George and Ginger are climbing in the dustbin   (MK-E1;6)
       F: they're looking for food
       C: cats
       F: that's cats, yeah
       C: *a kaķis*
           'a <u>cat</u>'
       F: there's a cat, a black cat
(25) C: *Piglet čuč*   (MK-E1;9)
           Piglet <u>sleep</u>-PRES-3
           'Piglet's sleeping'

　　　F: Piglet?
　　　F: Piglet going to sleep?
　(26) C: *(that) his leg's (um um) salocīts*   (MK-E2;1)
　　　　　'(that) his leg's (um um) bent'
　　　F: what's wrong with it, Maij?
　　　C: *(um) it's (um) salocīts*
　　　　　'(um) it's (um) bent'
　　　F: bent, isn't it?

Number (25) is one of 14 examples of lexical mixing with a Latvian verb; 12 of the 14 Latvian verbs are fully marked for tense and person and two are unmarked, as the one in (27) below:

　(27) C: *Maija zīm this one*   (MK-E1;9)
　　　　　Maija draw+unmarked this one
　　　　　'Maija draw this one'
　　　F: yes, Maija's drawn on the book, yeah

As with Māra, unmarked Latvian verb forms are rare in Maija's data. Analysis of the first nine months (1;3–1;11) of Maija's verb use in un-mixed utterances, reveals only five tokens of unmarked verb forms in her Latvian data, out of a total of 81 verb types and 462 tokens (for further discussion of Maija's morpho-syntactic development, see Sinka & Schelletter 1998; for details of the development of her functional categories, see Garman, Schelletter and Sinka 1999). Example (27) could be seen either as a desire on Maija's part to accommodate English, by producing an unmarked Latvian verb form, or as a performance error.

　　　The 37 utterances containing lexical mixing during Latvian sessions include uses of English exclamations and formulas; two examples are given here:

　(28) C: *happy birthday dear mammiņa!*   (MK-L1;11)
　　　　　'happy birthday dear mummy!'

　(29) C: *es teicu   ouch!*   (MK-L2;0)
　　　　　I   say-PAST-1s ouch!
　　　　　'I said ouch!'

There are also three uses of English adverbs. Two examples are given below: in (30), Maija is chatting to her mother and in (31), Maija is building a little house:

　(30) C: *mammīte neraud now*   (MK-L1;9)
　　　　　mother-FEM-NOM-SING-DIM not-cry-PRES-3 now
　　　　　'mummy isn't crying now'

M: *neraud tagad, nē*
'isn't crying now, no'

(31)   C: *tur,   ne down there*   (MK-L2;0)
'there, not down there'

C: *priekšā*
front-FEM-LOC-SING
'in front'

The remaining 26 utterances with mixes consist mainly of English nouns incorpo-
rated into otherwise Latvian utterances.

Morphological mixing. There is one example of morphological mixing in Maija's
data. This occurs in a conversation with her mother at age 2;1. At this point, both
mother and daughter are making things out of plasticine; Maija has made a face
but is not very happy with the result:

(32)   M: *un   kāpēc Maijai   čupu   lūpa?*   (MK-L2;1)
and why   Maija-DAT pile-FEM-GEN-PLU lip-FEM-NOM
'and why is Maija pouting?'

C: *(m) es uztaisijusi (m)*   a *sejiņas*
(m) I   make-past participle-FEM-SING a *face-FEM-GEN-SING
like that!
like that
'(m) I (have) made a face like that!'

As well as the language mixing in this utterance, there are two errors in the
Latvian. Firstly, the auxiliary *esmu* ('am') is missing before the past participle,
though the participle itself is correctly marked for number and gender. Secondly,
sejiņas ('face') is in the genitive case instead of the accusative, although the
gender is correct.

I have categorised this utterance as an example of morphological mixing
because of the presence of the indefinite article 'a' before the Latvian noun. If a
determiner other than an indefinite or definite article had been used (for example
a demonstrative, possessive or quantifier) then this could have been classified as
a lexical mix, as these determiners also exist in Latvian. Maija has certainly
applied appropriate grammatical restrictions of a kind here, in that 'a' is used to
premodify a singular count noun; however, as Latvian does not have any articles,
and the use of determiners is optional, Maija has introduced a category which is
not necessary in the Latvian utterance. Whether the Latvian noun here has the
status of N or of DP headed by a null determiner (Radford 1997) is beyond the

scope of this paper but will need to be addressed in future publications.

Syntactic mixing. There are no examples of syntactic mixing in Maija's Latvian sessions but there are 14 such examples in conversations with her father. Altogether there are five types: examples (33), (34) and (35) appear only once; example (36) occurs three times and example (37) eight times. The last two types, representing 11 out of the 14 syntactic mixes, appear in the same sample, at age 2;2.

(33)   C: _klēpītī_   sit   (MK-E1;10)
              lap-LOC-SING sit
              'in your lap sit'
        F: you're sitting on daddy's lap, yeah, okay?

(34)   C: that *ones play   (MK-E1;11)
        F: yeah, you've finished your crocodile now, yeah?
        C: yes

(35)   F: have you finished?   (MK-E2;0)
        C: no
        F: no?
        C: more some
        F: some more?

(36)   C: what they is?   (MK-E2;2)

(37)   C: what that is?   (MK-E2;2)

In all five instances, Maija has imposed freer Latvian word order on English utterances (there is also a lexical mix in (33)). In (33), the prepositional phrase precedes the verb instead of following it; in (34), Maija produces OV order instead of VO; in (35), the DP order is switched, so that the noun is followed by the determiner and in both (36) and (37), the *wh*-questions are formulated in CSV order and not CVS. The utterances represented by (36) and (37) seem also to be rather repetitive in nature, as though Maija has focused on a certain formula which she then repeats constantly during the recording session:

(38)   C: (what do) what they is?   (MK-E2;2)
        F: that's just a little jigsaw tin, Snoopy tin

(39)   C: what they is?   (MK-E2;2)
        F: what?
        C: what they is?
        F: well, that's a different jigsaw

(40)   C: what that is?   (MK-E2;2)
        F: that's a 'L' for 'Lija', isn't it?
        C: what that is?
        F: that's a ('U' for 'umbrella') 'U' for 'umbrella'

Additionally, well before this recording at 2;2, Maija has shown that she can form *wh*-questions correctly. At 1;11, there are 21 well-formed *wh*-questions and no errors in the COMP system. Here are just three examples:

(41)   C: who is this?   (MK-E1;11)

(42)   C: what was that?   (MK-E1;11)

(43)   C: where's Crocodile?   (MK-E1;11)

Table 8 summarises the above information for Maija. The three types of mixed utterances are presented as i) percentages of the total number of mixed utterances in the three corpora (English, Latvian and combined total) and ii) percentages of the total number of complete and intelligible utterances in the three corpora.

Table 8. *Maija's mixed utterances*

Utterance focus	L	M	S	Corpus
No. mixed	61	0	14	English sessions
% mixed	81.3%	0%	18.7%	
% C&I	2.2%	0%	0.5%	
No. mixed	37	1	0	Latvian sessions
% mixed	97.4%	2.6%	0%	
% C&I	1.25%	0.05%		
Total mixed	98	1	14	Whole corpus
% mixed	86.7%	0.9%	12.4%	
% C&I	1.7%	0.05%	0.25%	

L – lexical, M – morphological, S – syntactic

3.   Discussion

An in-depth analysis of all Māra's and Maija's utterances (mixed and unmixed) is beyond the space available in this chapter. However, I have attempted to present the children's mixed utterances against the background of their total utterances, giving information about their unmixed utterances where it has been possible to do so. There is an obvious need for this: if, for example, discussion concerns the lack of inappropriate morphological marking in mixed utterances, we need to provide adequate information regarding the emergence of appropriate morphological marking in unmixed utterances.

What, therefore, can be said about the mixed utterances in Māra and Maija's data and the nature of any cross-linguistic influences in their language? Throughout the chapter so far, I have concentrated on presenting the mixed utterances according to lexial, morphological and syntactic categories. Before returning to these, I would like to provide an overview of a slightly different kind. Table 9 shows a breakdown of all the mixed utterances according to whether they are whole clauses, as in the case of the syntactic mixes discussed above, phrases, exclamations or formulas (eg 'ouch' or 'happy birthday'), or single insertions of determiners, adjectives, nouns, pronouns, verbs and adverbs.

Table 9 reveals that the most dominant category mixed for both children is single nouns. They account for 60% of all mixed utterances for Māra (31 types, 40 tokens) and 42% of all mixed utterances for Maija (32 types, 47 tokens). If phrases and clauses are excluded, then nouns represent 77% of all single word mixes for Māra and 54% of all single word mixes for Maija.

Table 9. *Breakdown of mixed utterances*

	Māra		Maija	
Clauses	2	(3%)	14	(12%)
Phrases	13	(19%)	12	(11%)
Exclamations/formulas	0		14	(12%)
Determiners	0		1	(1%)
Adjectives	3	(5%)	6	(5%)
Nouns	40	(60%)	47	(42%)
Pronouns	0		3	(3%)
Verbs	7	(10%)	11	(10%)
Adverbs	2	(3%)	5	(4%)
Total tokens	67	(100%)	113	(100%)

These figures are a little higher than those reported by Vihman (1998) and Redlinger & Park (1980). Vihman found 39% noun types switched in comparison to other elements (43% if sentences were excluded) in Raivo and Virve's language and Redlinger & Park reported 40% noun switches, excluding phrases, for two to three year-olds. However, the percentages of nouns in Māra and Maija's mixed data is still below the 75% (85% without phrases) reported by Lindholm & Padilla (1978) for their two to six year-olds.

The picture presented by both children is remarkably similar, except for the use of clauses and exclamations/formulas by Maija. 11 of Maija's 14 mixes at clause level occur in one sample and are discussed in detail in the section on syntactic mixing in Maija's data, above. Her use of exclamations and formulas as mixes is apparent in both languages (seven in her English sessions and seven in her Latvian) and runs across the whole data set, with at least one use at each monthly age sample except for 1;8 and 1;9.

Returning to the lexical, morphological and syntactic distinction, it is clear that, for both girls, mixing primarily concerns the mixing of lexical categories, chiefly nouns, as reported above. The evidence from the data also shows that the types of language contact do not differ greatly across the data collection period. This compares with Lanza's (1997b) account of Siri's language development and language mixing from 2;0 to 2;7. Lanza reports a slight decrease in mixing over time but finds that the *type* of mixing remains the same. Although the percentage of mixed utterances in Māra and Maija's data is in general very small (cf Tables 5–8), there is evidence of some lexical mixing throughout. With regard to morphological and syntactic mixing, however, there are only four examples in Māra's data out of 5,342 utterances; in Maija's data there are 15 such utterances out of a total of 5,650. This leads us to question why there are so few cross-linguistic structures in the language of these two Latvian-English bilinguals.

In the data, there appears to be no evidence of 'fusion', defined by Meisel (1989: 37) as the "inability to separate two grammatical systems"; both subjects clearly separate the two linguistic systems at the level of grammatical competence: language-appropriate morphological markings for tense, person, gender, case and number are evident from the first recordings and there is little evidence of bound morphemes of one language being attached to elements from the other language. Given the data presented here, I concur with Meisel (1989) who suggests that there is insufficient evidence of fusion being prominent in bilingual development.

It is also interesting to note that the morphological and syntactic mixes that do occur in Māra and Maija's data, do so *after* the acquisition of functional categories in both children, contrary to claims made by Meisel (1994) and Köppe & Meisel (1995) that this type of mixing would occur *before* the acquisition of functional categories. However, it may be that the set of such mixes in these data is too small (less than 0.1% in Māra's case and 0.3% in Maija's) to be of great significance; neither should one discount the possibility that these examples may be performance errors.

The *lack* of morphological and syntactic mixing for both Māra and Maija, on the other hand, support further Sinka & Schelletter (1998) and Garman, Schelletter & Sinka's (1999) findings that functional categories develop early in the language of the Latvian-English bilingual child. Garman, Schelletter & Sinka investigated the development of five functional categories in two bilingual children: Sonja, a German-English bilingual and Maija, the Latvian-English bilingual reported on in this chapter. For Maija, detailed examination of all unmixed complete and intelligible utterances led to the observation that functional categories were seen to be developing on average some three months earlier in Latvian (from age 1;4 for Tense, Agreement and Case) than in English. These findings then in turn support Meisel (1994) and Köppe & Meisel's (1995) claim that once functional categories are in place, syntactic constraints will not be violated — hence the lack of morphological and syntactic mixing in the data presented here.

As discussed above, Latvian and English differ in their structural realisations and morphological complexity; it seems, therefore, that the diverse nature of the two languages enables the child to separate the two language systems from an early stage and prompts her to produce language-specific structures whilst acquiring Latvian and English simultaneously.

Acknowledgments

I am grateful to Professor Michael Garman of The University of Reading for his helpful comments on this chapter and generally for his unstinting support and encouragement. I also acknowledge the support of our research team and the ESRC for grant no. R000222072, awarded to Michael Garman, Christina Schelletter and Indra Sinka; the resulting project, "Functional Categories in Bilingual Child Language: Evidence from English, German and Latvian", paved the way for further research into Latvian-English child language acquisition.

References

Arnberg, Lenore. 1987. *Raising Children Bilingually. The Pre-school Years*. Clevedon: Multilingual Matters.
Bolinger, Dwight & Donald A. Sears. 1981. *Aspects of Language*. New York: Harcourt Brace Jovanovich.
De Houwer, Annick. 1990. *The Acquisition of Two Languages from Birth: A Case Study*. Cambridge: Cambridge University Press.

De Houwer, Annick. 1995. "Bilingual language acquisition". In P. Fletcher & B. MacWhinney (eds), *The Handbook of Child Language*. Cambridge, MA: Basil Blackwell, 219–250.

Döpke, Susanne. 1992. *One Parent — One Language*. (Studies in Bilingualism 3) Amsterdam: John Benjamins.

Fantini, Alvino E. 1985. *Language Acquisition of a Bilingual Child: A Sociolinguistic Perspective*. Clevedon: Multilingual Matters.

Garman, Michael, Christina Schelletter & Indra Sinka. 1999. "Three hypotheses on early grammatical development". In M. Perkins & S. Howard (eds), *New Directions in Language Development and Disorders*. London: Plenum Press, .

Gawlitzek-Maiwald, Ira & Rosemarie Tracy. 1996. "Bilingual bootstrapping". *Linguistics* 34: 901–926.

Köppe, Regina & Jürgen M. Meisel. 1995. "Code-switching in bilingual first language acquisition". In L. Milroy & P. Muysken (eds), *One Speaker, Two Languages: Cross-Disciplinary Perspectives on Code-Switching*. Cambridge: Cambridge University Press, 276–301.

Lanza, Elizabeth. 1997a. *Language Mixing in Infant Bilingualism: A Sociolinguistic Perspective*. New York: Oxford University Press.

Lanza, Elizabeth. 1997b. "Language contact in bilingual two-year-olds and code-switching: language encounters of a different kind?'. *The International Journal of Bilingualism* 1 (2): 135–162.

Lindholm, Kathryn J. & Amado M. Padilla. 1978. "Language mixing in bilingual children". *Journal of Child Language* 5: 327–335.

Meisel, Jürgen M. 1989. "Early differentiation of languages in bilingual children". In K. Hyltenstam & L. Obler (eds), *Bilingualism Across the Lifespan: Aspects of Acquisition, Maturity and Loss*. Cambridge: Cambridge University Press, 13–40.

Meisel, Jürgen M. 1994. "Code-switching in young bilingual children: the acquisition of grammatical constraints". *Studies in Second Language Acquisition* 16: 413–439.

Miller, Jon F. & Robin S. Chapman. 1996. *Systematic Analysis of Language Transcripts*. University of Wisconsin, Madison.

Muysken, Pieter. 1995. "Code-switching and grammatical theory". In L. Milroy & P. Muysken (eds), *One Speaker, Two Languages: Cross-Disciplinary Perspectives on Code-Switching*. Cambridge: Cambridge University Press, 177–198.

Myers-Scotton, Carol. 1997. *Duelling Languages: Grammatical Structure in Codeswitching*. Oxford: Clarendon Press.

Paradis, Johanne & Fred Genesee. 1996. "Syntactic acquisition in bilingual children: autonomous or interdependent?" *Studies in Second Language Acquisition* 18 (1): 1–25.

Radford, Andrew. 1997. *Syntactic Theory and the Structure of English: A Minimalist Approach*. Cambridge: Cambridge University Press.

Redlinger, Wendy & Tschang-Zin Park 1980. "Language mixing in young bilinguals". *Journal of Child Language* 7: 337–352.

Sinka, Indra & Christina Schelletter. 1998. "Morphosyntactic development in bilingual children'. *The International Journal of Bilingualism* 2 (3): 301–326.

Taeschner, Traute. 1983. *The Sun is Feminine: A Study on Language Acquisition in Bilingual Children*. Berlin: Springer.

Vihman, Marilyn M. 1985. "Language differentiation by the bilingual infant". *Journal of Child Language* 12: 297–324.

Vihman, Marilyn M. 1998. "A developmental perspective on codeswitching: conversations between a pair of bilingual siblings". *The International Journal of Bilingualism* 2 (1): 45–84.

Volterra, Virginia & Traute Taeschner. 1978. "The acquisition and development of language by bilingual children". *Journal of Child Language* 19: 311–326.

Beyond 'One System or Two?'

Degrees of Separation Between the Languages of French-English Bilingual Children

Johanne Paradis

McGill University

1. Introduction

The degrees of separation and interconnectivity between the two languages of a bilingual has been the subject of much research on adult bilinguals. Evidence from neuropsychological and psycholinguistic investigations demonstrate the complex nature of inter-lingual representation and processing in bilingual speakers (e.g., Cutler, Mehler, Norris & Segui 1989; De Groot 1993; Kroll & De Groot 1997; Paradis 1997). An interactional perspective on language representation in adult bilinguals is succinctly summarized by Grosjean (1995: 259): "Bilinguals are not the sum of two complete or incomplete monolinguals but have a unique and specific linguistic configuration". Thus, one cannot consider a question like 'Do bilinguals have one language system or two?' to be sufficiently nuanced to adequately capture the relationship between an adult bilingual's two languages.

In contrast, much of the research on simultaneous bilingual children has focused on the rather narrow theme of 'one system or two'. Initially, researchers argued that children acquiring two languages simultaneously began by establishing a unitary language system which later differentiated into two systems between the ages of two to three years (e.g. Leopold 1949/71; Volterra & Taeschner 1978; Redlinger & Park 1980). More recent empirical findings have convincingly demonstrated that bilingual children have differentiated language systems at least by the age of two, if not earlier. Researchers have shown early differentiation in pragmatic abilities (Lanza 1992; Genesee, Nicoladis & Paradis 1995; Nicoladis & Genesee 1996), in the organization of the lexicon (Pearson, Fernandez & Oller 1995; Quay 1995), in the acquisition of morphosyntax (Meisel 1989; Paradis & Genesee 1996) and, to a more limited extent, in the acquisition of phonology

(Schnitzer & Krasinski 1994, 1996; Paradis 1996; Johnson & Lancaster 1998).

Since most researchers now assume early differentiation, some have recently been considering more subtle questions about the relationship between a bilingual child's linguistic systems (Hulk & van der Linden 1996; Hulk 1997; Hulk & van der Linden 1998; Döpke 1998; Müller 1998; contributors to this volume). More specifically, researchers are now going beyond the 'one system or two?' dichotomy and are examining the degrees of separation and interaction between the developing languages of bilingual children. For example, the German-English bilingual children studied by Döpke (1998) showed English-like verb placement in a substantial number of their German utterances over a period of several months, a phenomenon which she claims is unattested in monolingual German children. Such systematic error patterns in the bilingual children's German syntax suggests crosslinguistic interaction in acquisition. Similarly, Müller (1998) found that some, but not all, children acquiring German together with either French, English or Italian demonstrated error patterns in their use of subordinate clauses in German which resembled the word orders of the other languages. Finally, Hulk (1997) and Hulk & van der Linden (1996, 1998) found that a French-Dutch bilingual girl showed evidence of Dutch word order, for example the object placed before the verb, in some of her French utterances. In French, the object typically follows the verb.

The common thread joining these investigations is the notion that the dual linguistic representations of a bilingual child are probably not hermetically sealed — that systematic interplay between them should be expected. Since the research on adult bilinguals indicates that some overlap between the final-state systems is typical, there is all the more reason to assume interaction in development. The research discussed in this chapter has been chosen to address the following three issues concerning the investigation of interaction effects in bilingual acquisition. The data have been selected from longitudinal observational studies on the acquisition of morphosyntax in French-English bilingual two year olds (Paradis & Genesee 1996, 1997), and from a cross-sectional experimental study on phonological processing, also conducted with French-English two year olds (Paradis 1998, in print).

1.1 How can one determine if interaction is taking place?

In order to investigate whether interaction is taking place in the bilingual acquisition of two languages, it is necessary to draw comparisons with monolingual children. What may seem like a crosslinguistic influence could be nothing more than a typical stage in monolingual development. For example, the placement of subjects post-verbally is an attested phenomenon in monolingual child French, even though SVO is the dominant word order in adult French (Pierce 1992). If a child were acquiring French together with a language with VS word order, the appearance of VS structures in the child's French might be mistakenly attributed solely to transfer from the VS language. Accordingly, the studies on morphosyntax and phonology presented in this chapter include reference to empirical findings for monolingual children acquiring the target structures in each language. In fact, the study on phonology includes monolingual children directly as control groups in the experiment.

1.2 What determines when and in what direction interaction might take place?

If one assumes that bilingual children possess two language systems, then one would expect crosslinguistic structures to emerge in a limited and systematic way. After all, widespread and seemingly random crosslinguistic interaction would undermine the assumption of differentiated systems. Both Döpke (1998) and Müller (1998) suggest that crosslinguistic transfer may occur for structures for which there is inter-language ambiguity in the input. For instance, English has fixed, verb-object word order and German has rule-governed but variable word order, with verb-object as one possibility in certain constructions. Thus, the superficial similarity may lead German-English bilingual children to misuse the verb-object word order in German until they acquire the appropriate German rules for sentence word order. The directionality is determined by the fact that no evidence exists in English for the other word orders available in German, such as object-verb, so no ambiguity is present and transfer would not be predicted. In order to test the inter-language ambiguity hypothesis, the morphosyntactic and phonological data selected for discussion in this chapter involve structures for which some ambiguity could be construed.

1.3 Would interaction be expected to occur in all subcomponents of the grammar?

In their account of the differentiation process, Volterra & Taeschner (1978) suggest that the subcomponents of the grammar separate at different times. More precisely, they propose that the lexicon differentiates into two systems before the syntactic component. It is equally possible that crosslinguistic interaction in acquisition might be more prevalent in one subcomponent than another. The studies presented in this chapter are based on different subcomponents of the grammar, and the findings indicate evidence for crosslinguistic effects on the level of phonology, but not for morphosyntax. Possible reasons for this discrepancy and how the results on morphosyntax can be reconciled with other studies arguing for crosslinguistic effects at this level are discussed in the final section of this chapter.

2. Acquisition of syntax

In Paradis & Genesee (1996), we examined whether French-English bilingual children were acquiring two syntactic systems autonomously and like that of monolinguals. In so doing, we presented data which bear on the question of crosslinguistic interaction in acquisition. In order to look at the potential for crosslinguistic interaction, two contrasting aspects of French and English morpho-syntax were studied: verb movement with respect to negation and the distribution of pronominal subjects and finite verbs. Verb movement and negation was also examined in the syntactic acquisition of French-English bilingual in Paradis & Genesee (1997), and those data will be discussed here as well.

2.1 *Verb movement and negation in monolingual children*

In French, all finite verbs, thematic and non-thematic, move to the left the negator *pas* 'not' (Pollock 1989, for example). This process is shown below in (1a) for verbs in the present tense, for the auxiliary verb *avoir* 'have' in (1b) and for the modal *pouvoir* 'can' in (1c). Note that in (1b) and (1c), the thematic verb is in the non-finite form, and thus appears to the right of the negator. On the contrary in English, thematic verbs are always placed to the right of the negator. Non-thematic verb forms bear the tense features in negative constructions and appear to the left of the negator. These verb forms include do-support DO, shown in (1d), auxiliary HAVE, as in (1e), and the modal *can* , as in (1f).

(1)   a.   *Le lion (ne) voit   pas l'éléphant.*
            the lion   see-PRES not the elephant
            'the lion does not see the elephant'

        b.   *Le lion (n') a   pas vu   l'éléphant.*
            the lion   have not see-PAST PART. the elephant
            'the lion did not see the elephant'

        c.   *Le lion ne peut pas voir   l'éléphant.*
            the lion   can not see-INFIN the elephant
            'the lion cannot see the elephant'

        d.   The lion does not see the elephant.

        e.   The lion has not seen the elephant.

        f.   The lion cannot see the elephant.

Since the true contrast between French and English is only demonstrated through the simple tenses, as shown in (1a) and (1d), the similarity between the other negative constructions across the languages could act as a source of inter-language structural ambiguity. Such ambiguity could lead children acquiring French and

English simultaneously to temporarily produce crosslinguistic structures, as illustrated in (2). In (2a), the English finite thematic verb is placed to the left of the negator and in (2b), the finite thematic verb in French is placed to the right of the negator.

(2)   a.   *The lion sees not the elephant.
        b.   *Le lion (ne) pas voit   l'éléphant.
            the lion   not see-PRES the elephant

Crosslinguistic studies of French or English-speaking monolingual children show that these children obey the language-specific rules for verb placement *vis à vis* the negative marker early on (Pierce 1992; Déprez & Pierce 1993). This phenomenon is particularly demonstrable due to the use of nonfinite verb forms in root clauses (ie. optional root infinitives, Wexler 1994) at the early stages of syntactic acquisition. The examples in (3) illustrate French or English-speaking children's sensitivity to verb placement in negative constructions (examples from Déprez & Pierce 1993; Pierce 1992). In (3a), the child used a non-finite thematic verb in French and correctly placed it to the right of the negator. In (3b), he used a finite verb and thus placed the verb to the left of the negator. The example in (3c) shows an English-speaking child placing the thematic verb to the right of the negator. Given the language-specific accuracy of monolinguals with respect to verb placement, the presence of utterances like those in (2) in the speech of French-English bilingual children could easily be considered the result of crosslinguistic interaction in acquisition.

(3)   a.   *Pas chercher les voitures.*   (Philippe 2;1)
            'not look for the cars'
        b.   *Ça tourne pas.*   (Philippe 2;1)
            'that isn't turning'
        c.   Me no go home.   (Peter 2;1)

2.2 *Pronominal subjects in monolingual children*

In French, pronominal subjects, such as *je* 'I', *tu* 'you', or *il* 'he', are clitics rather than NP's like their true pronoun counterparts in English (Kayne 1975). In the Quebec French dialect the children in these studies were acquiring, subject clitics have the properties of person agreement morphology (Cummins & Roberge 1993; Auger 1995). Two types of evidence put forth in Auger (1995) to support this analysis are subject doubling and clitic repetition in coordinated constructions. Examples of subject-doubled constructions are given in (4a) and (4b). In these constructions a lexical subject or strong pronoun appears with a co-referential clitic with no accompanying pause in between, indicating that the clitic does not occupy an argument position. Quebec French speakers produce utterances of this type most of the time (Auger 1995). The examples in (4c) and (4d) show a contrast between Standard French and Quebec French. In the former, the clitic does not have to be repeated in the coordinated phrase, (4c), but in Quebec French, it is strongly preferred to repeat the clitic, (4d). This preference is an indication of the bound-morpheme properties of subject clitics.

(4)   a.   *Annie elle fume.*
              Annie 3SG FEM-smokes
              'Annie smokes.'
       b.   *Moi j'aime   la   bouffe mexicaine.*
              me 1SG-like the food   Mexican
              'I like Mexican food.'
       c.   *Je mange du pain   et   bois   du   vin.*
              CLITIC-eat some bread and drink some wine
              'I am eating bread and drinking wine.'
       d.   *Je mange du pain et je bois du vin.*

The evidence that pronominal subjects belong to a different morphosyntactic category in French and English is not apparent in all constructions. In both languages, constructions with a solitary pronominal subject followed directly by a finite verb would be common in the input. Thus, it is possible that this surface overlap in the distribution of clitics and pronouns may act as a source of inter-language structural ambiguity for French-English bilingual children. What would be an indication of crosslinguistic effects regarding the status of pronouns and clitics in bilingual acquisition? Pierce (1992) found that the clitic/pronoun distinction between pronominal subjects is evident in the speech of French and English-speaking monolingual children by the distribution of these pronominal subjects and finite verbs. In French, there is a contingency between clitics and finite verbs, while in English pronouns can appear with either a finite or non-finite thematic verb. Examples in (5a) and (5b) show that a clitic subject can appear with a finite verb and a lexical subject can appear with a nonfinite verb in French. As shown in (5c), French-speaking children do not produce clitics with nonfinite verbs. In contrast, English-speaking children can produce pronouns with non-finite verbs, for example (5d). Examples are from Pierce (1992). This contingency is expected because as agreement morphology, clitics should only appear with finite or moved verbs. Therefore, if the clitic/finite verb contingency is not very strong or is non-existent in the French syntax of bilingual children, this could be interpreted as crosslinguistic influence. Alternatively, the presence of a pronoun-finite verb contingency in bilingual children's English could also be interpreted as crosslinguistic influence.

(5)   a.   *Elle dort.*   (Daniel 1;8)
               'she sleeps'

          b.   *La poupée dormir.*   (Natalie 2;1)
               'the doll sleep'

          c.   **Elle dormir.*
               'she sleep'

          d.   I washing.   (Naomi 1;10)

2.3 *Participants and procedure*

Spontaneous speech data from five French-English bilingual children are discussed in this section. This group of children has been combined from the three children studied in Paradis & Genesee (1996) and the two children studied in Paradis & Genesee (1997). All the children were observed longitudinally from approximately the ages of 2;0 to 3;0 years. The criteria for inclusion in both studies was that the children each had one French-speaking and one English-speaking parent, had been exposed to both languages from birth, and were spontaneously using both languages during the observation period. It was not required that the children be balanced bilinguals as dominance or preference for one language is a typical aspect of early bilingual development (De Houwer 1995).

The children were observed over the one year period at various intervals. The children studied in Paradis & Genesee (1996) were observed once every six months and the children studied in Paradis & Genesee (1997) were observed at two month intervals on average (except for a gap of 7 months between the penultimate and final observation for Mathieu, shown in Table 2). At each observation interval, the children were video- and audio-taped in naturalistic play sessions with their parents lasting about 45 minutes. Each interval consists of three play sessions: child and mother alone, child and father alone, and child with both parents together. Twenty to thirty minutes of each tape was transcribed and coded for the presence of the morphosyntactic items, such as finite and nonfinite root clauses, clitic and pronoun subjects and negative markers. Transcription, coding and analyses were based on the CHAT/CLAN system (MacWhinney 1991).

The children's ages, MLU's in words (MLU = mean length of utterance) and speech sample sizes for each observation interval are given in Table 1 (from Paradis & Genesee 1996) and Table 2 (from Paradis & Genesee 1997). The data from Paradis & Genesee (1997) are taken from two instead of three play sessions, and thus the sample sizes are smaller.

Table 1. *Ages, sample sizes and MLU's (from Paradis & Genesee 1996)*

Interval 1

Child	Age	Sample[a]	French MLU	English MLU
William	2;2	314	1.26	1.29
Gene	1;11	351	1.92	2.04
Olivier	1;11	261	2.32	1.55

Interval 2

Child	Age	Sample	French MLU	English MLU
William	2;10	557	1.35	1.54
Gene	2;7	528	2.12	2.17
Olivier	2;6	424	2.59	2.18

Interval 3

Child	Age	Sample	French MLU	English MLU
William	3;3	960	1.60	2.19
Gene	3;1	598	2.36	2.44
Olivier	2;10	676	2.40	2.31

[a] Numbers are averaged over three sessions. The number of utterances equals the total number of French, English, and mixed utterances.

2.4 *Verb movement and negation in bilingual children*

2.4.1 *French*
For this analysis, I discuss findings from all five French-English bilingual children. For William, Gene and Olivier, it was calculated that 91% of all their negative utterances in French consisted of a finite verb placed to the left of the negative marker, which is in adherence to the rules of the adult grammar. Mathieu and Yan used only one finite negative utterance in French each, but in both cases the finite verb was appropriately followed by the negative marker. Examples of finite negative utterances from each child are given in (6). There were just two

Table 2. *Ages, sample sizes and MLU's (from Paradis & Genesee 1997)*

Yann

Age	Sample[a]	English MLU	French MLU	Combined MLU[b]
1;11	134	1.16	1.4	1.26
2;3	151	1.49	1.58	1.57
2;5	277	1.45	1.43	1.46
2;7	207	1.33	1.39	1.39
2;10	454	1.55	1.47	1.57
3;0	556	1.44	1.96	1.80

Mathieu

Age	Sample	English MLU	French MLU	Combined MLU[a]
1;9	162	1.071	1.58	1.27
1;11	185	1.25	1.49	1.37
2;1	310	1.45	1.58	1.59
2;3	349	1.22	1.60	1.36
2;11	432	1.96	1.50	1.90

[a] Numbers are averaged over two sessions. The number of utterances equals the total number of French, English, and mixed utterances.
[b] Combined MLU is calculated from the total of French, English and mixed utterances.

utterances consisting of a nonfinite verb appearing with a negative marker, produced by Mathieu and William, and the verb was correctly placed to the right of the negative marker in each one.

(6) a. <u>people</u> *là, va pas là.* (William 2;10)
'people (emphasis) don't go there'

b. *Je peux pas dire quoi.* (Gene 2;7)
'I cannot say what'

c. *Je veux pas parler à Papa.* (Olivier 2;6)
'I don't want to talk to Daddy'

d. *(y) n'a plus.* (Mathieu 2;11)
'there's no more' (*plus* = negative marker)

e. *Bouge pas.* (Yan 3;0)
'don't move'

In spite of the uneven frequencies between children, it appears that on the whole their French negative utterances display language-specific patterns. However, Gene produced two utterances which did not follow the expected language-specific pattern, given in (7). In (7a) and (7b), the finite thematic verb has been placed to the right of the negative marker, as in the hypothetical example in (2b). Could these utterances be considered crosslinguistic structures? Because these structures comprise a marginal proportion of Gene's output and because they occurred in the speech of just one child out of five, the examples in (7) do not constitute evidence for a phenomenon as robust as that reported in Döpke (1998). Thus, I could only suggest that these examples are the result of episodic/ 'on-line' interference rather than systematic crosslinguistic transfer from English to French, and that their presence may not be a typical characteristic of the bilingual acquisition of French and English.

(7) a. Il pas joue dehors.   (Gene 1;11)
     b. Pas il va là.   (Gene 2;7)

2.4.2 English

None of the five children produced sentences like the example in (2a) with a thematic verb to the left of the negative marker. Since the majority of the children's English utterances during this period contained non-finite verbs, the majority of their English negative utterances contained a negative marker + thematic verb sequence. Examples from Mathieu and Yan are given in (8a) to (8d). The utterance in (8e) illustrates that when finite non-thematic verbal elements emerge in English, they are correctly placed to the left of the negator.

(8) a. The truck no go.   (Mathieu, 2;11)
     b. No working.   (Mathieu, 2;11)
     c. No eat my raisin.   (Yan, 2;10)
     d. No need that.   (Yan, 2;10)
     e. We don't take xxx. (unintelligible)   (Mathieu, 2;11)

2.5 Pronominal subjects in bilingual children

In order to ascertain whether the children had correctly classified English pronominal subjects as pronouns and French pronominal subjects as clitics, the distribution of pronominal subjects with finite and non-finite verbs was calculated for William, Gene and Olivier together. The results of this calculation are presented in Table 3. The percentages in Table 3 represent the number of pronominal subjects appearing with finite or nonfinite verbs, in French or English, out of the total number of pronominal subjects used. This analysis indicates that while pronominal subjects are nearly evenly divided between finite and non-finite verbs in English, there are almost no pronominal subjects appearing with non-finite verbs in French. A Chi-square analysis confirmed that this unequal distribution is significant ($X^2 = 22.7$, $p < .005$). Thus, the patterns displayed in their use of pronominal subjects suggests that the children understand the distinction between the status of pronominal subjects in their two languages. In addition, there is no evidence of crosslinguistic influence in their pronominal subject use. For example, there is a virtual absence of French clitics appearing with non-finite verbs, and no indication that pronouns are being restricted to use with finite verbs in English.

Table 3. *Percentage of finite and non-finite utterances in English and French with pronominal subjects (from Paradis & Genesee 1996)*

Language	Finite[a]	Non-finite
English	23.72%	20.71%
French	55.22%	0.35%

Note: $X^2 = 22.7$, $p < .005$
[a]Percentages are calculated out of the total number of utterances with pronominal subjects in both languages from all of the children.

2.6 Conclusion

The results of these morphosyntactic analyses suggest that for verb movement and classification of pronominal subjects, these bilingual children are acquiring French and English according to the patterns established by monolingual children. They demonstrate that even at the outset of syntactic acquisition, bilingual children have language specific knowledge operative in their language production. In contrast, the crosslinguistic influences predicted above were not systematically apparent in the language of these five children. However, the marginal number of English-influenced negative constructions in one child's French might indicate that for other French-English children, systematic and sustained use of crosslinguistic structures could occur.

3. Acquisition of phonology

In Paradis (1998; in press), one of the issues I addressed was whether bilingual children's phonological processing showed crosslinguistic effects. In contrast to the studies of morphosyntax presented above, I found evidence for such effects. This study consisted of a non-word repetition task given to three groups of children: monolingual French, monolingual English and French-English bilingual two year olds. The French and English nonsense words contrasted on the level of metrical properties distinct to each language. Thus, as with the aspects of morphosyntax investigated, language-specific effects were expected in the children's productions of these words. What is presented in this chapter is a subset of the data and analyses from Paradis (1998b, in print).

3.1 *Truncation and target language prosodic structure*

The non-word repetition task used in Paradis (1998, in press) was designed to elicit syllable omission or truncation patterns. It has been observed that when young children attempt to produce polysyllabic or long adult words, they often omit some of the syllables, for example, the word 'banana' is often reduced or truncated to 'nana' (Allen & Hawkins 1980). This phenomenon has also been observed in children acquiring languages other than English, for example, Dutch (Wijnen, Krikaar & den Os 1994), Spanish (Gennari & Demuth 1997) and Sesotho (Demuth 1996). In English, researchers have found that syllables which are perceptually salient, like stressed syllables and syllables in word final position, are more likely to be preserved than less salient syllables, such as initial or weak syllables. Thus, they argue that perceptual biases underlie the process of truncation (Echols & Newport 1992; Echols 1993; Hura & Echols 1996). However, other researchers have noted that syllable omission patterns also show the effects of prosodic biases or constraints in production (Allen & Hawkins 1980; Gerken, Landau & Remez 1990; Gerken 1994a, 1994b; Wijnen et al 1994; Schwartz & Goffman 1995; Demuth 1996; Pater & Paradis 1996; Gennari & Demuth 1997; Johnson Lewis & Hogan 1997; Pater 1997a; except see Kehoe & Stoel-Gammon 1997, for a unified prosodic-perception account). Specifically, it has been claimed that English-speaking and Dutch-speaking children have a 'trochaic bias' in their selection of which syllables to omit and which to retain in a truncated production (Allen & Hawkins 1980; Gerken, Landau & Remez 1990; Gerken 1994a, 1994b; Wijnen et al 1994; Schwartz & Goffman 1995). Trochaic rhythm refers to SW (S = stressed, W = weak) foot structures as opposed to iambic (WS) foot structures. For example, the disyllabic word 'monkey' is trochaic while the disyllabic word 'giraffe' is iambic. Since trochaic rhythm is the dominant, although not exclusive, rhythmic pattern for nouns in English and Dutch, these researchers argue that such a trochaic bias in children's truncation patterns indicates a sensitivity to this language-specific prosodic property (except see Allen & Hawkins 1980).

How does the trochaic bias work? Gerken (1994a) found that when truncating words with SWWS and WSWS structures, children preserved the two weak syllables in each word type differentially; they preserved the weak syllable right-adjacent to the first strong syllable in the words more often than the other weak syllable, so that their outputs corresponded to a SW template. Such differential preservation of non-final weak syllables cannot be explained straightforwardly by perceptual biases alone. One important aspect of Gerken's design is the use of four-syllable long words as stimuli. In two and three syllable words, the effects of perceptual saliency factors, like stress and final position, are difficult to disassociate from prosodic constraint factors. For example, in WSW words, the second weak syllable is also a final syllable, so if it is preserved in truncation, it is ambiguous whether perceptual or prosodic factors are responsible.

If English-speaking children's truncation patterns demonstrate sensitivity to language-specific prosodic structure, then children acquiring languages with contrasting prosodic structure should show different truncation patterns, beyond the predictions of perceptual salience. French contrasts with English on many aspects of word-level stress patterns (see also Pater 1997b). English is a trochaic language with variable placement of primary stress and stress alternations within words (Dresher & Kaye 1990; Hayes 1982; Kenstowicz 1994). The majority of English words are disyllabic and begin with an initial strong syllable (Cutler & Carter 1987), although iambic-like patterns can also be found, as in the word 'giraffe' (WS). In contrast, French is a language with fixed word-level stress on the final syllable (Bullock 1994; Dresher & Kaye 1990; Fletcher 1991; Hoskins 1994; Kenstowicz 1994). French is traditionally considered to have no rhythmic alternations within a word (Dresher & Kaye 1990; Kenstowicz 1994); however, this is currently being debated (Hoskins 1994; Paradis & Deshaies 1990). If stress alternations exist at all in French, they do not seem to be as consistent and prominent as stress alternations in English. The traditional analysis of French words as having only one prominent syllable was adopted for the stimuli presentation in this study (see Table 4). See Paradis (in print) for a discussion of possible interpretations of the results assuming the presence of secondary stress in French.

3.2 *Non-word stimuli*

Two aspects of prosodic organisation were compared in Paradis (1998b, in print): dominant word rhythm patterns and quantity-sensitivity. I only discuss the word rhythm analyses in this chapter. Nonsense words for French and English created to test the children's sensitivity to these two aspects of prosodic structure are presented in Table 4 and Table 5, respectively.

There are only six English stimuli given because the other six stimuli used in the study are relevant mainly to the quantity-sensitivity analyses. A detailed description and rationale for the segmental and syllabic content of the stimuli are discussed in Paradis (in press). Concerning word rhythm types, there is only one type for French, WWWS. There are two word rhythm types from English, representing common patterns found for nouns. The WSWS words were created to compare differential preservation of non-final weak syllables. Also, WSWS words have an iambic or French-like pattern and were included to provide a context for structural ambiguity. SWSW words were chosen because this is the archetypal English pattern, corresponding to two trochaic templates, and should not be ambiguous.

Table 4. *French nonsense words used in repetition task*

IPA[a]	Orthography	Word Rhythm
kotimatœ	quotimateux	WWWS
melapoli	mélapolie	WWWS
pelymatan	pélumatane	WWWS
ʀamɛlinoz	ramelinose	WWWS
panofaldɛ̃	panofaldin	WWWS
tumataskɛ̃	toumatasquin	WWWS
kʀabyldomi	crabuldomie	WWWS
maʀɪlgopã	marilgopant	WWWS
byltupamœ	bultoupammeux	WWWS
kazgumajõ	casgoumaillon	WWWS

[a]IPA = International Phonetic Alphabet

3.3 Predictions for bilinguals

First, let us consider how the contrast in prosodic organisation between French and English might produce language specific effects in bilingual children's phonological processing. Based on prior research by Gerken (1994a, 1994b), we could predict that English-speaking children would truncate target words in accordance with a trochaic production template, and that French-speaking children would truncate target words in accordance with an iambic production template. This would indicate a preference for preservation of the second weak syllable over the first weak syllable in W_1SW_2S English words, and a preference for the third weak syllable over the other weak syllables in the $W_1W_2W_3S$ French words. Concerning the SWSW words, we can make two predictions. First, when these words are

Table 5. *English nonsense words used in repetition task*

IPA[a]	Orthography	Word Rhythm
Type 1		
ləpætɪmun	lapatimoon	WSWS
fɑjimətæk	fahjeematak	WSWS
məlubɪkɑn	maloobikon	WSWS
Type 2		
koɷmigændə	koameeganda	SWSW
pækimoɷktə	pakeemoakta	SWSW
baɷdikulpə	bowdeekoolpa	SWSW

[a] IPA = International Phonetic Alphabet

truncated, we expect a preference for either the first or the second SW foot in the children's output because either one conforms to a trochaic template, which a WSW output does not. Second, lower overall rates of syllable omission for the SWSW English words in comparison with the other words could be expected because the target fits two template sequences exactly. Finally, for all the words, we expect stressed syllables and final syllables, whether weak or strong, to be preserved frequently due to perceptual factors. It is the preservation of non-final weak syllables that is indicative of language-specific prosodic biases.

Regarding crosslinguistic effects, we could predict that transfer would take place at points of structural ambiguity between the two languages. For the stimuli used in this study, the English WSWS words might provide such a point of ambiguity with the WWWS French words. If $W_1S_2W_3S_4$ words were treated as French words, we might see a preservation bias towards the third and four syllables, to satisfy a WS template. If they were treated as English words, we might see a greater bias towards preservation of the second and third syllables, in line with a trochaic template.

3.4 *Participants and procedure*

There were three groups of participants in this study: 18 monolingual French-speaking children with a mean age of 2;8; 18 monolingual English-speaking children with a mean age of 2;5 and 17 bilingual French and English-speaking children with a mean age of 2;5. The criteria for inclusion in the bilingual group was that the children had to have been exposed to both French and English consistently from birth, or within the first six months of life, and that they spontaneously produced utterances in both languages at the time of testing.

Whether our criteria for bilingualism were met was ascertained through language background questionnaires and through observations by the experimenters on the initial visit before testing started. It was not required that the children be balanced bilinguals as dominance or preference for one language is a typical aspect of early bilingual development (De Houwer 1995). For this study, dominance was equated with the language of greatest exposure, as indicated in the language background questionnaire. Seven of the children were French dominant, 9 were English dominant and 1 was considered to be a balanced bilingual. This informal measure of dominance plays a role in post-hoc analyses of crosslinguistic effects.

Two bilingual experimenters met with each child individually. One experimenter interacted with the child and the other took notes and operated an audiotape recorder. The children were shown stuffed toys and picture books of unfamiliar animals. Each of the toys and pictures had a nonsense-word name. When the children were introduced to a creature, they were provided with its name and asked to repeat it, for example, "This is a 'patoolfiga'. Can you say 'patoolfiga'?". Bilingual children were tested twice, once in each language, on separate occasions. The experimenter who interacted with the child spoke the language of the session, French or English, natively.

The children's repetitions of the words from the audio recordings were transcribed and compared to the notes made during the session. Comparison with the notes made during the sessions yielded agreement rates of 88% for French words and 83% for English words. After transcription, the children's productions were coded for preservation of target syllables. Syllables were coded as preserved if they were identical to the target, or if at least the vowel of the target syllable was preserved, without the target onset or coda. Minor mispronunciations and common substitutions of the onset consonants were disregarded.

Preservation scores were calculated for each syllable (first, second, third, fourth) of each target word for each child. The denominators consisted of the number of times each target word was produced by that child and the numerator consisted of the number of times that particular syllable was included in the child's production. The rationale for the choice of denominator was that each time the word was produced, there was an opportunity to produce all four syllables.

3.5 *Position analyses*

3.5.1 *French WWWS words*
The mean proportions of syllables preserved as a function of position in the target word are shown in Table 6 for both the monolingual and bilingual groups. Two one way within-language group ANOVA's with syllable position as a factor (4

levels: first, second, third and fourth) revealed that for both the monolinguals and bilinguals, the effect of syllable position in the target word had a significant effect on preservation (Monolinguals: F (3,17) = 25.927, $p < .0001$; Bilinguals: F (3,16) = 47.020, $p < .0001$). A two-way ANOVA with language group as a between factor and syllable position as a within factor showed no differences between the bilingual and monolingual groups ($F(3,99) = 1.548$, $p > .05$). The results of post-hoc Fisher LSD tests for the one-way ANOVA's are presented in Table 6. The preservation patterns for both groups are as follows: Syllables in fourth position were retained more than those in third position, in second position, and in first position. Syllables in third position were retained more than syllables in second position and first position. There was no difference in preservation between syllables in second and first position.

The differential preservation of weak syllables in third position over those in second and first is consistent with an iambic template bias in truncation.

Table 6. *Mean proportions of syllable preservation by position for the monolingual and bilingual groups for French WWWS words*

Position Contrasts	Monolinguals		Bilinguals	
	Means	*t* value	Means	*t* value
4–3	.92–.71	3.97*	.93–.60	5.12*
4–2	.92–.45	6.97*	.93–.24	10.66**
4–1	.92–.37	8.04**	.93–.32	9.36**
3–2	.71–.45	2.99*	.60–.24	5.55**
3–1	.71–.37	4.06*	.60–.32	4.24*
2–1	.45–.37	2.13 ns	.24–.32	1.31 ns

Note: 4,3,2,1 = syllables in fourth, third, second and first position respectively, i.e., $W_1W_2W_3S_4$
* $p < .05$
** $p < .01$

3.5.2 *English WSWS words*
The mean proportions of syllables preserved as a function of position in the target are shown in Table 7 for both the monolingual and bilingual groups. Two one way within-language group ANOVA's with syllable position as a factor (4 levels: first, second, third and fourth) revealed that for both the monolinguals and bilinguals, the effect of syllable position in the target word had a significant effect on preservation (Monolinguals: F (3,17) = 56.011, $p < .0001$; Bilinguals: F (3,16) = 24.745, $p < .0001$). A two-way ANOVA with language group as a between

factor and syllable position as a within factor showed a significant interaction effect, indicating that the monolinguals and bilinguals did not treat these words in the same way ($F(3,99) = 4.550$, $p = .005$). The results of post-hoc Fisher LSD tests for the one-way ANOVA's are presented in Table 7. The preservation pattern for the monolingual group is as follows: Syllables in fourth position were retained more than those in third position and in first position. Syllables in second position were also retained more than those in third position and in first position. Syllables in third position were retained more than those in first position. There was no difference in preservation between syllables in second and fourth position. The preservation pattern for the bilingual group is as follows: Syllables in fourth position were retained more than those in third position, in second position and in first position. Syllables in second position were retained more than those in first position. Syllables in third position were also retained more than those in first position. Syllables in second position were not retained more than those in third position. Post-hoc comparisons of the between-language group means from the two-way ANOVA showed that there was a significant difference between the mean preservation rates for the second syllable between the monolinguals and bilinguals (89% versus 55%, $t(7) = 4.238$, $p < .005$). No other inter-language comparisons between syllable positions were significant.

The differential preservation of non-final weak syllables in third position over those in first position shown by both the monolinguals and the bilinguals is consistent with a trochaic template bias in truncation. In contrast, the equal preservation of strong syllables in second position and weak syllables in third position shown by the bilinguals could indicate an influence from French, where weak syllables in third position, left-adjacent to a final strong syllable, are preferred over other weak syllables. It was predicted that the English WSWS words might produce such crosslinguistic effects due to the inter-language structural ambiguity of these forms.

In addition to structural ambiguity, the bilingual children's language dominance could also have played a role in determining the preservation patterns for WSWS words. On the one hand, the equal preservation of syllables in second and third position may have been the result of the children's vacillation between French and English in processing these forms. On the other hand, it is possible that the equal preservation of syllables in second and third position is a 'flattening' effect caused by two different preservation patterns brought on by dominance. In other words, the English dominant children may have been treating these words as English words, while the French dominant children were treating them as French words. In order to investigate this possibility, the preservation scores for syllables in second and third position for WSWS words were divided into two groups:

scores of the English dominant and the French dominant groups. The results of this recalculation support the possibility of a dominance effect. English dominant bilinguals preserved syllable two 64% of the time, and syllable three 41% of the time. The French-dominant bilinguals showed the opposite trend: 36% of syllables in second position were preserved while 57% of syllables in third position were preserved. Thus, the French-dominant group may have shown a tendency to treat English WSWS words like French words.

Table 7. *Mean proportions of syllable preservation by position for the monolingual and bilingual groups for English WSWS words*

Position Contrasts	Monolinguals		Bilinguals	
	Means	*t* value	Means	*t* value
4–3	.89–.51	5.35*	.87–.47	4.52**
4–2	.89–.89	.13 ns	.87–.55	3.63*
4–1	.89–.11	11.03**	.87–.11	8.60**
3–2	.51–.89	5.35*	.47–.55	.89 ns
3–1	.51–.11	5.81**	.47–.11	4.08*
2–1	.89–.11	11.16**	.55–.11	4.97**

Note: $4,3,2,1 = $ syllables in fourth, third, second and first position respectively, i.e., $W_1S_2W_3S_4$
* $p < .05$
** $p < .01$

3.5.3 *English SWSW words*
The mean proportions of syllables preserved as a function of position in the target are shown in Table 8 for both the monolingual and bilingual groups. Two one way within-language group ANOVA's with syllable position as a factor (4 levels: first, second, third and fourth) revealed that for both the monolinguals and bilinguals, the effect of syllable position in the target word had a significant effect on preservation (Monolinguals: F $(3,9) = 19.144$, $p < .0001$; Bilinguals: F $(3,12) = 17.280$, $p < .0001$). Note that the number of subjects is smaller for this comparison because some subjects in both groups did not truncate the words of this type (see *Length* below). A two-way ANOVA with language group as a between factor and syllable position as a within factor was not significant, indicating that the monolinguals and bilinguals treated these words in the same way overall $(F (3,63) = 1.424, p > .05)$. The results of post-hoc Fisher LSD tests for the one way ANOVA's are presented in Table 8. The similar preservation patterns for both groups are as follows: Syllables in fourth and third position were

preserved more often than those in second position and first position. There were
no significant differences between the preservation rates for syllables in third and
fourth position. The groups differed with respect to syllables in first and second
position. The monolinguals preserved the syllables in first position more than
those in second position, but the bilinguals preserved them equally. This difference is not directly relevant to the consideration of a trochaic template bias, and
was not significant in the two-way, mixed ANOVA.

The preservation patterns for the truncated productions of SWSW words
appear to indicate that the children in both groups most frequently preserved the
final SW foot and thus, are consistent with a trochaic template bias.

Table 8. *Mean proportions of syllable preservation by position for the monolingual and
bilingual groups for English SWSW words*

Position Contrasts	Monolinguals		Bilinguals	
	Means	*t* value	Means	*t* value
4–3	.81–.85	.34 ns	.96–.67	2.35 ns
4–2	.81–.11	6.13**	.96–.17	6.38**
4–1	.81–.39	3.64*	.96–.35	4.95**
3–2	.85–.11	6.47**	.67–.17	4.032*
3–1	.85–.39	3.98*	.67–.35	2.60*
2–1	.11–.39	2.49*	.35–.17	1.44 ns

Note: 4,3,2,1 = syllables in fourth, third, second and first position respectively, i.e.
$W_1S_2W_3S_4$
* p < .05
** p < .01

3.6 *Length analyses*

Truncation rates were compared between the language groups and between the
individual words for each language. First, the average output length in syllables
for all the words combined for each language group was similar (French monolinguals = 2.77; English monolinguals = 2.85; Bilinguals-French = 2.68; Bilinguals-
English = 2.67). With respect to the individual words, both the monolingual and
bilingual children truncated the items in the French stimuli set equally (Monolingual: $F(9,25) = 1.250$, $p > .05$; Bilingual: $F(9,28) = 1.192$, $p > .05$). In contrast, the
monolingual and bilingual children did not truncate all the English words equally
(Monolingual: $F(11,28) = 4.596$, $p < .001$; Bilingual: $F(11, 25) = 1.795$, $p = .054$).
This difference is only marginally significant for the bilingual children. (The

analyses for the English words include the six stimuli items used for the quantity-sensitivity analyses which not discussed in this chapter). Following our hypothesis, planned contrasts were performed on the monolinguals' and bilinguals' truncation rates of the SWSW words versus the other word types combined in English (WSWS, WSWW). As predicted, both the monolinguals and the bilinguals truncated the SWSW words significantly less than the other word types, although the differences were smaller for the bilinguals (Monolinguals: $F(1, 308) = 50.99$, $p < .01$; Bilinguals: $F(1, 275) = 15.875$, $p < .01$). Fewer truncations of the SWSW words provides further support for the operation of a trochaic bias in syllable omission patterns.

3.7 *Conclusion*

The results of the non-word repetition task suggest that, like the morphosyntactic analyses, the bilingual children perform in language-specific ways and like monolingual children on the whole. Both the bilingual and monolingual children showed the same patterns in non-final weak syllable preservation and output length for the English WSWS and SWSW words and for the French WWWS words in accordance with predicted language-specific trochaic and iambic biases. In contrast, group differences appeared in the performance of the children on the WSWS English words in the comparison of preservation rates for the second and third syllables. The bilingual children seemed to show evidence for both the French and English preservation patterns for the second and third syllables. Because the English WSWS words are similar to the French words, and thus could be considered structurally ambiguous, this group difference could be attributed to the operation of crosslinguistic influences in the children' phonological processing. The post-hoc analyses of the WSWS results suggest that dominance could play a role in determining children's strategies with respect to structurally ambiguous input.

4. Why are there differences between syntactic and phonological acquisition?

In both the morphosyntactic and phonological studies, structures in French and English that could be construed as ambiguous crosslinguistically were examined in the speech of bilingual two year olds. The results of these studies are divergent in that the children showed evidence of crosslinguistic influence on the level of phonology, but not on the level of syntax. Let us consider two potential reasons for this discrepancy.

A striking potential difference is methodology. One study is based on experimental manipulation and the other is observational. Experimental procedures may be more sensitive and thus may capture more subtle interactions between the two languages. In fact, an experimental task might be sensitive enough to determine if English-influenced word order in negative constructions in French is a systematic phenomenon in some French-English bilingual children. But, we cannot conclude that experimental procedures are necessary for finding crosslinguistic effects because other observational studies have found evidence for such effects in spontaneous speech (e.g. Hulk & van der Linden 1996; Hulk 1997; Hulk & van der Linden 1998; Döpke 1998; Müller 1998).

Another potential reason for the absence of interaction at the level of syntax is language pair. The above-mentioned studies involved language pairs including one V2 language like Dutch or German with relatively variable word order. It is possible that bilingual acquisition of one or more variable word order language provides a greater number of ambiguous surface forms to lead children astray, and in turn, the effects of crosslinguistic interactions may be more noticeable in the acquisition of such language pairs.

In conclusion, when one takes into account the emerging body of research on crosslinguistic interaction in acquisition, the answer to the question posed above, 'Would interaction be expected to occur in all subcomponents of the grammar?' is yes. In spite of the null results for the aspects of morphosyntax investigated with French-English bilinguals, positive results have been found for children acquiring other aspects of syntax in other language pairs. However, the null results for French-English morphosyntax raise an important point: Crosslinguistic interactions may not be found everywhere an ambiguity exists across a language pair. Future challenges for researchers in this field include predicting more precisely how and when crosslinguistic effects take place.

Acknowledgments

I would like to thank Isabelle Fonte, Jessica Little and Sophie Petitclerc for their invaluable assistance in creating the stimuli, and in collecting, transcribing and coding the data for the phonological study. I would also like to thank Fred Genesee, Elena Nicoladis and Joe Pater for helpful discussion of ideas related to the morphosyntax and phonological studies. This research was supported financially by the Social Sciences and Humanities Research Council of Canada (research grant: 410–95–0726) and by FCAR (Fonds pour la formation de chercheurs et l'aide à la recherche, doctoral fellowship: 963612), for which I am grateful.

References

Allen, G. & Hawkins, S. 1980. "Phonological rhythm: Definition and development". In G. Yeni-Komishan, J. Kavanagh & C. Ferguson (eds), *Child phonology: Vol. 1. Production*. New York: Academic Press, 227–256.

Auger, J. 1995. "Les clitiques pronominaux en français parlé informel: Une approche morphologique". *Revue québécoise de linguistique 24(1)*: 21–60.

Bullock, B. 1994. "Does the French syllable have weight?" In Mazzola, M. (ed), *Issues and theory in Romance Linguistics*. Washington DC: Georgetown University Press, 3–18.

Cummins, S. & Y. Roberge. 1993. "A morphosyntactic analysis of romance clitic constructions". In M. Mazzola (ed), *Issues and theory in Romance linguistics*. Washington, D.C: Georgetown University Press, 239–257.

Cutler, Anne, & D.M. Carter. 1987. "The predominance of strong initial syllables in the English vocabulary. *Computer Speech and Language*, 2: 133–42.

Cutler, Anne, Jacques Mehler, Dennis Norris & Juan Segui. 1989. "Limits on bilingualism". *Nature* 340: 229–230.

De Groot, Annette. 1993. "Word-type effects in bilingual processing tasks: Support for a mixed-representational system". In R. Schreuder & B. Weltens (eds.), *The Bilingual Lexicon*. Amsterdam and Philadelphia: John Benjamins, 27–52.

De Houwer, Annick. 1995. "Bilingual language acquisition". In P. Fletcher and B. MacWhinney (eds.), *Handbook on Child Language*. Oxford: Blackwell.

Demuth, Katherine. 1996. "The prosodic structure of early words". In J. Morgan and K. Demuth (eds), *Signal to Syntax*. Mahwah, NJ: Lawrence Erlbaum, 171–186.

Déprez, Viviane, & Amy Pierce. 1993. "Negation and functional projections in early grammar". *Linguistic Inquiry 24(1)*: 25–67.

Döpke, Susanne. 1998. "Competing Language Structures: The Acquisition of Verb Placement by Bilingual English-German Children," *Journal of Child Language* 25(3): 555–584.

Dresher, E. & J. Kaye. 1990. "A computational learning model for metrical phonology". *Cognition* 34: 137–195.

Echols, C. 1993. "Perceptually-based model of children's earliest productions". *Cognition* 46: 245–296.

Echols, C. & E. Newport,. 1992. "The role of stress and position in determining first words". *Language Acquisition* 2: 189–220.

Fletcher, J. 1991. "Rhythm and final lengthening in French". *Journal of Phonetics* 19: 193–212.

Genesee, Fred, Elena Nicoladis, & Johanne Paradis. 1995. "Language differentiation in early bilingual development". *Journal of Child Language* 22: 611–631.

Gennari, S. & Katherine Demuth. 1997. "Syllable omissions in the acquisition of Spanish". In E. Hughes, M. Hughes and A. Greenhill (eds.), *BUCLD 21 Proceedings*, 182–193.

Gerken, L. 1994a. "A metrical template account of children's weak syllable omissions from multisyllabic words". *Journal of Child Language* 21: 565–584.

Gerken, L. 1994b. "Young children's representation of prosodic phonology: Evidence from English-speakers' weak syllable productions". *Journal of Memory and Language* 33: 19–38.

Gerken, L., R. Remez & B. Landau. 1990. "Function morphemes in young children's speech perception and production". *Developmental Psychology* 26: 204–216.

Grosjean, François. 1995. "A psycholinguistic approach to code-switching: The recognition of guest words by bilinguals". In L. Milroy & P. Muysken (eds), *One speaker, two languages: Cross-disciplinary perspectives on code-switching*. Cambridge: Cambridge University Press, 259–275.

Hayes, B. 1982. "Extrametricality and English stress". *Linguistic Inquiry* 13: 227–276.

Hoskins, S. 1994. "Secondary stress and stress clash resolution in French: An empirical investigation". In Mazzola, M. (ed), *Issues and theory in Romance Linguistics* . Washington DC: Georgetown University Press, 35–47.

Hulk, Aafke C. 1997. "The acquisition of French object pronouns by a Dutch/French bilingual child". In A. Sorace et al (eds), *Proceedings of GALA '97*, 512–526.

Hulk, Aafke C. & Elisabeth van der Linden. 1996. "Language mixing in a French-Dutch bilingual child". In E. Kellerman, B. Weltens & T. Borgaerts (eds), *Toegepaste taalwetenschap in Artikelen* 55 (EUROSLA 6, A selection of papers): 89–103.

Hulk, Aafke C. & Elisabeth van der Linden. 1998. "Non-selective access and activation in child bilingualism". Paper presented at the 11th Biennial *International Conference on Infant Studies*, Atlanta, Georgia.

Hura, S. & C. Echols. 1996. "The role of stress and articulatory difficulty in children's early productions". *Developmental Psychology* 32: 165–176.

Johnson, C. & P. Lancaster. 1998. "The development of more than one phonology: A case study of a Norwegian-English bilingual child". *International Journal of Bilingualism* 2(3): 265–300.

Johnson, J., L. Lewis & J. Hogan. 1997. "A production limitation in syllable number: A longitudinal study of one child's early vocabulary". *Journal of Child Language* 24: 327–349.

Kayne, R. 1975. *French Syntax: The Transformational Cycle*. Cambridge: MIT Press.

Kehoe, M. & C. Stoel-Gammon. 1997. "Truncation patterns in English-speaking children's word productions". *Journal of Speech, Language and Hearing Research* 40: 526–541.

Kenstowicz, M. 1994. *Phonology in Generative Grammar*. Cambridge, MA: Blackwell.

Kroll, J. & Annette De Groot. 1997. "Lexical and conceptual memory in the bilingual: Mapping form to meaning in two languages". In A. de Groot & J.F. Kroll (eds) *Tutorials in Bilingualism: Psycholinguistic Perspectives*. Mahwah, NJ: Lawrence Erlbaum, 169–200.

Lanza, Elizabeth. 1992. "Can bilingual two-year-olds code-switch?" *Journal of Child Language* 19: 633–658.

Leopold, W. 1949/71. *Speech Development of a Bilingual Child: A Linguist's Record*. (Vols. 1–4). New York: AMS Press.

MacWhinney, Brian. 1991. *The CHILDES project. Tools for analyzing talk*. Mahwah, NJ: Lawrence Erlbaum.

Meisel, Jürgen M. 1989. "Early differentiation of languages in bilingual children". In K. Hyltenstam & L. Obler (eds), *Bilingualism across the Lifespan: Aspects of Acquisition, Maturity and Loss*. Cambridge: Cambridge University Press, 13–40.

Müller, Natascha. 1998. "Transfer in bilingual first language acquisition", *Bilingualism* 1(3): 151–171.

Nicoladis, Elena & Fred Genesee. 1996. "A longitudinal study of pragmatic differentiation in young bilingual children". *Language Learning* 46(3): 439–464.

Paradis, C. & D. Deshaies. 1990. "Rules of stress assignment in Quebec French: Evidence from perceptual data". *Language Variation and Change* 2: 135–154.

Paradis, Johanne. 1996. "Phonological differentiation in a bilingual child: Hildegard revisited". In A. Stringfellow, D. Cahana-Amitay, E. Hughes & A. Zukowski, (eds), *BUCLD 20 Proceedings*, 528–539.

Paradis, Johanne. in print. "Do bilingual two year olds have separate phonological systems?" *International Journal of Bilingualism*.

Paradis, Johanne. 1998. "Prosodic phonology in bilingual two year olds: One system or two?" Paper presented at the 11th Biennial *International Conference on Infant Studies*, Atlanta, Georgia.

Paradis, Johanne & Fred Genesee. 1996. "Syntactic acquisition in bilingual children: autonomous or interdependent?" *Studies in Second Language Acquisition* 18: 1–25.

Paradis, Johanne & Fred Genesee. 1997. "On continuity and the emergence of functional categories in bilingual first language acquisition". *Language Acquisition* 6(2): 91–124.

Paradis, Michel. 1997. "The cognitive neuropsychology of bilingualism". In A. de Groot and J.F. Kroll (Eds.), *Tutorials in Bilingualism: Psycholinguistic Perspectives*. Mahwah, NJ: Lawrence Erlbaum, 331–354.

Pater, Joe. 1997a. "Minimal violation and phonological development". *Language Acquisition* 6(3): 201–353.

Pater, Joe. 1997b. "Metrical parameter missetting in second language acquisition". In S.J. Hannahs & M. Young-Scholten (eds), *Focus on Phonological Acquisition*. Philadelphia and Amsterdam: John Benjamins, 235–261.

Pater, Joe & Johanne Paradis. 1996. "Truncation without templates in early child phonology". In A. Stringfellow, D. Cahana-Amitay, E. Hughes & A. Zukowski, (eds.), *BUCLD 20 Proceedings*, 540–551.

Pearson, Barbara, Sylvia Fernandez, & D. Kimbrough Oller. 1995. "Cross-language synonyms in the lexicons of bilingual infants: One language or two?" *Journal of Child Language* 22: 345–368.

Pierce, Amy. 1992. *Language Acquisition and Syntactic Theory*. Dordrecht: Kluwer.

Pollock, Jean-Yves. 1989. "Verb movement, universal grammar and the structure of IP". *Linguistic Inquiry* 20: 365–424.

Quay, Suzanne. 1995. "The bilingual lexicon: Implications for studies of language choice". *Journal of Child Language* 22: 369–387.

Redlinger, Wendy E. & Tschang-Zin Park. 1980. "Language mixing in young bilinguals". *Journal of Child Language* 7: 337–352.

Schnitzer, M. & E. Krasinski. 1994. "The development of segmental phonological production in a bilingual child". *Journal of Child Language* 21: 585–622.

Schnitzer, M. & E. Krasinski. 1996. "The development of segmental phonological production in a bilingual child: A contrasting second case". *Journal of Child Language* 23: 547–571.

Schwartz, R. & L. Goffman. 1995. "Metrical patterns of words and production accuracy". *Journal of Speech and Hearing Research* 38: 876–888.

Volterra, Virginia & Traute Taeschner. 1978. "The acquisition and development of language by bilingual children". *Journal of Child Language* 5: 311–326.

Wexler, Kenneth. 1994. "Optional infinitives, head movement and the economy of derivations". In D. Lightfoot and N. Hornstein (eds.), *Verb Movement*. Cambridge, MA: Cambridge University Press.

Wijnen, Frank, E. Krikhaar. & E. Den Os. 1994. "The (non)realization of unstressed elements in children's utterances: Evidence for a rhythmic constraint". *Journal of Child Language* 21: 59–83.

Cross-Linguistic Structures in the Acquisition of Intonational Phonology by German-English Bilingual Children

Ulrike Gut

University of Bielefeld

1. Introduction

This chapter is concerned with cross-linguistic structures in the acquisition of intonational phonology by German-English bilingual children. It will be argued that prior to explaining cross-linguistic structures in psycholinguistic terms, it is necessary to identify them reliably. Both these aims are currently difficult to achieve in the area of the acquisition of phonology. After a brief review of prejudices and attitudes that have influenced research in cross-linguistic structures and bilingualism in general (Section 2), the current conception of bilingual speech processing and language representation in both language learners and adult speakers will be discussed (Section 3). I will show that cross-linguistic structures can be explained as either slips of the tongue or fillers of a gap in the slower developing language. The difficulty of identifying cross-linguistic structures will be exemplified with data from the acquisition of segmental phonology (Section 4). The specific task of a German–English bilingual learner acquiring the intonational phonology of both languages will be outlined in Sections 5 and 6. In Section 7, data on cross-linguistic structures in the phonetic realisation of pitch accents by a bilingual child will be presented. Section 8 focuses on the acquisition of the intonational phonology of questions of the same child. In Section 9, it is suggested that intonational phrasing may help to identify the nature of semantic or syntactic cross-linguistic structures.

2.   Attitudes towards cross-linguistic structures

Early research on "language mixing" or cross-linguistic productions by speakers of more than one language (and indeed on bilingualism in general) seems to have been considerably influenced by preconceived ideas and intense emotional involvement. Cross-linguistic productions were seen as an indication of an imperfect command of the respective languages, and terms such as "limited bilingualism" and "semilingualism" were coined (Cummins 1976). In a similar vein, the detrimental effects of childhood bilingualism were stressed by several authors (Jones & Stewart 1951; Tireman 1955; Macnamara 1966). This was followed by a counter phase during which researchers tried to prove the cognitive superiority of bilingual children (Ianco-Worrall 1972; Scott 1973; Ben-Zeev 1977; Lambert 1977; Kessler & Quinn 1982).

Cross-linguistic productions during bilingual language acquisition were either considered a stage that had to be outgrown, or their existence was denied altogether. The first view was proposed by Volterra & Taeschner (1978) and many others (Redlinger & Park 1980; Vihman & McLaughlin 1982; Grosjean 1982; Saunders 1982; Taeschner 1983; Vihman 1985; Arnberg 1987,), who described bilingual language acquisition as a progression from a single undifferentiated system to two separate systems. Denial of cross-linguistic productions has been the approach of supporters of the Independent Development Hypothesis (Bergman 1976; Padilla & Lindholm 1984), who assume a completely separate acquisition of the two languages from the beginning.

It is only recently that a new view of bilingualism has been proposed that dispenses with the metaphor of one or two language systems. Instead of primarily comparing bilingual language processing and representation with that of monolinguals, current research recognises them as subjects for scientific investigation in their own right (de Houwer 1990; Tracy 1995). It is now assumed that a bilingual is not the sum of two more or less complete monolinguals but a language user with highly specific processing and representation mechanisms.

3.   Bilingual speech processing and language representation

Unfortunately, knowledge about bilingual language processing and storage is only just beginning to emerge. In terms of language representation, there is some evidence that the two languages of a bilingual speaker are stored in the same area of the brain (Paradis 1992), although this is sometimes disputed (e.g. Shanon 1982). Psycholinguistic experiments show that the two lexicons of a bilingual are closely connected. Stimulus material in one language results in a parallel low level activation of the other language. In the Stroop test, where subjects are asked to name the colour of the letters of a word, which in itself constitutes a colour term, cross-language interference occurs (Segalowitz 1977; Ehri & Ryan 1980). A double activation of both languages for visual word recognition was proposed by Grainger (1993).

This simultaneous activation of the two languages has been called the "bilingual mode" (Lattey 1981; Hoffmann 1991; Grosjean 1995). In speech to monolinguals, it is usually suppressed. In conversation with other bilinguals, in contrast, output control is relaxed and speakers are in the bilingual mode, where code-switching can occur.

In terms of language processing, bilinguals seem to have to make subtle adjustments in both perception and production in order to accommodate the two languages. Cutler (1994) assumes that certain perceptual strategies facilitate speech perception. A strategy for English would be to take a stressed syllable as a signal for the beginning of a word. In French, segmentation would be based on the syllable, and in Japanese on the mora. Bilinguals, she claims, can only use one strategy (Cutler et al. 1992). French–English bilinguals were presented with the same perception task as corresponding groups of French and English monolinguals in earlier studies. When the subjects were divided into English- or French-dominant speakers, Cutler et al. could show that the French-dominant bilinguals used syllable-based segmentation strategies in French and the English-dominant bilinguals used stress-based segmentation with English. In short, in the dominant language each group resembled monolingual speakers, whereas in the non-dominant language they did not. However, segmentation in the non-dominant language was not imperfect or inferior in any way. The subjects simply fell back on general, less language-specific strategies.

Watson (1991) found that the articulation of certain phonemes by bilinguals may differ from that of monolinguals, yet without being perceptually noticeable. The French/English bilinguals he studied showed a systematic difference in onset frequency of the first formant in vowels following voiced and voiceless stops in both languages; a feature which is produced only by English but not French monolinguals. He also found greater aspiration in French voiceless velars in his bilingual data compared to monolingual average values. Each production, however, was well within the acceptable monolingual range. Bilinguals thus may have different production routines for some phonemes to reduce the processing load. At the level of everyday perception, however, they will stay well within mono-lingually acceptable limits.

If that is the case, children acquiring two languages need to develop these specifically bilingual linguistic abilities. They must acquire two systems of language representation, which have to be kept apart should the situational context require it. Furthermore, they must acquire perceptual and articulatory skills which are within monolingual boundaries but at the same time may incorporate modifications in order to reduce the processing load.

Given the need for a certain degree of interlinguistic assimilation, cross-linguistic productions during language acquisition can be expected. These should not be seen as an indication of imperfect development. Instead they offer us a unique opportunity to study the specific bilingual acquisition process. Cross-linguistic productions that reflect cross-linguistic *representations* (ie. lasting acquired structures) during language acquisition are probably very rare. Only an exclusive production of a particular cross-linguistic structure in all conversational settings, including monolingual ones, may be taken as evidence for a cross-linguistic representation. In all other cases, it will be assumed that the cross-linguistic productions are of a *transitory character* and occur on a performance level either due to imperfect "suppression" strategies of code-switching, which could be considered slips of the tongue (de Houwer 1995) or a means of filling gaps in one language with the structures of the other (Tracy 1995). In segmental phonology, for example, Hoffmann (1985) observed in her Spanish/German subject "borrowing" of the uvular roll from German and its usage as a replacement for the Spanish apical roll. However, the identification of cross-linguistic structures in both segmental and suprasegmental phonology poses many problems, as the following section will show.

4.   Identification of cross-linguistic structures in the acquisition of phonology

Research in the acquisition of segmental phonology by bilingual children has been highly influenced by the debate on one or two representational systems discussed above. On the one hand, Burling (1959) and Schnitzer & Krasinski (1994) as well as Leopold (1947) adduced evidence for an initially undifferentiated consonant system in the bilingual children they studied. On the other hand, no such evidence was found by Deuchar (1989), Ingram (1981), Oksaar (1970), and Raffler-Engel (1965), which led these authors to assume two separate phonological systems from the beginning.

One reason for this apparent contradiction could be that many of the proposed "undifferentiated systems", are in fact misinterpretations of regular features of phonological acquisition. This is most probably the case in the above cited studies which found evidence for an initial cross-linguistic consonant system: Schnitzer & Krasinski (1994) reported that their Spanish-English subject showed a phase in which the appropriate vowels were produced in each language, but only one consonant system seemed to exist. This was interpreted as evidence for a "mixed" stage. Deuchar & Clark (1996), however, offer a phonetic explanation for this pattern of acquisition. The voice onset time (VOT) for the Spanish stops /p/, /t/, and /k/ nearly equals those of the English stops /b/, /d/, and /g/ — they are produced by a short lag after the release. This means that the contrast between "voiced" and "voiceless" stops in Spanish is realised by voicing lead versus short lag, whereas in English it is realised by short vs. long lag. At 1;11, Deuchar & Clark's subjects did not achieve a perceptible voicing contrast in either language. At 2;3, the English contrast was acquired. In Spanish, however, it was hardly perceptible and produced within the short lag. These findings are in line with evidence from monolingual studies which report that Spanish children acquire voicing lead much later than English children acquire their corresponding contrast. Thus, whilst English/Spanish bilingual learners may temporarily sound as if they are using the same consonants in their Spanish and English utterances, Deuchar & Clark's study presents clear evidence of a parallel and asynchronous phonological acquisition. Thus, many conclusions of a mixed system could be due to the lack of sophisticated acoustic measurements in child language data analysis.

Similar examples for the difficulty of identifying cross-linguistic structures in the acquisition of segmental phonology can be cited for English–German bilingual children. Consider the following examples from Adam, an English–German bilingual child growing up in Germany.

(1)   [3;6]   [weːt] for *red*

(2)   [4;4]   [hæp] for *have*

Example (1) shows final devoicing of the /d/ and could be considered an instance of a cross-linguistic production where the German final devoicing rule is applied to an English lexical item. However, data from monolingual children acquiring English also show final devoicing (Wode 1988; cf. Ingram 1989). Example (2) again might be assumed to be a cross-linguistic mix of the German [haːb] and the English [hæv]. Yet, other productions by Adam show that he systematically replaces labiodental fricatives with bilabial stops in English (examples 3 and 4):

(3)   [4;4]   [əʊbə] for *over*

(4)   [4;4]   [muːb] for *move*

Moreover, this substitution has also been recorded for monolingual children.

Identification of cross-linguistic structures in phonology should therefore be made with great care. This applies even more to the area of intonational phonology, where not much is known about the adult systems and acquisition data is scarce.

5.   The acquisition of intonational phonology

It was discussed in Section 4 that certain productions by bilingual children in the area of segmental phonology may have been misinterpreted as cross-linguistic structures, firstly, because very little was known about the monolingual acquisition of the respective languages and, secondly, because auditory analysis was not complemented by acoustic measurements. This difficulty also presents itself in the area of intonation — in fact to an even greater extent.

The term "intonation" refers to the use of the phonetic features pitch, length, loudness and pause for various linguistic purposes. In narrow definitions, it comprises only the systematic and distinct pitch movements during an utterance or intonational phrase (IP). These pitch movements are associated with stressed syllables, of which the last one, the nucleus, has a special status. It is usually aligned with the most important word of the utterance and carries a perceptually distinct pitch movement, which can contribute to its meaning. Wider definitions of intonation include phenomena such as stress, emphasis, and the segmentation of utterances and texts (cf. Crystal 1969; Cruttenden 1986). A stressed syllable in English and German, for example, shows a longer and louder vowel than an unstressed one. Emphasis in English is achieved by higher pitch and a prolongation of the vowel; in German, an increase of loudness and possibly higher pitch and a longer vowel are produced for emphasis (Gut 1995).

Intonation can be analysed auditorily and transcribed in a unilinear fashion using symbols for the various significant pitch movements (cf. O'Connor & Arnold 1973). The most recent approach, Intonational Phonology (see Ladd 1996 for an introduction), assumes two levels of representation: the phonological level, where the intonation system of any language can be described in terms of a series of high (H) and low (L) tones associated with stressed syllables (pitch accents), and high and low boundary tones at the end of an utterance. A set of language-specific phonetic realisation rules leads to the actual speech production in which the phonological level is mapped onto the physical level. In this approach, intonational analysis is based on instrumental analysis, which measures the fundamental frequency (F0) for pitch, amplitude for loudness and frequencies for spectrographic analyses. This is complemented by an auditory analysis. A widely used transcription system is ToBI (Silverman et al. 1992; Beckman & Ayers 1993) for English and German ToBI for German (Batliner & Reyelt 1994; Mayer 1995).

All of the studies concerned with the monolingual acquisition of intonation use a unilinear description system and do not differentiate between a phonetic and a phonological level (Galligan 1987; Marcos 1987; Robb & Saxman 1990; Flax et al. 1991). To my knowledge, only two studies are presently carried out in the acquisition of intonational phonology, both of them with bilingual children (Gut 1999; Grabe, Post & Watson in prep). These studies are concerned with the acquisition of intonational features on both the phonetic and phonological level. For a bilingual learner, the acquisition of two intonation systems comprises several tasks: Firstly, the identification of two separate systems in his or her ambient languages, and secondly the acquisition of the phonological representations and phonetic realisation rules of each of these. Theoretically, each task provides ample opportunity for the production of cross-linguistic structures. The phonological systems may be temporarily or permanently merged on a representational level, and the phonetic production routines may be simplified so that only one "hybrid" strategy is used in both languages. The following section discusses these processes in detail for the case of English–German bilingual language learners.

6. The acquisition of intonational phonology by German–English bilingual learners

In the preceding section, it was pointed out that bilingual acquisition of intonation entailed the separate representation of two phonological systems and the acquisition of two different phonetic realisation strategies. For a German–English bilingual learner, this task seems formidable: Grabe (1998) compared the intonational phonologies of German and English, using a reduced inventory of pitch accents and boundary tones based on Gussenhoven (1984). She recognises only two categories of underlying phonological pitch accents: H*+L and L*+H. Boundary tones are either H% (high) or 0% (level). On the underlying phonological level, she concludes, German and English intonation is identical, and even most of the phonetic realisations of the pitch accents are similar. A bilingual learner seems to be presented with the difficulty of differentiating two such similar systems at an early stage.

Differences between the two systems can be found in the phonetic realisation of the non-final H*+L pitch accent. Whereas in English the peak of the rise in F0 is reached within the stressed vowel, in German it is aligned with the right edge of the vowel (Figures 1a and b in the Appendix). In contrast, the dip of the F0 in the non-final L*+H in German occurs at the middle of the stressed vowel, in English at the right edge of the syllable rhyme (Figures 2a and b). However, experiments showed that these phonetic differences are not perceived reliably and that bilingual subjects could not categorise them correctly. This means that a bilingual speaker has the option of using only one phonetic production strategy in both languages without noticeable deviance from a monolingual speaker. Section 7 is concerned with the strategy adopted by Laura, the bilingual English-German subject I have studied.

A difference between the German and English intonation systems lies in the use of pitch movements for different linguistic purposes. The association of a particular type of nuclear pitch movement with a particular type of utterance is not congruent in both languages. In English, the majority of *wh*-questions seem to be associated with falling pitch movements and the majority of yes-no questions with rises. In German, however, all kinds of questions are more likely to be produced with a rising movement. The possibility exists for a bilingual learner to misapply structures in either language, which could be interpreted as an imperfect representation of the respective phonological systems. Section 8 will deal with this.

7. Laura's phonetic realisations of pitch accents

Laura is the second-born child of a German mother and an English father from a middle-class background. She has lived in Southern Germany all her life. Her English input is restricted to a few hours a week with her father and holidays in the UK. Laura addresses both of her parents and her elder brother predominantly in German. There are 26 phonetically and intonationally transcribed recordings with Laura, covering the ages 2;5,10 to 4;3,12. They range in length from 30 to 180 minutes and comprise between 44 and 502 child utterances each. Approximately half of these had an exclusively English-speaking investigator, the other half a German-speaking one. Of the total of 6121 utterances, 498 utterances from across all recordings were selected for an instrumental analysis using ESPS/x-waves for spectrograms and the transcriber programme for a ToBI labelling of the pitch movements.

The phonetic realisations of Laura's nuclear H*+L and L*+H pitch accents in both languages at the ages of 2;5 and 4;2 are compared in Table 1.

At 2;5, only H*+L pitch accents could be measured in English. All of Laura's final (ie. where the nucleus falls on the last syllable of the utterance) H*+L show a rise of F0 within the vowel — a small one on the lexical item "tea", and a distinct one on "horse" (Figure 3 in the Appendix). As Figure 3 illustrates, the fundamental frequency at the beginning of the vowel (marked by the left-hand

Table 1. *Laura's phonetic realisations of pitch accents in English and German at 2;5 and 4;2*

age	language	pitch accent			
		L*+H final	L*+H non-final	H*+L final	H*+L non-final
2;5	German	variable	variable	variable	tendency to align rise in F0 with right edge of vowel
2;5	English	none	none	variable	rise before drop (long vowel)
4;2	German	none	no dip	straight fall none	level (short vowel); rise aligned with right edge of vowel (long vowel)
4;2	English	variable	variable		variable

vertical line) is on 450 Hz. It then rises to about 510 Hz before falling to 300 Hz at the end of the vowel (right-hand line). In non-final H*+L pitch accents (ie. where one or more unstressed syllables follow the nucleus), F0 either rises before the drop on a long vowel or stays level before dropping in short vowels. Unfortunately, the small number of examples precludes any conclusion other than the observation that Laura's phonetic realisations of pitch accents in English at this age are highly variable and do not show any systematic tendencies.

In German, Laura's phonetic realisations of final H*+L pitch accents are equally variable. Out of five instances, two straight falls of F0, one level F0 plus subsequent drop, and two rises of F0 within the vowel can be observed. The productions do not show systematic variation, and there is no correlation of a particular pattern with vowel length. The non-final H*+L shows a less heterogeneous picture: in half of the cases, the rise of F0 is aligned with the right edge of the vowel, both on short ("essen") and long ("deinen") vowels. Other phonetic realisations include: the peak of the rise within the vowel, a level F0 plus subsequent drop, and a rise aligned with the right edge of the syllable. In the production of German final L*+H pitch accents, Laura shows both straight rises or dips of F0 within the vowel. In the non-final L*+H, only a slight dip and an alignment of the rise with the right edge of the vowel can be observed.

In summary, Laura's productions of pitch accents at 2;5 in both English and

German are characterised by a great variety. The only clearly discernible tendency is the alignment of the F0 rise in German non-final H*+L pitch accents with the right edge of the vowel. Thus, only a small correspondence with the adult data reported by Grabe (1998) can be noted.

A look at productions at 4;2 does not reveal any significants developments since she was 2;5. In English, no tendency in the phonetic realisations of any of the pitch accents can be established. In German, non-final H*+L is either associated with no F0 movement (level) on short vowels or a rise aligned with the right edge of the vowel in long vowels. There is only one instance of a final H*+L, which is realised as a straight fall. Laura's L*+H pitch accents in German show no dip in F0 at 4;2.

It can be concluded that Laura does not use a stable production strategy for any of the pitch accents in either language even at 4;2. Tendencies for language-specific differences can be observed in so far as rises of F0 are more likely in English H*+L than in corresponding German productions. Equally, the rise of F0 in a non-final H*+L is aligned with the right edge of the vowel only in German. However, much more data are needed in order to consolidate the tendencies found in this study. In particular monolingual data are needed in order to decide whether Laura's unstable productions are typical for children of her age or whether they reflect her specific bilingual acquisition process, which might result in a cross-linguistic hybrid phonetic production strategy.

8.   Laura's acquisition of the intonation of questions

In Section 6 it was suggested that the intonation systems of English and German differ in the way nuclear pitch movements are used to mark different types of questions and that this therefore constitutes an area where cross-linguistic productions might occur. This section investigates this hypothesis by describing Laura's path of acquisition of intonation in questions.[2]

In the 26 transcribed recordings, Laura produced a total of 583 questions, 120 in English and 445 in German, with 18 questions containing lexical items or structural elements of both languages. Due to the quality of the recordings, only a small number[3] of these questions was selected for an acoustic analysis. In total, there are 115 instrumental analyses of questions by Laura.

Figure 4 (next page) gives an overview of Laura's acquisition of questions on various linguistic levels in both German and English. The syntactic development of Laura's questions shows initial syntactic simplifications (VP structure) in both languages. A comparison of the two languages, however, shows that English lags behind considerably. Whereas Laura has adult-like syntax in German by 3;0, it takes her another ten months to achieve the same level in her English questions. However, the sequence of acquisition that Laura shows in other areas is remarkably similar. The order of acquisition for question words is the same in both languages: "what" and "where" are followed by "why", "which", and "who". Only the pace of acquisition differs. Whereas Laura's acquisition in German is continuous, she remains at a very early level in English for a long time until, at 3;10, a sudden spurt of acquisition occurs on all linguistic levels.

This asynchrony in her acquisition is most striking in her use of nuclear pitch movements. At 2;5, Laura produces only one phonological category of nuclear pitch accents in her German questions: a H*+L. Of the 20 questions, the majority (16) end in a low boundary tone (L%), three give the auditory impression of a fall ending midway, and only one ends in a high tone (H%). Thus, Laura's questions at this point are clearly associated with a final falling pitch movement. This is, however, not due to Laura's inability to produce a L*+H pitch accent. Two questions have them in a pre-nuclear position, as in examples 5 and 6.

(5)   *maɪn tɛdɪbeːɐ ɪs voː*
      L*+H   H*+L L%
    'my teddybear is where'

(6)   *voːz | tɛdɪbeːɐ*
    L*+H   H*+L L%
    'where's teddybear'

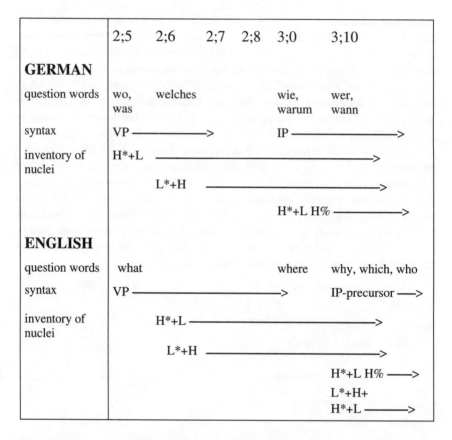

Figure 4. *Laura's acquisition of the intonation in questions from age 2;5 onwards. The production of question words, the state of her syntactic development and the inventory of her nuclear pitch patterns for both German and English*

Laura does not produce many English questions at 2;5. There are only two instances of an utterance beginning with "what". However, the following [izdes] cannot be assigned clearly to either German or English. The nuclear pitch accents produced in both cases are H*L .

At 2;6, Laura produces a nuclear L*+H for the first time in German questions. However, it is very rare in comparison to the H*+L pitch accent, which is still exclusively associated with a L%. Differentiated usage of pitch accents in *wh*-questions and yes/no questions cannot be observed. In English, most of her six questions are direct imitations of the input. She produces two H*+L pitch accents with H% and three L*+H nuclear pitch accents.

At 2;7, Laura produces a fixed pitch movement pattern with some of her German questions. This pattern is not only phonologically but sometimes even phonetically identical. The utterance is the German question [vas Is des] ("What's this?"). The pitch movement and pitch height of some of the renditions of [vas Is des] seem to have become fixed as can be taken from Table 2.

Table 2. *F0 height in Hz of the vowels in some of the renditions of [vas Is]*

/a/	(%H)	/I/	(L*+H)	/e/	(H%)
	365.3		281		427.5
	356.5		308.1		435.4
	355.5		305.8		454.8
	350.9		272.7		442.7
	372.9		287.5		445.3

The pitch pattern of the question is a %H at ~350 Hz, the L*+H at ~300 Hz and the boundary tone H% at ~440 Hz. These are only five instances from a total of 14 productions of this particular question in this recording, however, their perceptual similarity is very striking. Nevertheless, this nucleus pattern is not exclusively associated with this utterance and Laura also continues to use different patterns with this utterance. This intonational phenomenon, which ceases at 2;8, is exclusive to Laura's German. Laura never produces it in any of her English questions.

Another instance of asynchronous acquisition in both languages is the emergence of the nucleus + boundary tone combination H*+L plus H% in German. This pattern is firmly established at 3;0 when it is used with the majority of questions, both *wh*-questions and yes/no questions. In English, it only appears at 3;10. At this point, however, Laura also produces another pattern, that of a pre-nuclear L*+H pitch accent plus a H*+L nucleus, which is produced exclusively in *wh*-questions. This pattern never occurs in German. Thus, a clear separation of the phonological systems of intonation in their linguistic use for the marking of questions has been established at 3;10.

In summary, there is no conclusive evidence for the production of cross-linguistic structures in Laura's acquisition of the intonation of questions from 2;5 to 4;2. In a situation where the acquisition of one language considerably lags behind the acquisition of the other, opportunities to fill gaps with structures from the further developed language are high. However, Laura does not seem to make use of this option. At 2;7, when she begins to produce a new pattern in German, she does not make use of it in English, but instead she remains on the previous level. Not until ten months after the establishment of H*+L H% in German does she first produce it in English. Whether her acquisition path reflects her specific bilingual task again awaits confirmation by monolingual data.

9.   The intonation of cross-linguistic utterances

The investigation of the acquisition of intonational phonology by the English–German bilingual Laura did not yield convincing evidence for cross-linguistic productions that would point towards a temporary cross-linguistic representation of intonational phonology. However, bilingual children produce cross-linguistic structures in other linguistic areas: syntax, the lexicon and morphology. Can intonation help to determine the nature of these cross-linguistic productions? In the following, evidence for this suggestion will be drawn from mixed utterances produced by Laura and Hannah, another English–German bilingual child.

Most of Laura's speech in the early recordings (2;5,2 to 2;6,6) include elements of both her languages, as we can see in the following examples taken from interactions with an English speaker (German lexical items are underlined.

(7)   du: <u>bɪldən</u> nɔx bo:t
       'you build   still boat'

(8)   <u>vɪl</u> <u>aʊ</u> bɪg bɔət
       'I also want a big boat'

(9)   tɛdɪbɛə <u>tɪŋk</u>   ti:
       'teddy drinks tea'

(10)   maɪn <u>taʊə</u> ɪs <u>pa,pʊt</u>
       'my   tower is broken'

(11)   <u>ən</u> <u>də</u> tɔɪlət
       'in the toilet'

Whereas Laura shows the signs of acquiring syntax and morphology in her German, her English remains largely restricted to individual lexical items. She has only acquired rudimentary syntactic rules in English, and her speech can be characterised as predominantly German with a few double entries in her mental lexicon. These English entries seem to be treated as German ones and receive

German inflectional suffixes, as in example (7). Thus, her productions at this stage cannot be called cross-linguistic, as she does not seem to have a representation of the linguistic system of English yet.

From 2;7,2 on, Laura acquires her first rules in English syntax and morphology (cf. Gawlitzek-Maiwald 1997). The length of her utterances in general also increases. This co-occurs with a higher number of intra-utterance pauses. These pauses cannot be equated with intonational breaks produced by adult speakers in order to structure their discourse: They are longer and are not associated with other intonational features such as final-syllable lengthening and a subsequent readjustment of the intonation contour. Laura's pauses at this stage instead seem to be direct reflections of the processing load in her speech production.

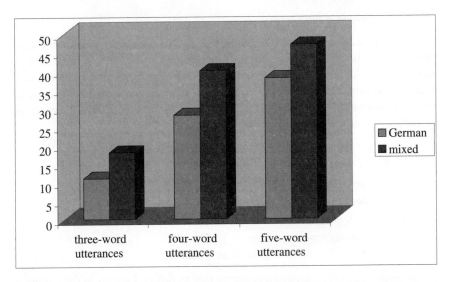

Figure 5. *Percentage of Laura's German and cross-linguistic 3-, 4- and 5-word utterances separated by an inserted pause at 2;7*

Figure 5 illustrates how the number of words an utterance contains correlates with the probability of the insertion of a pause for Laura at 2;7,2. This tendency holds true for her German and mixed utterances alike. The production of the latter, however, is consistently more likely to be interrupted by a pause than the former. Thus, the intonational break could be interpreted as evidence for a developing separation of Laura's mental lexicons and as a sign of an increase in the processing load.

Cross-linguistic productions decrease in number in Laura's subsequent language acquisition. Whilst they still made up a fifth of all her utterances at 2;7,2, only 16 utterances from a total of 192 contain cross-linguistic structures at 3;2. Of these, 6 have an inserted pause (transcribed with the vertical line 'I'), which, in the majority of cases, coincides with the "language switch" as exemplified in utterances 12 to 14:

(12)   gɔɪŋ|*um da aʊtʊ*
        'round the car'

(13)   ɪg I hap   ʃɔn|*tiː*
        'I I already have tea'

(14)   ɪç hab|*bɪg sp|spuːn*
        'I have a big spoon'

At 3;10, after a holiday in the UK, Laura's acquisition of English shows dramatic progress. First IP-precursors appear, she produces many *wh*-words, her lexicon has increased considerably, and many morphological rules have been mastered (for example the -ing and -s suffixes). Cross-linguistic productions are now extremely rare. Utterances 15 to 17 should therefore be considered slips of the tongue or examples of lexical items as fillers of lexical gaps.

(15)   əm *mit* jɛt wɔn
        'er with that one'

(16)   vaɪl hɪa ɪs maɪn tʃɪmnɪ
        'because here is my chimney'

(17)   *was*|hat sɪç als|als ʔə aɪn
        santaklɔz|gəgəl|fəklaidət
        'what I has dressed himself as a Santa Claus'

Furthermore, it could be argued that during this recording Laura is in the bilingual mode discussed earlier because she knows that the English-speaking investigator understands German. "Real", ie. intended code-switches, when Laura changes from English to German because it is easier for her to express herself in German, are always associated with an intonational break as can be seen in examples 18 and 19, produced at 4;3:

(18)   wɔn sliːpɪŋlən wɔn|*aɪnə|dɛə andəʁə bɛnjamiːn...*
        'one's sleeping| and one| one| the other Benjamin...'

(19)   bɪkɔ I *vaɪl dɛs bʁɛnt kʊk*
        'because| because that's burning look'

"Involuntary" or "unplanned" mixing, ie. the production of one or two lexical items in the other language because of relaxed control mechanisms does not occur in this recording, despite the presence of both a German-speaking and an English-speaking investigator.

In summary, it can be argued that intonation may help to identify the nature of cross-linguistic structures. In Laura's early speech, the segmentation of utterances by inserted pauses seemed to directly reflect her processing load, which was increased by both the number of words per utterance and, to an even greater extent, the production of utterances containing lexical items from both languages. Later mixed utterances are characterised by the fact that, should there be an inserted pause, it is likely to coincide with the point of language switch. This might be taken to indicate the growing separation of her syntactic and lexical systems. In her speech at 4;3, Laura uses intonational pauses to mark code-switches she produces for communicative purposes (examples 18 and 19). Other kinds of mixing are not separated by pauses and might therefore be interpreted as "unplanned" (examples 15 to 17) and produced in the bilingual mode.

The same indicative functions of intonational phrasing in mixed utterances can also be observed for Hannah. Hannah is the first-born child of an English mother and a German father, living in the South of Germany. Her mother speaks Southern British English and has an excellent command of German, which she acquired as a second language. Her father speaks Standard German and is equally fluent in English, which he acquired as a second language. Both parents spoke predominantly German with each other before Hannah was born. They then decided to address her in their respective mother tongues and to use English when speaking to one another. The parents estimate that, during her first year of life, Hannah was exposed to an equal amount of English and German. When she started talking, however, she showed little discrimination between the languages, using either of them with her parents and talking predominantly German. When Hannah started going to a crèche at 1;3, the parents changed their language policy and decided on English as the family language. Hannah's acquisition of both English and German is much more balanced and in synchrony than Laura's.

There are 14 video recordings made with Hannah between the ages of 2;0 and 2;9. During these recordings, which lasted between 30 minutes and an hour, an English-speaking investigator (her mother) and a German-speaking project member were present. Additionally, ten audio recordings were provided by her mother, which cover her ages 2;1 to 3;0. During these, she was addressed in English by both her mother and her father. Each contains between 100 and 200 child utterances.

Cross-linguistic productions by Hannah between 2;1 and 2;6 are relatively infrequent as the following table shows:

Table 3. *Percentage of mixed utterances of all of Hannah's utterances at each age.*

Age	Percentage of mixed utterances in all utterances
2;1	4.7%
2;2	7.8 &
2;3	8.5%
2;4	16%
2;6	8%

At 2;1 and 2;2, Hannah's cross-linguistic utterances rarely contain pauses; many of her mixed productions are fluent and without hesitations. Mixing consists mainly of lexical borrowing as shown in examples 20, 22, and 24.

(20) *ıç hapınən* kɔət
      'I haveıa cold'

(21) *maınə auaːllıtl*
      'my ouch llittle'

(22) *mama aʊx* kʊʃən
      'mummy also cushion'

(23) juːləs *aʊtl saː*
      'youl it offl so'

(24) mʌslıpəs *aʊf*
      'my slippers off'

However, if there is an inserted pause, it is often found at the point of language switch (examples 21 and 23). Length of utterance and likelihood of intonational breaks are closely connected also in Hannah's speech (see Gut 1999).

At 2;3, pauses are inserted in half of the cross-linguistic six-word and longer utterances Hannah produces. In (25), the intonational boundary occurs at the point of the language switch, in (26), it is impossible to decide whether [iːn] is a German or an English "in", but the pauses separate the cross-linguistic first part from the second and the German third part.

(25) *dı mama hɛlf mıə* ltap ıt iːn
      'mummy helps me lstrap it in'

(26) *dəs aıns* stwaːpl iːn ldı *puːpə*
      this is a strap l in lthe doll'

There is also a fair number of similarly disrupted cross-linguistic two-word utterances to be observed at 2;3. Hannah produces utterances such as utterances 27 and 28 where the words of each language are separated by an intonational break.

(27)   pʌpətslkʊkən
        'puppetslwatch'

(28)   guːgəːnltɛliː
        'watch ltelly'

At 2;4, the relative frequency of cross-linguistic utterances in Hannah's speech increases dramatically. An indication of this is that she produces an equal number of cross-linguistic utterances as English utterances. Hannah's language acquisition seems to be in a phase of restructuring. On a prosodic level, she frequently extends monosyllabic words with an unstressed syllable [ə] as illustrated for "ich" and "put" in (29):

(29)   ɪçə pʊtə   aɪnə handʃuː da dʁaʊf
        'I'm putting a   glove on there'

(30)   aʊf maɪn ɔvənlʊnt dan ɪ aɪ kʊkən vɛrɪ kɛəfʊlɪ
        'on my   ovenland then I   look very carefully'

(31)   ɪç hap gəmeɪd jʊ mʌtʃ bɛtə
        'I have made you much better'

On a morphological level, Hannah produces English verbs with German inflectional markers. The "-ən" suffix is added to an English verb in (30) [cook+en]; the "gə-" prefix for a German verb past participle is added to the English past participle in (31) [ge+made]. Mixed utterances containing structural mixing of this kind are fairly likely to be interrupted by intonational breaks. Those mixings that involve just a lexical borrowing are generally produced without intonational breaks. When they are interrupted by pauses, the majority of these intonational boundaries coincides with language switches as the following examples show:

(32)   da hast   I baːdɪ I aɪn aʊa I ɪn ju maʊf
        'there you have   bad(?) an outch in your mouth'

(33)   iːç maxlju ː mʌtʃ bɛtə
        'I make you much better'

(34)   ɪç kanə nɪçlwaʊnd də kɪtʃən
        'I can't round the kitchen'

As was the case for Laura, intonational features of Hannah's speech can help to determine the nature of her mixed utterances. In lexically mixed utterances,

Hannah is usually fluent and does not insert intonational breaks. If she does, however, they coincide frequently with the language switch and thus reflect processing load. In structurally mixed utterances, pauses are much likelier. This probably again reflects the processing load in a phase of structural reorganisation.

10. Summary

This paper is concerned with the identification of cross-linguistic structures in the acquisition of intonational phonology by English–German bilingual children. Bilingual language acquisition has now been recognised as a highly specific process, with cross-linguistic structures providing an opportunity to study it in detail and to evaluate issues such as the relative separation of the two language systems. The absence of cross-linguistic productions in Laura's acquisition of the intonation of questions suggests strongly that her two languages develop separately. Even in phases where the development of English lags considerably behind that of German, borrowing of structures does not occur. On a phonetic level, language-specific production strategies for pitch accent categories could not be found at either the ages 2;5 or 4;3. Only data from monolingual acquisition can help to decide whether this is a regular feature of the acquisition of intonation at this age or whether this reflects the specific bilingual acquisition process.

As a second point it was suggested that intonation may contribute to the determination of the nature of syntactic or lexical cross-linguistic structures. Lexically mixed utterances are likelier to be interrupted by intonational breaks than non-mixed ones, and the break often occurs at the point of the language switch. This was interpreted as an indication of separate language systems and as a reflection of the increased processing load.

Acknowledgments

My thanks go to Dr. Nolan and Dr. Hawkins of the phonetics laboratory in Cambridge for letting me perform some of my analyses there, and especially to Geoff Potter for his invaluable technical assistance.

Notes

1. The transcription system based on the British tradition (cf. O'Connor & Arnold 1973). See Gut (1999) for details.

2. The communicative intent "question" was determined with the help of the situational context and

the reactions of the child and her interlocutor. In Laura's speech, classification was based on pragmatic criteria. Syntax is still simplified up to 2;9.21 in German and even later in English, and questions do not always have, a question-word or inversion. For details see Gut (1999).

3. There was often background noise, wind, or many voices at once.

Appendix

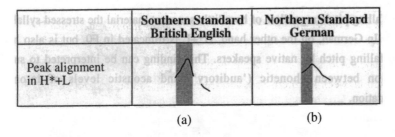

(a)   (b)

Figure 1. *The typical F0 movement on a nuclear H*+L pitch accent in English (a) and German (b). In English, the peak is reached within the vowel; in German, it is aligned with the right edge of the vowel. (From Grabe 1998, p. 145)*

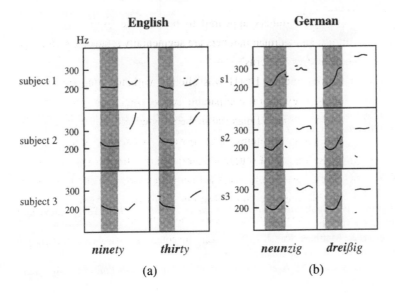

Figure 2. *F0 movements on a nuclear L*+H pitch accent in English (a) and German (b). (From Grabe 1998, p. 126)*

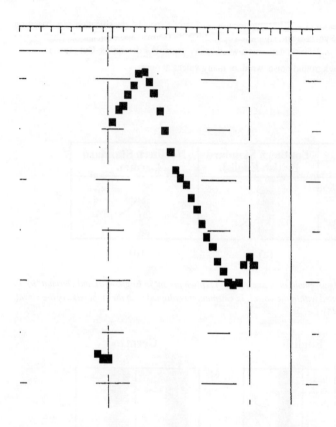

Figure 3. *Laura's phonetic realisation of the H*+L accent on "horse". (The bottom line is at 200 Hz, the top line at 500 Hz, with every one in between illustrating a step of 50 Hz)*

References

Arnberg, Lenore. 1987. *Raising Children Bilingually: The Pre-School Years*. Clevedon: Multilingual Matters.

Batliner, Anton & Matthias Reyelt. 1994. "Ein Inventar prosodischer Etiketten für VERBMOBIL". *Verbmobil Memo* 33.

Beckman, Mary E. & Gayle M. Ayers. 1993. *Guidelines for ToBI labelling*. Ms, Ohio State University.

Ben-Zeev, Sandra. 1977. "The influence of bilingualism on cognitive strategy and cognitive development". *Child Development* 48: 1009–1018.

Bergman, Coral A. 1976. "Interference vs independent development in infant bilingualism". In G. Keller, R. Teschner & S. Viera (eds), *Bilingualism in the Bicentennial and Beyond*. New York: Bilingual Press, 86–96.

Burling, Robbins. 1959. "Language development of a Garo and English-speaking child". *Word* 15: 45–68.

Cruttenden, Alan. 1986. *Intonation*. Cambridge: Cambridge University Press.

Crystal, David. 1969. *Prosodic systems and intonation in English*. Cambridge: Cambridge University Press.

Cummins, James. 1976. "The influence of bilingualism on cognitive growth: A synthesis of research findings and explanatory hypotheses". *Working Papers on Bilingualism* 9: 1–43.

Cutler, Anne. 1994. "Segmentation problems, rhythmic solutions". *Lingua*, 92: 81–104.

Cutler, Anne, Jacques Mehler, Dennis Norris & Juan Segui. 1992. "The Monolingual Nature of Speech Segmentation by Bilinguals". *Cognitive Psychology* 24: 381–410.

De Houwer, Annick. 1990. *The acquisition of two languages from birth: a case study*. Cambridge: Cambridge University Press.

De Houwer, Annick. 1995. "Bilingual Language Acquisition". In P. Fletcher & B. MacWhinney (eds), *The Handbook of Child Language*. Oxford: Blackwell, 219–250.

Deuchar, Margaret. 1989. *ESRC report on project "Infant bilingualism: one system or two?"* Unpublished Ms. Universität Hamburg.

Deuchar, Margaret & Angeles Clark. 1996. "Early bilingual acquisition of the voicing contrast in English and Spanish". *Journal of Phonetics* 24: 351–365.

Ehri, Linnea C. & Ellen B. Ryan. 1980. "Performance of bilinguals in a picture-word interference task". *Journal of Psycholinguistic Research* 9: 285–302.

Flax, Judy, Margaret Lahey, Katherine Harris & Arthur Boothroyd. 1991. "Relations between prosodic variables and communicative function". *Journal of Child Language* 18: 3–19.

Galligan, Roslyn. 1987. "Intonation with single words: Purposive and grammatical use". *Journal of Child Language* 14: 1–21.

Gawlitzek-Maiwald, Ira. 1997. *Der Erwerb von Infinitivkonstruktionen: Ein Vergleich monolingualer und bilingualer Kinder*. Tübingen: Niemeyer.

Grabe, Esther. 1998. *Comparative Intonational Phonology: English and German*. Doctoral dissertation. MPI Series in Psycholinguistics 7, Nijmegen, The Netherlands.

Grabe, Esther, Brechtje Post & Ian Watson. (in prep). "Intonational phonology in acquisition: phonetic variability and phonological category membership". To be submitted to *Journal of Child Language*.

Grainger, Jonathan. 1993. "Visual word recognition in bilinguals". In R. Schreuder & B. Weltens (eds), *The Bilingual Lexicon*. Amsterdam: John Benjamin, 11–25.

Grosjean, François. 1982. *Life With Two Languages: An Introduction to Bilingualism*. Cambridge, MA: Harvard University Press.

Grosjean, François. 1995. "A psycholinguistic approach to code-switching: the recognition of guest words by bilinguals". In L. Milroy & P. Muysken (eds), *One Speaker, Two Languages*. Cambridge: Cambridge University Press, 259–275.

Gussenhoven, Carlos. 1984. *On the Grammar and Semantics of Sentence Accents.* Dordrecht: Foris.

Gut, Ulrike. 1995. *The Intonation of German Learners of British English.* Unpublished M Phil dissertation, University of Cambridge.

Gut, Ulrike. 1999. *The Acquisition of Intonation by German-English Bilingual Children.* Universität Mannheim: PhD thesis.

Hoffmann, Charlotte. 1985. "Language acquisition in two trilingual children". *Journal of Multilingual and Multicultural development* 6: 479–495.

Hoffmann, Charlotte. 1991. *An Introduction to Bilingualism.* London: Longman.

Ianco-Worrall, Anita D. 1972. "Biligualism and cognitive development". *Child Development* 43: 1390–1400.

Ingram, David. 1981. "The emerging phonological system of an Italian-English bilingual child". *Journal of Italian Linguistics* 2: 95–113.

Ingram, David. 1989. *First Language Acquisition.* Cambridge: Cambridge University Press.

Jones, W. & W. Stewart. 1951. "Bilingualism and verbal intelligence". *British Journal of Psychology* 4: 3–8.

Kessler, Carolyn & Mary E. Quinn. 1982. "Cognitive development in bilingual environments". In B. Hartford, A. Valdman & R. Foster (eds), *Issues in International Bilingual Education: The Role of Vernacular.* New York: Plenum Press, 53–79.

Ladd, D. Robert. 1996. *Intonational Phonology.* Cambridge: Cambridge University Press.

Lambert, Werner. 1977. "The effects of bilingualism on the individual: cognitive and socio-cultural consequences". In P. Hornby (ed), *Bilingualism. Psychological, Social and Educational Implications.* New York: Academic Press, 15–28.

Lattey, Elsa. 1981. "Individual and social aspects of bilingualism." In H. Baetens-Beardsmore (ed), *Elements of Bilingual Theory.* (Study Series of the Tijdschrift van de Vrije Universiteit Brusel Nr. 6), 48–65.

Leopold, Werner. 1947. *Speech Development of a Bilingual Child.* New York: AMS Press.

Macnamara, John. 1966. *Bilingualism and Primary Education.* Edinburgh: Edinburgh University Press.

Marcos, Haydée. 1987. "Communicative functions of pitch range and pitch direction in infants". *Journal of Child Language* 14: 255–268.

Mayer, Jörg. 1995. *Transcription of German Intonation. The Stuttgart System.* Unpublished manuscript. University of Stuttgart.

O'Connor, J. & G. Arnold. 1973. *Intonation of Colloquial English.* London: Longman. (2nd edition)

Oksaar, Els. 1970. "Zum Spracherwerb des Kindes in zweisprachiger Umgebung". *Folia Linguistica* 4: 330–358.

Padilla, Amado & Kathryn Lindholm. 1984. "Child bilingualism: the same old issues revisited". In J. Martinez & R. Mendoza (eds), *Chicano Psychology.* Orlando: Academic Press, 369–408.

Paradis, Michel. 1992. "The Loch Ness Monster Approach to Bilingual Language Lateralization: A Response to Bergmeier and Ashton". *Brain and Language* 43: 543–537.

Raffler-Engel, Walburga. 1965. "Del bilinguismo infantile". *Arch. Glottologico Italiano* 50: 175–180.

Redlinger, Wendy E. & Tschang-Zin Park. 1980. "Language Mixing in Young Bilinguals". *Journal of Child Language* 3: 449–455.

Robb, Michael & John Saxman. 1990. "Syllable durations of preword and early word vocalizations". *Journal of Speech and Hearing Research* 33: 583–593.

Saunders, George. 1982. *Bilingual children: Guidance for the Family*. Clevedon: Multilingual Matters.

Schnitzer, Marc L. & Emily Krasinski. 1994. "The development of segmental phonological production in a bilingual child". *Journal of Child Language* 21: 585–622.

Scott, S. 1973. *The relation of divergent thinking to bilingualism: cause or effect?* Manuscript, McGill University.

Segalowitz, Norman. 1977. "Psychological perspectives on bilingual education". In B. Spolsky & R. Cooper (eds), *Frontiers of Bilingual Education*. Rowley, MA: Newbury House, 119–158.

Shanon, B. 1982. "Lateralisation in the perception of Hebrew and English words". *Brain and Language* 17: 107–123.

Silverman, Kim, Mary Beckman, John Pitrelli, Mari Ostendorf, Colin Wightman, Janet Pierrehumbert & Julia Hirschberg. 1992. "ToBI: a standard for labeling English prosody". *Proceedings, Second International Conference on Spoken Language Processing 2*. Banff, Canada, 867–70.

Taeschner, Traute. 1983. *The Sun is Feminine: A Study on Language Acquisition in Bilingual Children*. Berlin: Springer.

Tireman, L. 1955. "Bilingual child and his reading vocabulary". *Elementary English* 32: 33–35.

Tracy, Rosemarie. 1995. *Child Languages in Contact: Bilingual Language Acquisition (English–German) in Early Childhood*. Habililitationsschrift, Universität Tübingen.

Vihman, Marilyn M. 1985. "Language differentiation by the bilingual bnfant". *Journal of Child Language* 12: 297–324.

Vihman, Marylin M. & Barry McLaughlin. 1982. "Bilingualism and second language acquisition in children". In C. Brainerd & M. Pressley (eds), *Verbal Processes in Children. Progress in Cognitive Developmental Research*. Berlin: Springer, 35–58.

Volterra, Virginia & Traute Taeschner. 1978. "The Acquisition and Development of Language by Bilingual Children". *Journal of Child Language* 5: 311–326.

Watson, Ian. 1991. "Phonological processing in two languages". In E. Bialystok (ed), *Language Processing in Bilingual Children*. Cambridge: Cambridge University Press, 25–48.

Wode, Henning. 1988. *Einführung in die Psycholinguistik*. Ismanig: Hueber.

Concluding Remarks

Language Contact – A Dilemma for the Bilingual Child or for the Linguist?

Elizabeth Lanza
University of Oslo

1. Introduction

The contributions to this volume all illustrate quite successfully the need to examine crosslinguistic structures in the bilingual child's acquisition of two or more languages from infancy. Crosslinguistic structures include evidence of language contact in the morphosyntax and phonology as well as the lexicon of the bilingual child's developing systems. Each chapter is a timely addition to the ever-expanding field of bilingual first language acquisition which until recently has overlooked the value of such data. Prior to the late 1980's the main question on the research agenda for bilingual acquisition was whether the young child initially had one system, a fused system, or whether there was initial separate development. The one system hypothesis was indeed the reigning one with McLaughlin (1984: 29) even stating that "it seems unrealistic to suppose that the child differentiates the two languages from a very early age". An ever-increasing number of studies, however, have successfully illustrated that the bilingual child can, and does, differentiate between his or her two languages from very early on (cf. De Houwer 1995 and Lanza 1997a for an overview). Language contact is not a sign of confusion and hence the question is not whether there is one or two systems from the beginning, rather how do the languages interact in acquisition and use. Now that separate development is acknowledged as an overall theoretical premise, we can draw our attention to the structural, pragmatic, and cognitive motivations for language contact in the young bilingual child.

The articles in this volume address many issues concerning the role language contact may play in the child's language development. Particularly, how does the child utilise language contact in solving the puzzle of acquisition of his or her two languages? Or rather does the bilingual child encounter language contact as a challenge in his or her language development? Equally important is the focus on methodology and the linguist's attempts to grapple with this phenomenon of language contact in the child language data under analysis. What are the linguist's conceptualisation of the phenomenon and does it correspond with the reality experienced by the child? Are we as analysts employing the correct lenses for trying to view and understand what is really going on? Linguists working on bilingual first language acquisition indeed face the challenge of having to keep abreast of the growing literature in many fields, including linguistics, first language acquisition research and bilingualism research on language contact and code-switching. Staying up to date with the relevant literature in other fields presents a dilemma for the analyst. Indeed even when purportedly current literature on adult code-switching is cited, it is often not the most recent work available in the field.

In this chapter I will expand upon some of the issues presented in the chapters in this volume, namely the actual phenomenon of language contact in the bilingual child's language acquisition, as well as methodological issues the linguist must tackle in studying the matter at hand. We may ask whether language contact is a dilemma, or a challenge, for the child or rather simply for the linguist. In the following sections I will focus on the issues of language dominance, the importance of context for studying mixed utterances, the role of mixed utterances in the child's language development, and finally our conceptualisation of the bilingual child in relation to the more mature bilingual individual. Is the bilingualism in the bilingual child inherently different from that of the bilingual adult? In this final section I will relate the study of language contact in bilingual first language acquisition to more recent studies of synchronic language contact in more mature bilinguals as well as diachronic change in languages in bilingual communities.

2.   Language dominance or not: is that the question?

An immediate question in regards to crosslinguistic structures is whether the language contact can be considered an example of language transfer, or language dominance. The issue of dominance, that is, that one language is somehow stronger than the other and affects the processing of the other, has in fact been under fire in recent years in regards to bilingual first language acquisition. Although the notion of dominance is generally accepted in regards to older bilingual children and adults, there has been criticism of its validity among language-acquiring youngsters. DeHouwer (1998: 258) goes so far as to say that it "remains to be considered whether and to what extent the notion of 'dominance' is at all needed either as a descriptive or an explanatory concept with regard to very young bilingual children".

Paradis & Genesee (1996) discuss different ways in which language contact affects the acquisition process, whether the acquisition is autonomous or interdependent. As they clearly point out though (p. 3), "the notions of autonomy and interdependence presuppose the existence of two linguistic representations". Interdependence is potentially displayed through transfer of a grammatical property from one language to the other, acceleration of the acquisition of a certain grammatical property in one of the languages compared to acquisition in monolingual children, and delay in the acquisition of some grammatical property due to the fact of acquiring two languages. Although earlier studies noted some delay, more recent studies indicate that the rate of acquisition falls within the normal range for both languages. What is important for the current discussion is that both transfer and acceleration are most likely to occur when the child achieves a more advanced level of syntactic complexity in one of the languages. Paradis & Genesee state that transfer can occur because the grammatical property in question is also typically used in monolingual acquisition although perhaps not as frequently, or because the bilingual child is more *dominant* in one of the two languages.

The notion of transfer is a well-known term from research into second language acquisition. Müller (1998) applied it to bilingual first language acquisition to refer to a particular relief strategy used by the child when the input is ambiguous in that there is variation regarding one of the languages. The influence of the one language on the other is, therefore, indirect in that the child uses parts of the analysis of one language in order to sort out the ambiguous properties of the other. Müller's analysis concerns the acquisition of subordinate clauses in German, a language which presents such an ambiguity, acquired along with another language not containing such ambiguity, such as French, English, or Italian. The argument is that monolingual children acquiring German perform the same errors; however, bilingual children perform them more often. In this sense Müller's definition complies with the first type of transfer mentioned by Paradis and Genesee (1996), noted above. For now suffice it to say that the claim is that the notion of dominance cannot sufficiently address this particular type of language contact. Müller's emphasis is on the structural properties of the languages involved in the language contact situation, as an explanation for the "transfer".

In the following, I will argue for the importance of maintaining the notion of dominance in our investigations of early bilingualism, that some degree of language transfer, direct or indirect, can be attributed to dominance. However, I will also agree that the notion of dominance may not capture all aspects of crosslinguistic structures. There may be cases in which the structural properties of the languages involved will play an important role in transfer. The notion of dominance is closely related to the notion of a balanced bilingual, one who does not display evidence of any language dominance. It is in fact worth noting that the studies in this volume have not taken as a point of departure the notion of a balanced bilingual. Paradis (this volume) so clearly notes that the children in her study were not required to be balanced bilinguals "as dominance or preference for one language is a typical aspect of early bilingual development". Not only is it typical in development but also in language use among more mature bilinguals, including code-switching (cf. Bentahila & Davies 1992; Myers-Scotton 1999; Grosjean in press).

How has the issue of dominance been addressed more generally in the bilingual first language literature and specifically in this volume? Schlyter (1993: 289) addresses the case of bilingual children for whom "the two languages are not quite in balance during their development, but that, at least for periods of time, one of the languages is weaker". Her discussion focuses on the relationship between the weaker and stronger (that is, dominant) languages of children acquiring two languages simultaneously. As she notes, the stronger one exhibits all the aspects of normal first language acquisition, that is, core grammatical phenomena such as finiteness, word order, and placement of negation. In the weaker language, on the other hand, there is greater variation of these grammatical aspects, with development often lagging behind that of the stronger language. Schlyter also notes that some elements, for example, a pronominal subject, may be replaced by an element from the stronger language, when the child is speaking the weaker language. Hence we get a mixed utterance such as the following used by Siri who is 2;6 and acquiring Norwegian and English simultaneously (Lanza 1997b: 153):

(1)   *jeg* go there one day?
       'I'

Hence Schlyter's description of the weaker language implies that the bilingual child has less proficiency in that language as compared to the stronger language. Döpke (this volume) equates the notion of dominance with language development at unequal rates, similar to Tracy (this volume) who invokes the notion of unequal mastery. We will return to this issue of language proficiency below.

Genesee, Nicoladis & Paradis (1995) introduced another measure of dominance: the amount of "multi-morphemic utterances" MMU (utterances of two morphemes or more) used by a child in interaction. This measure apparently gave an accurate profile of the young French-English bilingual children in their study. However, an inherent problem with such a measure, particularly in a triadic interaction, is that potential interactional dominance by one of the parents can affect the child's MMU rate. For example, if the French-speaking parent spoke more often to the child than the other parent, there is chance for the child's MMU rate to be inflated in French.

In Lanza (1993, 1997a) I built on the work of Petersen (1988) and her dominant-language hypothesis and showed how the two-year-old bilingual girl Siri showed indications of dominance in her Norwegian, the majority language in her environment. This dominance was especially manifested through her directionality of mixing. Siri's language development was followed from the ages of 2;0 to 2;7. She acquired English and Norwegian in Norway in a family in which her mother was American and her father Norwegian. The parents claimed to stick to the 'one person-one language strategy' of interaction with the child. Siri essentially spoke English with her mother once she turned 2;1 and spoke Norwegian with her father.

Siri's general mixing pattern in her mixed utterances revealed that English lexical morphemes co-occurred with English and Norwegian grammatical morphemes; however, Norwegian lexical morphemes *only* co-occurred with Norwegian grammatical morphemes. In other words, Norwegian lexical morphemes did not co-occur with English grammatical morphemes. Hence items similar to (2) and (3) occurred but not (4):

(2)   English lexical with Norwegian and English grammatical:
        looke   and *looks*
            +INF

(3)   Norwegian lexical with Norwegian grammatical:
        klappe
        clap+INF
        '(to) clap'

(4)   *Norwegian lexical with English grammatical:
        klapps
        'claps'

These co-occurrence constraints indicated a prevalence of a Norwegian grammatical framework in Siri's speech. This pattern held for inflectional morphology but also for function words, including pronouns.

Siri's directionality of mixing was interpreted as but one indicator of her dominance and not the sole indicator. Her greater linguistic development in Norwegian, her language choice including more hesitation when speaking English, and furthermore, her parents' evaluation of her "stronger" language all converge as support for the claim of her dominance in Norwegian. What is important to point out here is that despite her dominance in Norwegian, Siri's English also developed and in many cases she did in fact have equivalent forms. Thus it is not merely lack of proficiency or unequal mastery of the weaker language that can explain the mixing patterns in her data. Note the exchange in (5). Siri at age 2;6

had both the Norwegian and English first person pronoun in her repertoire; however, she tended to use the Norwegian one. In this case we see where affect, a psycholinguistic variable, triggers the mixed utterance.

(5)   Siri's father is about to go out to visit some friends. Siri also wishes to go along, but is reminded that she had already been there earlier that day:
S: *I want to 'gain/*
       'want to/'
M: well, maybe another day
       you can go down there. Not — not tonight.
S: ((crying)) *jeg want to/*
       'I'
F: *Shh! jeg kommer snart tilbake.*
       'Shh! I will be back soon'.

Despite the attested directionality in Siri's language contact patterns, of mixing from Norwegian to English, I noted that there was some potential evidence for the opposite pattern, that is, influence from English to Norwegian. This occurred in the domain of her acquisition of negation (cf. Lanza 1997a: 157–160). In her one-word negation, Siri used the Norwegian *nei* and the English equivalent *no*. In the next stage instead of using the syntactic negator *ikke,* Siri persisted in using *nei* for some time in both her Norwegian utterances and her mixed utterances while in English she continued using *no,* similar to what monolingual children do in acquiring English. Notice the following examples:

(6)   *nei fits*   (2;1)
       'no'

(7)   *nei jeg kan do it*   (2;5)
       no I   can
       'I cannot do it'

(8)   *nei spise opp*   (2;3)
       'no eat   up'

(9)   *no laugh*   (2;4)

Although *no* and *nei* both function as discourse negation, it is important to point out that in adult language only the English *no* can function in phrasal negation (a type of syntactic negation), in a determiner position such as in *no food.* Unfortunately, there are few linguistic studies of the early acquisition of Scandinavian languages; however, there is some evidence that a monolingual Danish-speaking child used the negator *nej* similarly to Siri (Plunkett & Strömqvist 1992). Hence Siri's pattern represents a potential case of transfer from English to Norwegian, or can be interpreted within the Competition Model as a case of cross-language cue competition, as discussed by Döpke (this volume). The similarities across the two languages help the child deal with an intra-linguistic phenomenon. As Döpke states, "Cues which are frequently available, reliable and perceptually salient win over cues of lesser strength" (Döpke, this volume: 94).

But how does this relate to Siri's dominance? Döpke discusses the interface of language dominance, which she sees as environmental, and cognitive issues of language contact. She holds that the environmental factors, that is, the sociolinguistic situation, only influence the quantity with which cross-language phenomena appear, but are not the cause for their appearance. If the cross-language influences are bilateral, they could "not have been caused by the dominance of one language, but need to be seen as due to the cognitive challenges posed by the simultaneous exposure to two languages" (Döpke, this volume: 100).

It is important to point out that Siri's interesting case of negation does not refute the overall pattern of Siri's directionality of mixing. Hence it does not refute the claim of her language dominance in Norwegian, that is, it does not render the claim "untenable" that the bilingual child makes use of the syntactic structures of the stronger language when creating sentences in her weaker language. A claim of dominance and a claim of cross-language cue competition need not be exclusive. Just as we say that differentiation is manifested by the *majority* of child utterances being target-like, dominance can account for the *majority* of cross-linguistic structures in Siri's output. The case of her negation does not deny her dominance but rather can be explained by cognitive motivations. Moreover, dominance itself can be understood within a cognitive processing framework. The more frequently used language in the environment is usually the one which contributes to a bilingual child's purported dominance. What we use or hear more frequently has a high processing frequency and hence becomes "entrenched" in our cognitive processing, in the words of Langacker (1987, 1990). Similar structures across languages gain cue strength crosslinguistically as they offer the child a greater number of instantiations of the structure. This issue of frequency in the input needs to be explored more carefully. The Competition Model has been applied with success in both first and second language acquisition research (cf. Bates & MacWhinney 1989; and the review in MacWhinney 1997) and offers interesting insights for further exploration in the realm of bilingual first language acquisition.

As discussed above, dominance is not just a question of development but also of use. The notion of language development at unequal rates and unequal mastery are related to the issue of language proficiency, a term often applied to the competence of one or the other language in a bilingual child's repertoire. Although many scholars use the notion of "language proficiency" in speaking about simultaneous acquisition, De Houwer (1998: 258) questions it use and notes:

> The link between "dominance" and "proficiency" seems to be the most common one in the literature, but it still remains unclear whether indeed there is a consensus that "dominance" refers to *just* a child's greater proficiency in one language compared to another".

I have attempted to show above that dominance and language proficiency, or unequal mastery, are not to be equated although they may be related. In other words, unequal mastery may be a result of dominance. Moreover, I do not contend that dominance can explain *all* aspects of language contact. Lexical mixing, for example, may be exploited by the child for pragmatic reasons, illustrating the child's sensitivity to contextual demands. Difficulties in measuring the effect of language dominance or even the problem of ascertaining its presence in the language use of a bilingual infant should not lead us to doubting its existence nonetheless. Insufficient means of measuring the phenomenon should not lead us to denying the phenomenon. To invoke an old cliché, we shouldn't throw the baby out with the bath water.

I will contend that in order to discern different sources for language contact, we linguists will need to explore more carefully the actual context for the child's speech and how this may affect the child's processing and use of the two languages. Grosjean (in press: 7) brings in the notion of "dynamic interferences" which he defines as "speaker-specific deviations from the language being spoken due to the influence of the other deactivated language". These can be the effects of language dominance. As he so clearly points out, these interferences are difficult to separate from other forms of language mixing such as code-switching and borrowing when we do not take into account whether the speaker is in a monolingual or a bilingual mode. This is also the case for young bilingual children. In order to discern dominance patterns we will need to look more carefully at the variables of language mode and context. As Grosjean (in press: 21) states, "Future research will have to investigate the underlying mechanisms that make a stronger language 'seep through' despite the fact that it has been deactivated". Such research will also provide insights for the field of bilingual first language acquisition.

3. Language mode and context

Language mode is defined as "the state of activation of the bilingual's languages and language processing mechanisms at a given point in time" (Grosjean in press: 3). Hence activation of one language or both will influence cognitive processing. A bilingual, or a multilingual, will find himself or herself somewhere on a continuum between a monolingual and bilingual mode (cf. Grosjean 1998).What factors influence this positioning include those associated with language choice. Thus the sociolinguistic variable of context will trigger the psycholinguistic variable of language mode.

All too often it is assumed that the context of language use is simply the particular language used with the child. As Döpke (1992a) has clearly shown, however, different discourse strategies used by parents in interacting with their child will meet with different results in the use of the minority language. And as illustrated in Lanza (1997a), although adult interlocutors may only use one language with the child, an indication of comprehension of the other language may contribute to a bilingual context. In such a case, either language could possibly serve as the base or matrix language of an utterance, including the syntactic structure of that utterance. This underscores the need to carefully examine the context of language development and use, that is, the extent to which an interaction is monolingual or bilingual in nature, even when doing a grammatical analysis (Lanza 1998). As Duranti & Goodwin (1992) have pointed out, context is dynamic; language functions in context and as context.

In Lanza (1997a) I operationalised this monolingual — bilingual continuum through the use of various discourse strategies employed by the parent to open negotiations for a monolingual or a bilingual continuum.[1] In examining Siri's interactions from a discourse analytic perspective, I noted that her mother negotiated more of a monolingual context with her daughter than did the father. For example, her mother would often respond to Siri's lexical mixing with clarification requests while her father often moved on in the conversation thereby acknowledging comprehension of her English lexical contributions. This could explain the fact that Siri mixed lexically more often with her Norwegian-speaking father than she did with her English-speaking mother despite her attested dominance in Norwegian. Here we see another case in which dominance cannot explain all examples of language mixing. This analysis of Siri's mixing from a contextual perspective does not, however, refute the analysis of her mixed utterances which indicated a directionality of mixing, similar to that noted by Petersen (1988).

How do we determine which element is the mixed one in the bilingual child's utterance? From a language socialisation perspective, an interactional analysis of the context is vital for determining the communicative demands on the child. However, from a structural point of view, deciding what element is the mixed one involves determining the base or matrix language, and the guest or embedded language. Such an endeavour may be an impossible task on purely structural grounds given that many utterances are only composed of two morphemes. The issue of a matrix, or base, language has figured prominently in work on intra-sentential code-switching, and indeed is relevant in a discussion of language mixing in early bilingualism.

Tracy (this volume) notes that researchers typically assume that the base language can be determined either by the language of the interlocutor, or by sentence- or utterance-internal criteria. In this regard Myers-Scotton's Matrix Language Frame Model is invoked. It is important to point out that the frequency criterion mentioned by Tracy, that is, that the majority of words or morphemes can determine the matrix language, is a criterion that Myers-Scotton has abandoned in her most recent formulations (cf. Myers-Scotton 1993/1997, 1999). Rather the matrix language is identified implicationally through the operations of the model, through its System Morpheme Principle and the Morpheme Order Principle. In Lanza (1997b) through a language socialisation perspective, I showed how in conversations with Siri's mother the discourse dominant language was English while Norwegian was the matrix language of Siri's mixed utterances, a distribution which indicated her language dominance. Hence a contextual analysis as well as a linguistic analysis based on code-switching research was needed in order to understand Siri's mixing patterns.

A similar pattern to Siri's was found in another study of a two-year-old child, bilingual in Norwegian and English (Christiansen 1995). The child also had an American mother and a Norwegian father, similar to Siri. What Christiansen found was that of the 307 mixed utterances in the corpus, 215 (70%) involved the combination of Norwegian grammatical morphemes with English lexical morphemes. 92 mixed utterances (30%) involved the combination of English grammatical morphemes with Norwegian lexical morphemes. As Christiansen points out (p. 69), the general trend agrees with Petersen's (1988) *Dominant Language Hypothesis*, but one may be tempted to claim that the 30% utterances that apparently deviate from the pattern are a challenge. However, by looking at the use of these mixed utterances in interaction, she noticed that those involving Norwegian grammatical morphemes occurred in interactions with the father and the mother while those utterances involving English grammatical morphemes *only* occurred in interactions with the mother. Hence there is support for the claim that the child was dominant in Norwegian.

Why did the child use Norwegian lexical morphemes with his mother? An analysis of the parents' discourse strategies showed that both parents used response strategies that were bilingually oriented, that is, that opened up for lexical mixing and hence contexts in the code-switching mode. So the reason why Siri's data showed a clearer pattern in support of the *Dominant Language Hypothesis* was the mother's use of more monolingually oriented discourse strategies towards her daughter's mixing. Language dominance is essentially a psycholinguistic phenomenon closely intermeshed with sociolinguistic parameters, as we could see in Siri's data. Hence we see in Siri's data psycholinguistic, pragmatic and cognitive motivations for her crosslinguistic structures in language contact. No single analysis can provide the entire picture.

4. The role of mixed utterances

Although mixed utterances were in earlier research invoked as evidence for a stage of fusion, or evidence of a dilemma for the child, more recent work has shown that the use of mixed utterances rather illustrates the resourcefulness of the bilingual child. Deuchar & Quay (2000) have shown how the majority of the mixed utterances used by the very young child in their study were due to lexical gaps. As equivalents were acquired in both languages, the amount of mixed utterances decreased. Hence the child pooled her resources in order to communicate.

In Lanza (1997a) I performed an MLU analysis of Siri's English, Norwegian and mixed utterances similar to the analysis in Döpke (1992b), with a focus, however, on the mixed utterances. Of course, given that a mixed utterance is a combination of elements from both languages, mixed utterances are likely to contain two morphemes as a starting point. Hence we would expect a relatively higher value in MLU for the mixed utterances.[2] Similar to Döpke's results, the MLU's of Siri's mixed utterances surpassed those of the other language choices. Given that there were few mixed utterances in some of the interactions, particularly with her father, I tested the hypothesis that Siri was pushing the limit of her linguistic competence by comparing the MLU of her five longest utterances in each language for each sample with her five longest mixed utterances for that sample when possible. The data were broken down by samples as the analysis was also a language choice one. Wells (1985) found that the MLU's of the five longest utterances gives an indication of the child's upper limit for any sample; it corresponds to R. Brown's (1973) upper bound. In no samples were the MLU values of the mixed utterances lower than the MLU for both of the other language choices. This suggests then that the mixed utterance may be a resource, rather than an instance of confusion or a dilemma, for the child to push the limits of her grammatical competence. Hence we can see how the bilingual child can exploit mixing to meet communicative demands, even grammatical mixing as Siri did in order to communicate with her mother.

The discussion thus far on mixed utterances has focused on lexical mixing at the word level. Tracy (this volume) refers to a type of mixing she refers to as "crossover" phenomena in which the lexical items in an utterance come from one language but the overall structure is from the other. She calls for a new approach to language contact research to deal with them. Indeed this issue has not been seriously addressed before. However, recent work in code-switching and language contact (e.g. Bolonyai 1998; Myers-Scotton 1999; Türker 1999) have already addressed such an issue. Bolonyai's study is of particular interest as it concerns a case of early bilingualism. It documents the structural consequences of intensive language contact on a child's L1 and L2 language development in an L2-dominant environment. The young Hungarian child moved to the U.S. with her Hungarian parents when she was 1;5 and attended an English-medium nursery school from the age of 1;8. The data cover three different points over one and a half years at the ages of 3;7, 4;2, and 4;10. With a theoretical anchoring in the Matrix Language Frame Model (Myers-Scotton 1993/1997), Bolonyai illustrates how there is a turnover over time in the matrix language of the child's mixed utterances. The theoretical assumption is that lexical structure is abstract and complex with three levels of structure: the lexical-conceptual structure, predicate-argument structure, and morphological realisation patterns. She demonstrates that as a result of this turnover, abstract lexical structure can be "split" and "recombined" in such a way that surface structure is projected by an underlying grammatical system which in fact is composite. Such patterns are related to dynamic situations such as language shift, which is the case for the young Hungarian-English child in Bolonyai's study but also relevant in an immigrant setting (Türker 1999). Insights from newer approaches to language contact research may shed light on similar less common instances of mixed utterances such as those referred to as "crossover" phenomena.

Tracy brings up another vital issue in regards to the linguist's attempts to analyse mixed utterances. It concerns the ambiguity of expression with respect to language assignment, particularly in the case of languages which are very similar, such as Norwegian and English in the case of Siri. As Tracy so clearly notes, this problem is exacerbated by the fact that children during early language development experience instability both phonetically and phonologically. As noted by Tracy, in Lanza (1997a) I encountered this problem in my data with Siri with the forms [de] and [dæ] / [dæ:] which served a deictic function. I stated that the former form could be interpreted as the Norwegian deictic *det* or the English *there* while the latter could feasibly be attributed to the English *that* or the Norwegian *der*. However, this ambiguity was only relevant for the *first* sample under analysis. Moreover, the Norwegian *der* and its English equivalent *there* are pronounced with clearly different vowels, contrary to what is the case in German. Hence Tracy's comment that my orthographic rendering of the form *der* could have turned out to be *there* is not tenable.

This discussion, however, brings up an important issue and that is the necessity of including phonetic transcription. As I state in Lanza (1997a: 102), my working transcripts were phonetic when necessary; however, the interpretations were rendered in orthography in the book. A similar case in which a phonetic transcription could justify an interpretation concerns Gawlitzek-Maiwald's (this volume) rendering of a potentially ambiguous form. As an intermediate form between *gehen* and *going* we find the form *goen* which is interpreted as a combination of the English verb and the German suffix. Could this not have been the monolingual form usually rendered orthographically as *goin'*? Whether or not this variant is present in the dialect of English to which the child is exposed may provide a further clue towards disambiguation. Ambiguity in the data represents a dilemma for the linguist analysing bilingual children's mixed utterances. It is, however, important to point out that homonymy is a documented strategy in child language research: the child uses the limited number of forms in her repertoire to accomplish the greater number of meanings (Vihman 1981).

A final issue in regards to mixed utterances is one brought up by Döpke (this volume) and that involves the notion of the units of acquisition and language contact. The issue of the child's units in acquisition has been especially addressed in first language acquisition research particularly since Peters (1983). Sinka (this volume) classifies the bilingual child's use of the English *what that is?* as an example of a syntactic mix influenced by Latvian. However, one is left to wonder whether the child has extracted it from the larger *Do you know what that is?* The issue of chunks or formulas is an important one in cognitive linguistics, especially within cognitive grammar as articulated by Langacker (1990) who refers to such expressions as "composite expressions" (Langacker 1987: 29). Backus (1999) has recently applied this perspective to Dutch-Turkish code-switching and illustrated that in many cases the actual elements switched are expressions which have some lexical unity. This discussion is relevant for the issue of determining what the switched or mixed element in a mixed utterance is in early bilingual data.

5. Bilingualism across time: language development, language use and language change

Research in bilingual first language acquisition can be enriched through comparisons with other work in bilingualism and language contact. Van der Linden (this volume) has raised the issue of not divorcing young children's language behaviour from that of adults. The young child will after all grow into a fully competent member of his or her speech community. Moreover, language contact in acquisition, use and language change often illustrate similarities in expression.

The contributions to this volume have stressed the need to examine what happens in monolinguals, for what looks like transfer can in fact also occur in monolingual acquisition. A similar example can be found in a recent discussion of Treffers-Daller's (1999) work on borrowing and shift-induced interference in the bilingual communities of Brussels and Strasbourg. As Beecher (1999) points out, a purported example of Dutch influence in Brussels French is actually a structure that is prevalent in the spontaneous French spoken in France. She stresses that it is only through comparison with monolingual data that we can discern whether the contact situation can account for the change in language structure.

Furthermore, we also need to see what happens in more mature bilinguals. Both Döpke (this volume) and Müller (1998) suggest that crosslinguistic transfer might occur in structures for which there is ambiguity in the input concerning one of the languages. Hence one language may serve a catalyst function for an already existent option in the other language. This is a case in which the structure is also attested in monolingual acquisition while bilinguals use it more frequently, allegedly because of the catalyst support from the other language. In his work with Turkish in contact with other languages, Boeschoten (1998, 1999) notes that internal variation in the one language may correspond to basic patterns in the other and hence facilitate code-switching and language contact in general, and potentially lead to convergence from a diachronic perspective. Other synchronic evidence of language change based on natural language use and which reveals "covert influence" (Romaine 1989) from one language to another in a contact situation is reported on in Klein (1980). The grammatical markings in question are the use and distribution of the simple present and the progressive in a language contact situation involving English and Spanish in the U.S. Both languages mark progressivity; however, the distribution of the tense and aspect categories differ. Klein found that compared to monolingual Spanish speakers, the bilinguals used the progressive relatively more frequently; furthermore, they used the simple present less frequently than their monolingual counterparts in reference to time which included the specific moment of speech. A semantic shift was, therefore, in progress in the language system of these speakers since the simple present changed its meaning due to its more narrow range of use.

Another example of language change through language contact is found in Talmy (1982) who discusses the effects upon the semantic system of one language in contact with another. Focusing on Yiddish in contact with Slavic, Talmy presents "a framework for understanding the structured interaction of semantic systems" (p. 248). A particularly interesting principle he proposes is one for which we find a parallel in the data from a bilingual 7-year-old child (cf. Lanza in press). Talmy states that if a language borrows from an unparalleled donor morpheme class, the borrowing language does not assume the syntactic category but the meanings, and expresses these meanings with a native construction which is already semantically consonant with the donor language meaning. Yiddish did not borrow the Slavic suffix which indicated semelfactive aspect, but expressed it with its native periphrastic construction which already contained some of the donor language meaning. Similarly, the bilingual child did not import progressive aspect marked on the verb directly into her Norwegian, rather she expressed similar meanings through the use of native durative expressions in Norwegian.

Studying bilingualism across time through language development, language use, and finally language change surely poses a challenge to the linguist who has focused on bilingual first language acquisition. However, it is clear that insights from these fields can help us better understand the types of language contact and crosslinguistic structures we may experience in the early child language data.

6. Conclusion

There are many highly relevant issues that have been brought up in the contributions to this volume; moreover, there is an open invitation to explore the impact of other important issues. All of the articles concern bilingual development involving Indo-European languages, in most cases Germanic languages. In fact, in eight of the nine contributions, English is one of the languages in the pair, functioning as either a majority or a minority language, thus furnishing the possibility of examining the importance of ambient input. Sinka's article on Latvian-English acquisition provides data on a new language which contrasts with English in morphosyntactic complexity. Future studies will be welcome which combine typologically different languages in simultaneous acquisition. An issue in code-switching research has been whether or not typological differences in the languages in contact play a role in the degree to which the languages interact in use.

The issue of individual differences is also highly relevant. Paradis (this volume) points out that the crosslinguistic structures predicted within the domain of morphosyntax were not systematically apparent in the language of the five French-English bilingual children under study. However, she does not rule out this possibility in other children given the fact that one child did in fact have a marginal number of English-influenced negative constructions in his French. Moreover, the issue of dominance that I have highlighted is an individual phenomenon and difficult to measure or attest when individual differences are blurred in group figures and percentages. It is clear, however, that we will need theories that can capture the facts of individual differences in the expression of language contact.

It appears that language contact has not been a dilemma for the bilingual child, but rather one for the linguist, both methodologically and theoretically. The real challenge for the linguist working with bilingual first language acquisition is the need to be open to various explanations for the crosslinguistic structures evident in the data and not to be blinded by a preferred theory. Moreover, there is a necessity to bridge the gap between studies of more mature bilinguals and of children acquiring two languages. And this will require linking explanations based on psycholinguistic, sociolinguistic / pragmatic, and cognitive motivations for language contact phenomena.

Notes

1. Note that this analysis was employed in dyadic interactions only since audio data precluded access to eye contact, essential in determining language choice in triadic interactions. Tracy (this volume) in her discussion on determining the base language of a mixed utterance brings up my discussion and analysis in Lanza (1997a: 182) in which different baselines were used in the dyadic and triadic interactions. My discussion, however, was actually an analytic exercise in my critique of Redlinger and Park's (1980) analysis. I wanted to perform various approaches to analyzing mixed utterances and point out the problems with them, and to emphasize the importance of considering the theoretical assumptions underlying analytical procedures, as opposed to merely comparing "results".

2. Blends, however, only consist of one morpheme.

References

Backus, Ad. 1999. "Evidence for lexical chunks in insertional codeswitching". In B. Brendemoen, E. Lanza & E. Ryen (eds.), *Language Encounters Across Time and Space. Studies in Language Contact.* Oslo: Novus Press, 93–110.

Bates, Elizabeth & Brian MacWhinney. 1989. "Functionalism and the Competition Model". In B. MacWhinney & E. Bates (eds.), *The Crosslinguistic Study of Sentence Processing*. New York: Cambridge University Press, 3–73.

Beecher, Kate. 1999. "Update on spoken French". *Bilingualism: Language and Cognition* 2(2): 81–83.

Bentahila, A. & E. Davies (1992). "Code-switching and language dominance". In R.J. Harris (ed), *Cognitive Processing in Bilinguals*. Amsterdam: Elsevier, 443–458.

Boeschoten, Hendrik. 1998. "Codeswitching, codemixing, and code alternation: What a difference". In R. Jacobson (ed.), *Codeswitching Worldwide*. (Trends in Linguistics, Studies and Monographs 106). Berlin: Mouton de Gruyter, 15–24.

Boeschoten, Hendrik. 1999. "Equivalence and levels of analysis". In B. Brendemoen, E. Lanza & E. Ryen (eds.), *Language Encounters Across Time and Space. Studies in Language Contact*. Oslo: Novus Press, 63–72.

Bolonyai, Agnes. 1998. "In-between languages: Language shift/maintenance in childhood bilingualism". *International Journal of Bilingualism* 2(1): 21–43.

Brown, Roger. 1973. *A First Language. The Early Stages*. Cambridge, MA: Harvard University Press.

Christiansen, Karen M. H. 1995. *'Ka looking for du?' A study of language differentiation and the effect of context on language mixing*. Cand. Phild. thesis, University of Bergen, Norway.

De Houwer, Annick. 1995. "Bilingual language acquisition". In P. Fletcher & B. MacWhinney (eds), *The Handbook of Child Language*. Oxford: Basil Blackwell, 219–250.

De Houwer, Annick. 1998. "By way of introduction: Methods in studies of bilingual first language acquisition". *International Journal of Bilingualism* 2(3): 249–263.

Deuchar, Margaret & Suzanne Quay. 2000. *Bilingual Language Acquisition: Theoretical Implications of a Case Study*. Oxford: Oxford University Press.

Döpke, Susanne. 1992a. *One Parent One Language. An Interactional Approach*. (Studies in Bilingualism 3) Amsterdam and Philadelphia: John Benjamins.

Döpke, Susanne. 1992b. "A bilingual child's struggle to comply with the 'one parent-one language rule'". *Journal of Multilingual and Multicultural Development* 13(6): 467–485.

Duranti, Alessandro & Charles Goodwin. 1992. (eds). *Rethinking Context: Language as an Interactive Phenomenon*. Cambridge: Cambridge University Press .

Genesee, Fred, Elena Nicoladis & Johanne Paradis. 1995. "Language differentiation in early bilingual development". *Journal of Child Language* 22: 611–631.

Grosjean, François. 1998. "Studying bilinguals: Methodological and conceptual issues". *Bilingualism: Language and Cognition* 1(1): 131–149.

Grosjean, François. In press. "The bilingual's language modes". In J.L. Nichol (ed), *One Mind, Two Languages: Bilingual Language Processing*. Oxford: Blackwell.

Grosjean, François & Bernard Py. 1992. "La restructuration d'une première langue: L'intégration de variantes de contact dans la compétence de migrants bilingues". *La Linguistique* 27: 35–60.

Klein, F. 1980. "A quantitative study of syntactic and pragmatic indications of change in the Spanish of bilinguals in the U.S". In W. Labov (ed), *Locating Language in Time and Space.* New York: Academic Press, 69–82.

Langacker, Ronald. 1987. *Foundations of Cognitive Grammar. Vol. 1. Theoretical Prerequisites.* Stanford: Stanford University Press.

Langacker, Ronald. 1990. *Concept, Image, and Symbol: The Cognitive Basis of Grammar.* Berlin: Mouton de Gruyter.

Lanza, Elizabeth. 1992. "Can bilingual two-year-olds code-switch?" *Journal of Child Language,* 19 (3): 633–658.

Lanza, Elizabeth. 1993. "Language mixing and language dominance in bilingual first language acquisition". In E. Clark (ed), *The Proceedings of the Twenty-fourth Annual Child Langauge Research Forum.* Stanford University: Center for the Study of Language and Information Conference Series, 197–208.

Lanza, Elizabeth. 1997a. *Language Mixing in Infant Bilingualism: A Sociolinguistic Perspective.* Oxford: Oxford University Press.

Lanza, Elizabeth. 1997b. "Language contact in bilingual two-year-olds and code-switching: Language encounters of a different kind?" *International Journal of Bilingualism* 1 (2): 135–162.

Lanza, Elizabeth. 1998. "Cross-linguistic influence, input and the young bilingual child". *Bilingualism: Language and Cognition* 1(3): 181–182.

Lanza, Elizabeth. In press. "Temporality and language contact in narratives in bilingual first language acquisition: Some methodological and theoretical considerations". In L. Verhoeven & S. Strömqvist (eds), *Narratives in a Bilingual Context.* Amsterdam and Philadelphia: John Benjamins.

MacWhinney, Brian. 1997. "Second language acquisition and the Competition Model". In A. de Groot & J. Kroll (eds), *Tutorials in bilingualism: Psycholinguistic perspectives.* Mahway, New Jersey: L. Erlbaum, 113–142.

MacLaughlin, Barry. 1984. "Early bilingualism: Methodological and theoretical issues". In M. Paradis & Y. Le Brun (eds), *Early Bilingualism and Child Development.* Lisse: Swets & Zeitlinger B.V., 19–46.

Müller, Natascha. 1998. "Transfer in bilingual first language acquisition". *Bilingualism: Language and Cognition* 1(3): 151–171.

Myers-Scotton, Carol. 1993/1997. *Duelling Languages: Grammatical Structure in Code-switching.* Oxford: Oxford University Press. 1997 reprint with new "Afterword".

Myers-Scotton, Carol. 1997. "Code-switching". In F. Coulmas (ed), *The Handbook of Sociolinguistics.* Oxford: Blackwell, 217–237.

Myers-Scotton, Carol. 1999. "Putting it all together: The matrix language and more". In B. Brendemoen, E. Lanza & E. Ryen (eds), *Language Encounters Across Time and Space. Studies in Language Contact.* Oslo: Novus Press, 13–28.

Paradis, Johanne & Fred Genesee. 1996. "Syntactic acquisition in bilingual children: Autonomous or interdependent?" *Studies in Second Language Acquisition* 18: 1–25.

Peters, Ann. 1983. *The Units of Language Acquisition.* Cambridge: Cambridge University Press.

Petersen, Jennifer. 1988. "Word-internal code-switching constraints in a bilingual child's grammar". *Linguistics* 26: 479–493.

Plunkett, Kim & Sven Strömqvist. 1992. "The acquisition of Scandinavian languages". In D. Slobin (ed), *The Crosslinguistic Study of Language Acquisition*. Vol. 3. Hillsdale, N.J.: L. Erlbaum.

Redlinger, Wendy and T. Z. Park. 1980. "Language mixing in young bilingual children". *Journal of Child Language* 7: 337–352.

Romaine, Suzanne. 1989. *Bilingualism*. Oxford: Blackwell.

Schlyter, Suzanne. 1993. "The weaker language in bilingual Swedish-French children". In K. Hyltenstam & Å. Viberg (eds), *Progression & Regression in Language*. Cambridge: Cambridge University Press.

Talmy, Leonard. 1982. "Borrowing semantic space: Yiddish verb prefixes between Germanic and Slavic". *Proceedings of the Eighth Annual Meeting of the Berkeley Linguistics Society*. Berkeley Linguistics Society, University of California-Berkeley.

Treffers-Daller, Jeanine. 1999. "Borrowing and shift-induced interference: Contrasting patterns in French-Germanic Contact in Brussels and Strasbourg". *Bilingualism: Language and Cognition* 2(1): 1–22.

Türker, Emel. 1999. "Codeswitching and 'loan translations'". In B. Brendemoen, E. Lanza & E. Ryen (eds), *Language Encounters Across Time and Space. Studies in Language Contact*. Oslo: Novus Press, 111–124.

Vihman, Marilyn. 1981. "Phonology and the development of the lexicon: Evidence from children's errors". *Journal of Child Language* 8: 239–264.

Wells, Gordon. 1985. *Language Development in the Pre-School Years*. Cambridge: Cambridge University Press.

Author Index

Subject Index

In the series STUDIES IN BILINGUALISM (SiBil) ISSN 0298-1533 the following titles have been published thus far or are scheduled for publication:

1. FASE, Willem, Koen JASPAERT and Sjaak KROON (eds): *Maintenance and Loss of Minority Languages.* 1992.
2. BOT, Kees de, Ralph B. GINSBERG and Claire KRAMSCH (eds): *Foreign Language Research in Cross-Cultural Perspective.* 1991.
3. DÖPKE, Susanne: *One Parent - One Language. An interactional approach.* 1992.
4. PAULSTON, Christina Bratt: *Linguistic Minorities in Multilingual Settings. Implications for language policies.*1994.
5. KLEIN, Wolfgang and Clive PERDUE: *Utterance Structure. Developing grammars again.*
6. SCHREUDER, Robert and Bert WELTENS (eds): *The Bilingual Lexicon.* 1993.
7. DIETRICH, Rainer, Wolfgang KLEIN and Colette NOYAU: *The Acquisition of Temporality in a Second Language.* 1995.
8. DAVIS, Kathryn Anne: *Language Planning in Multilingual Contexts. Policies, communities, and schools in Luxembourg.* Amsterdam/Philadelphia, 1994.
9. FREED, Barbara F. (ed.) *Second Language Acquisition in a Study Abroad Context.* 1995.
10. BAYLEY, Robert and Dennis R. PRESTON (eds): *Second Language Acquisition and Linguistic Variation.* 1996.
11. BECKER, Angelika and Mary CARROLL: *The Acquisition of Spatial Relations in a Second Language.* 1997.
12. HALMARI, Helena: *Government and Codeswitching. Explaining American Finnish.* 1997.
13. HOLLOWAY, Charles E.: *Dialect Death. The case of Brule Spanish.* 1997.
14. YOUNG, Richard and Agnes WEIYUN HE (eds): *Talking and Testing. Discourse approaches to the assessment of oral proficiency.* 1998.
15. PIENEMANN, Manfred: *Language Processing and Second Language Development. Processability theory.* 1998.
16. HUEBNER, Thom and Kathryn A. DAVIS (eds.): *Sociopolitical Perspectives on Language Policy and Planning in the USA.* 1999.
17. ELLIS, Rod: *Learning a Second Language through Interaction.* 1999.
18. PARADIS, Michel: *Neurolinguistic Aspects of Bilingualism.* n.y.p.
19. AMARA, Muhammad Hasan: *Politics and Sociolinguistic Reflexes. Palestinian border villages.* 1999.
20. POULISSE, Nanda: *Slips of the Tongue. Speech errors in first and second language production.* 1999
21. DÖPKE, Susanne (ed.): *Cross-Linguistic Structures in Simultaneous Bilingualism.* 2000
22. SALABERRY, M. Rafael: *The Development of Past Tense Morphology in L2 Spanish.* n.y.p.